Salt Lake City

Welcoming the World

By Dick Nourse

✳

Photography Editing and Captions by François Camoin

✳

Profiles in Excellence by Barry Scholl

✳

Art Direction by Enrique Espinosa

URBAN
TAPESTRY
SERIES
TOWERY
Publishing, Inc.

LIBRARY OF CONGRESS CATALOGING-IN-PUBLICATION DATA

Nourse, Dick, 1940-
     Salt Lake City : welcoming the world / by Dick Nourse ; photography editing and captions by Fançois Camoin ; profiles in excellence by Barry Scholl.
          p.   cm. — (Urban tapestry series)
     Includes index.
     ISBN 1-881096-58-0 (alk. paper)
     1. Salt Lake City (Utah)—Civilization.   2. Salt Lake City (Utah)--Pictorial works.   3. Business enterprises—Utah—Salt Lake City.
4. Salt Lake City (Utah)—Economic conditions.   I. Camoin, François André, 1939-   . II. Scholl, Barry, 1962-   . III. Title.
IV. Series.
F834.S25N68   1998
979.2′258—dc21   98-34799
                                                                                                            CIP

Towery Publishing, Inc., 1835 Union Avenue, Memphis, TN 38104

PUBLISHER: J. Robert Towery
EXECUTIVE PUBLISHER: Jenny McDowell
NATIONAL SALES MANAGER: Stephen Hung
MARKETING DIRECTOR: Carol Culpepper
PROJECT DIRECTORS: Dean Daly, Linda Frank

EXECUTIVE EDITOR: David B. Dawson
MANAGING EDITOR: Michael C. James
SENIOR EDITORS: Lynn Conlee, Carlisle Hacker
EDITOR/PROFILE MANAGER: Brian Johnston
EDITORS: Mary Jane Adams, Lori Bond, Jana Files, Susan Hesson
ASSISTANT EDITOR: Rebecca Green
EDITORIAL ASSISTANTS: Sunni Thompson, Allison R. Wear

CREATIVE DIRECTOR: Brian Groppe
PROFILE DESIGNERS: Laurie Beck, Kelley Pratt, Ann Ward
DIGITAL COLOR SUPERVISOR: Brenda Pattat
DIGITAL COLOR TECHNICIANS: Jack Griffith, Darin Ipema, Jason Moak, Beverly Timmons
PRODUCTION RESOURCES MANAGER: Dave Dunlap Jr.
PRODUCTION ASSISTANTS: Geoffrey Ellis, Robin McGehee
PRINT COORDINATOR: Tonda Thomas

© FRANÇOIS CAMOIN

☙ CONTENTS ❧

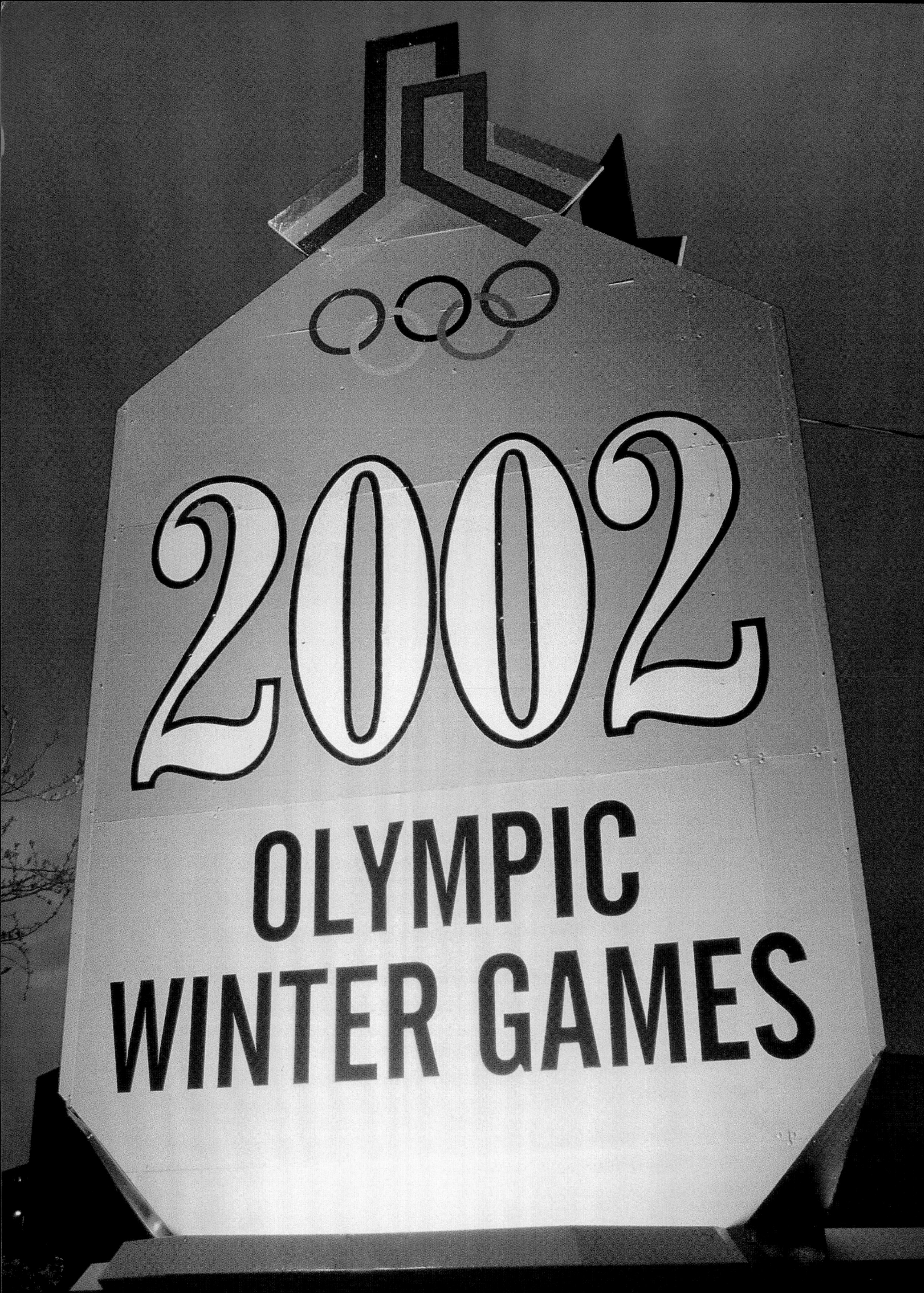

© KAY SHAW / HILLSTROM STOCK PHOTO

by Dick Nourse

W ITH STEVE YOUNG—THE NFL STAR AND former Brigham Young University quarterback—serving as master of ceremonies, the Olympic flag arrived in Salt Lake City the day after it had been lowered in Nagano, Japan, site of the 1998 Winter Games. "For the first time on Utah soil: the Winter Olympic flag," Young announced, as the white banner with five interlocking rings was unfurled.

The flag had been carried personally by Mayor Deedee Corradini, who received it in Nagano and brought it home to Salt Lake City, site of the XIX Olympic Winter Games to be held in 2002. At the ceremony, Corradini stated simply, "The eyes of the world now turn from Nagano to Salt Lake City."

A coveted symbol of the community's three-decade quest to bring the event to the mountainous Utah locale, the flag was transported after the ceremonies to the City and County Building, where it awaits the 2002 Olympics and serves as a reminder to all who come that The World Is Welcome Here—the slogan that has been used throughout the drive to bring the Winter Games to Utah.

I T TOOK 30 YEARS AND FOUR PREVIous international campaigns, but on June 16, 1995, Salt Lake City was awarded the XIX Winter Olympic Games. Come February 2002, the snowy slopes of the majestic Wasatch Mountains will be the stage for the first U.S.-based Winter Olympics since 1980.

But as significant as the Games may be, many were struck by the parallels to an event some 150 years earlier. This is not the first time that people have looked upon the Salt Lake Valley and proclaimed it an ideal location. Steve Young, in fact, is a living legacy of the area's original Mormon settlers. As pundits and Olympic boosters have proclaimed, the coming of the 2002 Winter Games is an affirmation that Salt Lake City is, in another sense, a promised land of sorts that, through the years, has enabled successive generations to rediscover its beauty, its spacious grandeur, and its living spirit.

© RICK McCLAIN

*I*N JULY 1847, BRIGHAM YOUNG—STEVE YOUNG'S great-great-great grandfather and then-president of the Church of Jesus Christ of Latter-day Saints—led a pioneer wagon train through a tiny canyon, looked out over the wide valley that nestles Salt Lake City, and proclaimed, "This is the right place." With these simple words, a community of faith that now spans the globe was established, and a spiritual home was born.

Brigham Young's words have continued to resonate throughout this community. Although they were meant to apply specifically to the band of Mormon immigrants and spiritual seekers who were looking to establish a new home where they could practice their faith in peace, the words "this is the right place" have become something of a slogan for this beautiful city bordered by the Wasatch Mountains to the east and the broad Great Salt Lake to the west.

And while the city has come to be regarded as one of the country's most beautiful, the area did not at first appear to be so desirable. Some in the haggard group of settlers who followed Brigham Young through the mouth of Emigration Canyon in the Wasatch Mountains and gazed upon the luscious green valley and the giant salty lake beyond expected more exultant surroundings and wanted to move on. They had been through much in the previous few years: persecution in Missouri, resettlement in Illinois, and the murder of their prophet and first president, Joseph Smith, at the hands of an angry mob.

MORE THAN A CENTURY AND a half ago, Brigham Young and his followers set their sights on the West and its promise of religious freedom. Along the trail they forged, Mormon pioneers left messages on buffalo skulls—important markers for those who would later travel the same path across the plains and into what is now known as the Wasatch-Cache National Forest.

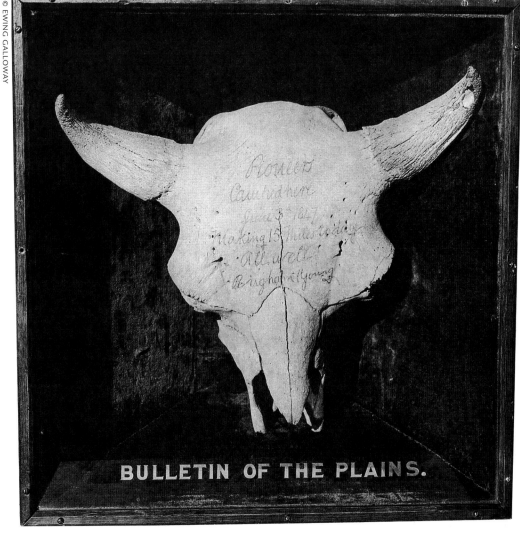

© EWING GALLOWAY

BULLETIN OF THE PLAINS.

Utah's infamous winter snows blanket Old Deseret, a pioneer village in This Is the Place State Park, where the Mormons first laid eyes on the Salt Lake Valley (ABOVE). Imagine their amazement when they first glimpsed the spectacular sunsets that occur over the Great Salt Lake (OPPOSITE).

Led by Brigham Young, a group of 170 Mormon pioneers volunteered to leave Illinois in search of their Zion, a place where their Church of Jesus Christ of Latter-day Saints could practice its religion without fear. The vanguard group made an 1,100-mile trek that began in 1846, ending up here in 1847. Surrounded by rushing streams and tall, green fir trees along the nearby Wasatch range, the group set about to make their new home on the edge of the desert blossom like a rose. And from here, the Mormons reasoned, their spiritual work would blossom forth throughout the world. The pioneers broke ground, planted seeds, and built homes. They developed new and innovative irrigation and cultivation techniques that helped tame the often harsh climate.

And in seemingly no time at all, they completed their mission. Over the next 20 years, some 80,000 Mormons would follow Brigham Young's advance party, and the Salt Lake Valley would rise as their home. In addition to establishing farms and growing food in the area, the Mormons built a number of other towns in the Wasatch canyons and throughout what is known today as Utah. ❧

A MONUMENT IN TEMPLE SQUARE commemorates the thousands who pushed their worldly belongings across the country in handcarts at a time when the Mormon church couldn't afford wagons (RIGHT). In the aftermath of their difficult journey, the pioneers built the Salt Lake City Temple, the spiritual center of the Church of Jesus Christ of Latter-day Saints (OPPOSITE).

But foremost among their accomplishments was the establishment of Salt Lake City itself, the seat of their church. Here, Brigham Young laid out broad streets, wide enough so that a wagon and its team of four oxen or horses could be turned completely around without backing up and making a second pass. Today, you can still do this, although the police take a dim view of U-turns, whether by automobile or covered wagon.

Within four days of arriving in the area, Brigham Young also chose the site for the Temple, a soaring granite structure with six spires that took some 40 years to build and has become the home of the Church of Jesus Christ of Latter-day Saints.

Today, the four-block Temple Square, enclosed by imposing 15-foot walls, remains for Mormons what the Vatican is for Roman Catholics. It is the site of the Temple (reserved for religious purposes only), the Tabernacle (a 6,500-seat-auditorium with a soaring dome and near-perfect acoustics), and the Assembly Hall (a smaller granite structure used for lectures and meetings).

W HILE SALT LAKE CITY IS HEADQUARTERS for the Mormons, some 60 other denominations and religions practice here. Visitors are sometimes surprised to learn what a tolerant and diverse place Salt Lake City is, and how accepting the predominantly Mormon population is of other religious viewpoints.

Visitors are also surprised to learn what a grown-up, modern, cosmopolitan city this is. No, we're not talking about a clone of Seattle or Atlanta. Salt Lake City does have a frontier town aura about it, a small-town feeling that residents

cherish. But this valley along the Great Salt Lake is today home to about 76 percent of the state's 2 million residents and is expected to absorb almost 80 percent of an estimated million new Utahns by 2020.

What's more, the area is being noticed and lauded for its desirable lifestyle and business community. Salt Lake City is on *Time* magazine's list of the "Top 5 Hottest Places" in the United States for job growth. We've been on *Fortune* magazine's top 10 list of best cities in America for business. *Newswatch* cites us as the "number one city with the best environment for business." *Adweek* says that Salt Lake is "poised to become the city of the future." And *Town & Country* magazine calls us "a vibrant, vigorous, and still a visionary city."

THE FACES OF UTAH: ONCE populated almost exclusively by Northern European immigrants who attempted to erase all traces of Native American culture, Salt Lake City is rapidly becoming a cosmopolitan intersection of people and lifestyles—an ongoing celebration of the area's modern-day diversity.

THE NATURAL SPLENDOR OF THE Salt Lake area carries over into the heart of the city, making brief escapes from the daily grind all the more enjoyable— whether you're lunching at an outdoor café or relaxing in the recesses of City Creek Park.

For businesses looking for the prestige, connections, entertainment, and cultural activities of an urban center, Salt Lake City has much to offer without sacrificing its abundance of open space and decidedly friendly atmosphere. Add to all this the city's highly favorable commercial rental rates, and it's clear why it has been so attractive to companies of all sizes, from industry giants to smaller, emerging businesses. In 1997 alone, unemployment remained at a low 3 percent, and 42,000 new jobs were created in a number of diverse economic sectors, making the local economy more resilient than others that rely on a single industry or product.

If Salt Lake City does have a dominant industry, it's tourism. More than 8 million people a year visit the city and its environs. And with the Olympics on the horizon, those figures are expected to double, and even triple, as the Games draw near. ☞

*T*HE CITY'S MAIN TOURIST DRAW, TEMPLE Square, logs more than 5 million visitors a year. Yet Salt Lake City has plenty of other attractions and surprises. A dozen national parks, as well as monuments and recreation areas throughout the state, attract visitors in the millions. A glance at a map will show that Utah is dotted with national parks and forests, and that Salt Lake City—located in the north central part of the state—is ideally situated for access to almost all of them.

Winter sports are among the area's popular draws. Less than an hour's drive from downtown Salt Lake City are nine major ski areas, three cross-country ski areas, and the nation's only recreational ski-jumping and bobsledding complex. Some 60 percent of the skiers and winter sports enthusiasts in Salt Lake City each year are from out of state, attracted by the surrounding mountains, which get an average of nearly 60 inches of dry powder each winter. The dry consistency is created as storms pass over the Great Salt Lake, which pulls moisture from the snow, providing especially good skiing.

*S*EE AND SKI: SALT LAKE AFFORDS the perfect home base for exploring the wonders of Utah. Located some 200 miles southeast of the city, Arches National Park dazzles visitors with its spectacular sandstone formations, created by centuries of wind and ice erosion (OPPOSITE). Closer to home, winter sports enthusiasts can swoosh along the powdery slopes at any of the area's nine world-class ski resorts.

Once one of the West's most popular tourist attractions, there's sustained interest in the old Great Salt Lake, keeping it a favorite haven for picnickers, swimmers, sailors, even commercial fishermen out to catch the brine shrimp that thrive there. Located some 16 miles west of downtown Salt Lake City, and measured at 92 miles long and 48 miles wide, the Great Salt Lake is the second-largest saltwater lake in the world.

Throughout the decades, tourists by the millions have thrown themselves in— and floated. The lake is so salty that you literally can't sink. Visitors and locals alike enjoy swimming and floating in the briny water, exploring the seven islands in the lake, or hiking and biking on the improved trails along the 100-mile shoreline. There is a new Saltair Resort and Pavilion (named after a popular Moorish-style resort originally built in 1893) that is the site for musical concerts and dances that take place in the huge ballroom.

Time has taken its toll, though, on the famous Bonneville Salt Flats, once a land-speed racing mecca. The dwindling salt supply (at the hands of industry) has so deteriorated the flats that the distance and speed today's jet-powered cars require is no longer possible, making any challenge to existing records or the speed of sound difficult. Efforts to restore the flats are under way, though, and it appears that the supersonic cars will continue to push the envelope here.

Just to the south of the Great Salt Lake lies Bingham Canyon, home to Kennecott Utah Copper, one of the world's largest open-pit copper mines and the source for 15 percent of all the copper consumed in the United States. Twice as deep as the world's tallest building and nearly two and a half miles wide, the Bingham Canyon Mine (as it's popularly known) is also something of a tourist draw. Digging at the mine commenced around the turn of the 20th century, and is still going strong, yielding copper, gold, and other minerals. ☞

PREHISTORIC LAKE BONNEVILLE once covered much of western Utah, as well as portions of Idaho and Nevada. Today, its lasting legacy is the Great Salt Lake.

WHILE TOURISTS FIND MUCH TO ENTICE THEM in the Salt Lake vicinity, there are also many qualities that appeal to those of us who live here. Things that make the place a great home. Things that we're happy to share with visitors and newcomers, but that we're also happy to have as our own.

For one thing, the area's an affordable place to live. A growing population and the availability of sufficient land are both factors in the construction boom taking place in the Salt Lake Valley. The real estate market has seen sizable increases, especially when it comes to new homes. Ownership of homes is common; in fact, two out of three residents along Wasatch Front communities own their own homes.

The cost of living in general is relatively low, especially for a community with as much to offer as Salt Lake City. It's possible to live here and raise a family more economically than in other communities.

As the urban heart of the state of Utah and the crossroads of the Intermountain West, Salt Lake City is well equipped with transportation facilities. Salt Lake City International Airport is closer to the heart of the city it serves than any other U.S. airport. From this facility, at least half of America's population can be reached within a two-and-a-half-hour flight aboard one of the eight major airlines and three regional carriers that serve the area. For those who prefer pavement and steering wheels, Interstate Highways 15 and 80 intersect in the Salt Lake Valley. ☛

© OWEN "R" BLACK

INCREDIBLE VISTAS NOTWITHSTAND-ing, Salt Lake is known for its family-oriented atmosphere, and at least two of the city's residents have developed a rather unique method of bridging the generation gap.

We like to dine out as well as folks in San Francisco or Boston, but without having to put up with crowds and high prices. There are 300 restaurants in Salt Lake City, 75 of which are located downtown within walking distance of Salt Palace Convention Center and the Delta Center Arena. That's in addition to numerous nightclubs.

Nightclubs? Well, it's not widely known, but yes, despite widespread fear and rumor among those visiting Salt Lake City, alcoholic beverages can be served with meals in restaurants and hotels. And mixed drinks alone are available in private clubs, where visitors are welcome to purchase temporary memberships

at a nominal fee. Liquor can also be purchased in state-run stores, including two excellent wine merchants located in the Salt Lake area.

We like our professional and college sports here. Salt Lake is home to four professional sports teams: the wildly popular Utah Jazz NBA basketball team and the WNBA's Utah Starzz; the Salt Lake Buzz Triple-A baseball club; and the Utah Grizzlies, members of the International Hockey League. Our University of Utah and Brigham Young University in Provo offer sports fans plenty of thrills with nationally ranked teams in practically every major collegiate sport. ☞

THE EXPANSE THAT IS SALT Lake City comes alive under the evening skies.

THE ARTS THRIVE IN SALT Lake City, from the world-renowned Utah Symphony to the area's three major dance companies—Ballet West, the Ririe-Woodbury Dance Company, and the Repertory Dance Theatre.

Our applause is not confined to athletic feats. Salt Lake is an excellent destination for patrons of the performing arts, as well, and we like the variety and diversity of artistic offerings here. Among them are Ballet West, the Utah Opera Company, the Ririe-Woodbury Dance Company, the Repertory Dance Theatre, the Utah Symphony, and numerous theater groups. Undoubtedly the best-known performing arts organization here is the world-renowned Mormon Tabernacle Choir, which draws crowds to rehearsals each Thursday evening and to performances on Sunday mornings. This majestic choir, formed shortly after the founding of the city, is composed entirely of volunteers, and is accompanied by an awe-inspiring 11,623-pipe organ.

We like the museums that dot the city, especially downtown, where 15 art galleries also make their home. The Museum of Natural History, the Utah State Historical Society, and the Utah Museum of the Fine Arts are favorites for residents and visitors alike. ☞

Like most other folks, we love to shop, and Salt Lake offers a broad array of opportunities to tune up our pocketbooks. Patrons can shop to their heart's content at two giant indoor malls, both within walking distance from the Salt Palace Convention Center and the Delta Center. The ZCMI Center Mall and Crossroads Plaza offer both major department stores and specialty shops. Trolley Square—the restored historic transportation hub from the early 1900s that's just a short shuttle ride from downtown Salt Lake City—boasts its own specialty stores and restaurants.

We like our access to the best health care facilities in the West. Salt Lake City is known as a healthy place to live for lots of reasons. For example, the predominant culture stresses clean and healthful living, the climate is dry and temperate, the air is pure, access to health care facilities is easy, and community health programs (such as forums sponsored by the Salt Lake Area Chamber of Commerce) are numerous and effective. As a result, the cost of health care is some 26 percent lower than the national average. Major health care facilities include the University of Utah's Hospital and School of Medicine, and Primary Children's Medical Center (which has been singled out as one of the top 10 children's hospitals in the country). ☞

TWO OF SALT LAKE'S BETTER-known occupants are the Zion Cooperative Mercantile Institution (ZCMI), founded by Brigham Young to facilitate trade in the early days of the colony, and Primary Children's Hospital, located near the University of Utah campus.

*T*HIS IS THE RIGHT PLACE." BRIGHAM YOUNG'S prophetic statement turns out to be just as solid and just as far-sighted today as it was more than a century and a half ago. ◻ As 2002 nears, long-held promises are turning into reality: a newly remodeled stadium for opening and closing Olympic ceremonies, a new hockey arena, new downhill ski slopes, and a new Winter Sports Park, complete with ski-jumping hills and a bobsled/luge track. All of these facilities are located within minutes of the metropolitan area, and all are waiting to welcome the world to the area we consider to be so special.

Like the early settlers who followed Brigham Young in search of paradise, today's newcomers and visitors—the throngs who travel here each year, and the immense crowds who will come to partake of the Winter Olympics—will find Salt Lake City to be everything they dream it to be. There is, after all, a spirit of growth and enterprise, of spaciousness and freedom, and of the natural magnificence of this right place. ◻

*T*EMPLE SQUARE'S SEAGULL Monument does more than celebrate the Utah state bird. Legend has it that in the early days of the Mormon settlement, as a plague of crickets threatened to wipe out the first year's crop, thousands of seagulls swooped down to save the day. Since then, millions of modern-day settlers have come to the Salt Lake area, where the view from Ensign Peak reveals a city that has spread its own wings and taken flight (OPPOSITE).

EVEN UNDER AN EVENING SKY, the treasures of Utah are illuminated. At 45 feet high and 33 feet wide, Delicate Arch poses as the state's most recognizable feature (OPPOSITE). Back in the heart of the city lies an equally stunning, man-made attraction—the four-block Temple Square, headquarters for the Mormon Church. One of the square's more frequented public buildings is the North Visitor Center, known for its murals and 11-foot-tall replica of Bertel Thorvaldsen's *Christus* (TOP). Creating a visual impact of its own through its star and laser shows is the Hansen Planetarium, opened in 1965 (BOTTOM).

The valley that takes its name from the Great Salt Lake is witness to countless wonders, from salt-encrusted tumbleweed sculptures along the northern shoreline to the sweeping snows of Antelope Island State Park, where the elk, deer, and buffalo roam (PAGES 36 AND 37).

DINOSAURS OF EMERY COUNTY, UTAH   150

© FRANK JENSEN

Among its lesser known qualities, the Salt Lake area is fertile ground for dinosaur hunters. The Utah Museum of Natural History, located on the University of Utah campus (BOTTOM AND OPPOSITE), and Ogden's George S. Eccles Dinosaur Park (TOP) are two prime places for rediscovering the state's archaeological roots.

© TERRY NEWFARMER / UNIVERSITY OF UTAH

WHILE THE SALT LAKE-Egypt connection is a bit unclear, sphinxlike carvings stand guard at various points around the city, including the Masonic Temple, built in 1926 (OPPOSITE). More impressive in stature is outsider artist Thomas B. Childs' monumental likeness of Joseph Smith, founder and first prophet of the Mormon Church (TOP). From its perch in Gilgal Gardens—an eccentric blend of sculpture, landscaping, and theology—the stone carving has moved many to ponder.

Climb its pyramid of stairs and the Delta Center will lead you to the city's human sphinx, Karl "the Mailman" Malone, spiritual leader of the NBA Utah Jazz (BOTTOM). More recently, the center also became home to the WNBA's Utah Starzz, who captured the hearts of local basketball fans in their 1997 inaugural season.

LEGEND HAS IT THAT ON JULY 24, 1847, Brigham Young stopped the first wagon train bringing the Mormons west, looked down on the valley spread out below, and declared, "This is the right place." Now known as This Is the Place State Park, the 1,600-acre site is home to Old Deseret, a pioneer village that includes Young's farmhouse (OPPOSITE BOTTOM). Even under a blanket of snow, the historic park is the perfect spot for an old-fashioned Mormon wedding (TOP AND OPPOSITE TOP).

I N THE SHADOW OF THE WASATCH Mountains, the areas north and west of Utah's Great Salt Lake are some of the most sparsely populated in the state. And while the advent of modern energy has made its way even here, the occasional lilting windmill still rises as a reminder of earlier times.

Back in the city, historic homes are part and parcel of Salt Lake's urban landscape. Brigham Young's Beehive House, so named because of the decorative element on its highest point, represents the Mormon ideals of order, cooperation, and industriousness. Originally built in 1902 for mining magnate Thomas Kearns, the Kearns Mansion today is home to Utah's governor (PAGE 47).

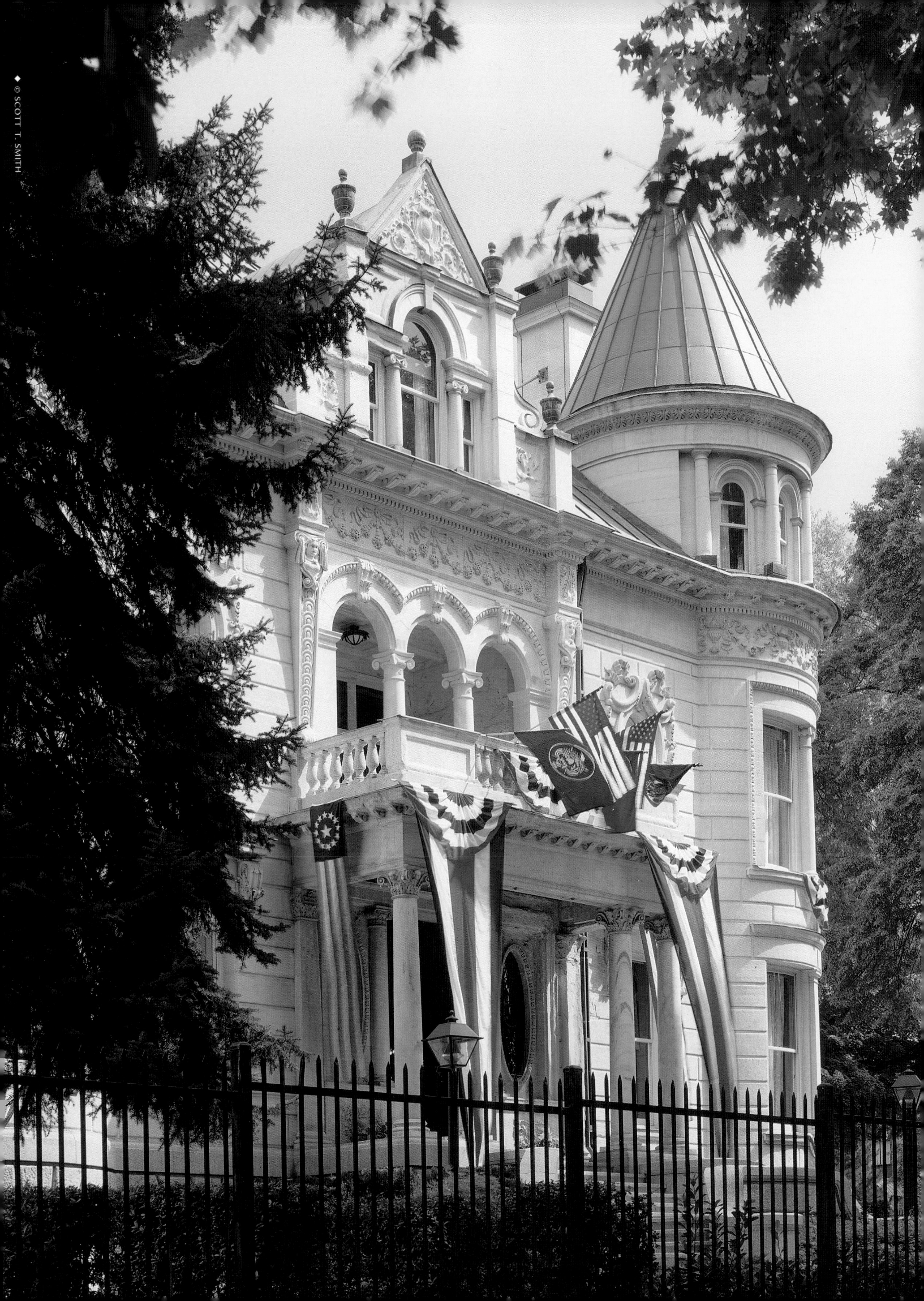

© SCOTT T. SMITH

DEVERAUX MANSION (TOP), completed in 1857, currently functions as a restaurant, but was once called home by former Mayor William Jennings. Built by one of Utah's first millionaires, railroad contractor Alfred McCune, the McCune Mansion (OPPOSITE) stands where Main Street begins its long climb to the State Capitol. And while it may never have housed the rich and famous, this small frame cottage in the Marmalade District (BOTTOM) typifies yet another version of the area's eclectic architecture.

ORT DOUGLAS, LOCATED JUST
east of the University of
Utah campus, was originally
built in 1862 to help keep the road
to California open during the Civil
War. The historic site has a somewhat
dubious past, thanks to its first com-
mander, Colonel Patrick Connor,
who felt that his job was to help
bring more Gentiles to Utah to dilute
the area's Mormon influence. On a
more welcoming note, plans are under
way to incorporate the fort as part of
the Olympic Village for the 2002
Winter Games.

Reminders of Utah's war veterans cast long shadows on the area's past. To walk through Salt Lake City Cemetery is to stroll through history, spelled out on the sandstone, granite, and marble headstones that honor the soldiers, as well as nine Mormon Church presidents, several notorious gunmen, and the inventor of the traffic light (OPPOSITE). Built to commemorate Mormon Church members who fought for the United States in the Mexican War of 1846, the bronze and granite Mormon Battalion Monument stands on the grounds of the State Capitol (LEFT).

ALTHOUGH IT CURRENTLY houses several upscale restaurants, the New York building started life as the New York Hotel, perhaps so named to evoke dreams of the exotic East Coast city in the minds of Salt Lake natives and weary travelers (OPPOSITE TOP). A meeting place for the Volunteer Firemen's Association since 1900, Ottinger Hall today is a museum of the early history of firefighting in Salt Lake City (LEFT). Portions of that history are no doubt shared with neighboring Park City, some 30 miles east of Salt Lake, where an 1898 fire destroyed much of downtown Main Street. In keeping with the old mining town's pioneer spirit, most of the buildings, including City Hall (OPPOSITE BOTTOM), were quickly rebuilt.

O NCE A PROVINCIAL CAPITAL built of brick, sandstone, and granite, Salt Lake is becoming a city of glass and steel monoliths, where the reflections of its older structures juxtapose the past and the present in a shifting panorama.

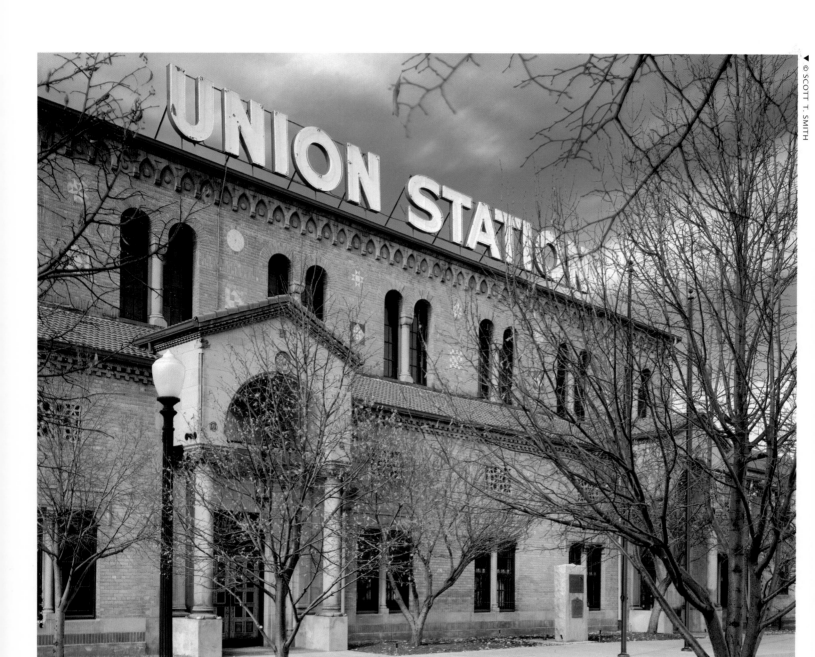

CONSTRUCTED IN 1924 AFTER the original depot was destroyed by fire, Ogden's Union Station, with its Spanish-influenced architectural style, now houses museums, an art gallery, a gift shop, and the Ogden/Weber Convention and Visitors Bureau (OPPOSITE). Parisian in concept, if not in execution, Salt Lake's Union Pacific Depot, completed in 1909, raises its mansard roof above the city's west side. The building's fate now lies in the hands of the planners and developers who are reinventing this once-bustling area in time for the 2002 Olympics.

LOUD NOISE, INTRICATE MACHIN-
ery, the smell of coal and oil
and steam, the rapture of
long-distance travel—trains still fas-
cinate us. On quiet nights in Salt
Lake, it's possible to hear the engines
whistle and the freight cars shuffle as
they pass through on a long run to
Las Vegas or Los Angeles.

THE YEAR WAS 1931 WHEN Utahn Ab Jenkins drove his Mormon Meteor to unheard-of speeds just short of the Nevada border 100-odd miles from Salt Lake. Since then, the Bonneville Salt Flats have attracted speed enthusiasts and tourists alike, many of whom come just to witness a 44,000-acre stretch of land so flat you can actually see the curvature of the earth (OPPOSITE).

Before the automobile entered the scene, the area made history of another —albeit slower—kind in 1869, as two locomotives met at Promontory Summit to inaugurate the age of transcontinental railroad travel. A replica serves as a reminder of the historic event from its splendid isolation at the Golden Spike National Historic Site (ABOVE).

JUST AS TRAINS OPENED UP THE West for more rapid settlement, the automobile made possible the modern-day freedom of individual travel, giving rise to countless businesses that today stand only as a memorial to earlier times.

KNOWN LARGELY FOR ITS Mormon population, Salt Lake City is fast becoming an ethnically diverse community. The colorful dress and traditions of other cultures have been woven into the local fabric through events like Native American powwows (OPPO-SITE LEFT) and Croatian folk dances (OPPOSITE RIGHT). But whether wrapped in the hopeful gaze of a Somalian refugee (LEFT) or the festive polka sounds of an accordion player in Jordan Park's International Peace Gardens, the future holds great promise for the city's development.

IN SALT LAKE CITY, STARCHED shirts and business suits sometimes give way to more intriguing costumes. During the annual Fort Douglas Scottish Festival, a group of fiercely proud Scots pay tribute to their heritage (TOP AND OPPOSITE TOP). Perhaps less common but no less eye-catching are these exotic dancers, colorfully filling the stage with their Middle Eastern moves (BOTTOM AND OPPOSITE BOTTOM).

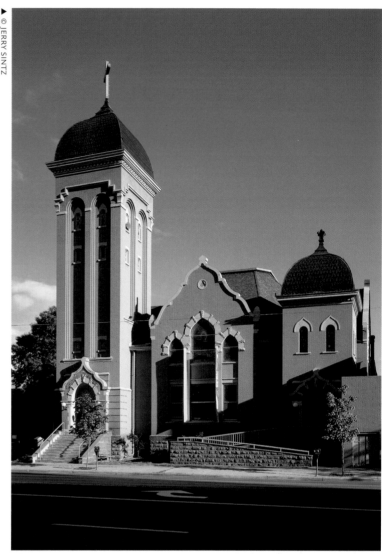

Diverse denominations flourish in Salt Lake City, where many of the area's faithful seek inspiration in their architecturally magnificent sanctuaries. The First Presbyterian Church, anchored by a square tower that could have graced a Norman castle (OPPOSITE); the Cathedral Church of Saint Mark, with its bell tower reminiscent of a California mission (LEFT); and the softly curved rooflines of the First United Methodist Church (RIGHT) all speak to the abundant influences that have made a mark on the city.

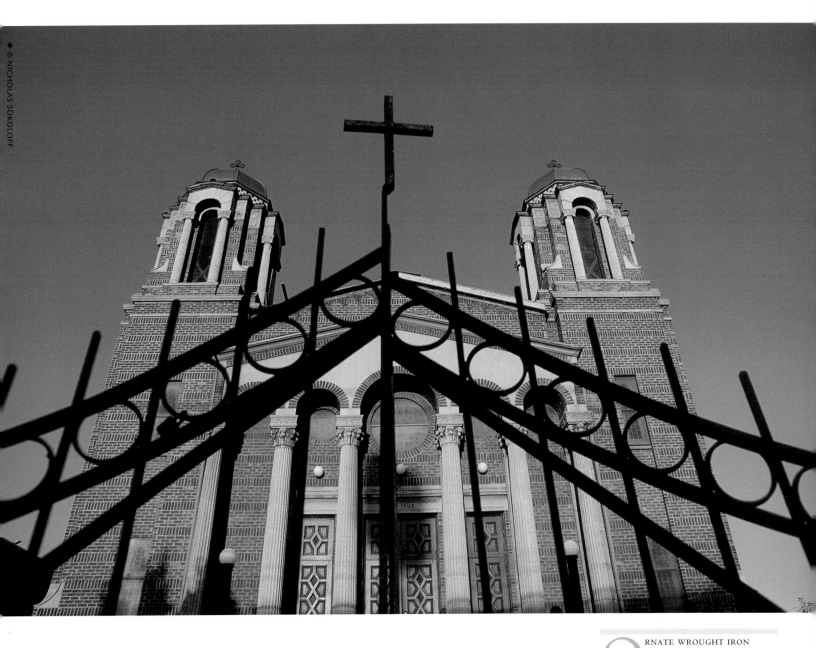

ORNATE WROUGHT IRON
guards the entrance to two
of Salt Lake City's other
religious landmarks, the Temple of
the Church of Jesus Christ of Latter-
day Saints (OPPOSITE) and the Holy
Trinity Greek Orthodox Church.

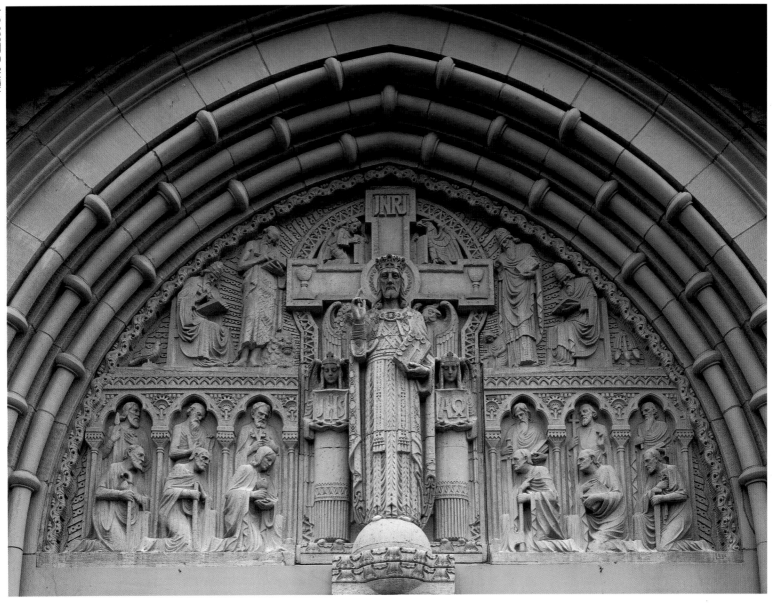

ELABORATE STONE DETAILS, including intricately carved iconography and grotesque gargoyles, mark the exterior of the Cathedral of the Madeleine, begun in 1899 and completed in 1926. The Roman Gothic structure is replete with stained glass and other fine artwork.

the Church will
Praise Thee O Lord
Ps. 21, 23
I have cried to Thee O Lord
me hearken to my voice
Ps. 140, 1
EXIT
EXIT
EXIT

THE OLD AND THE NEW SHARE the limelight in Salt Lake, where the circular stained-glass patterns in the historic Cathedral of the Madeleine are repeated in the skylight of the new Salt Palace Convention Center, completed in 1996.

© RICHARD CUMMINS / PHOTOPHILE

THE INTERIOR OF THE CATHE-dral of the Madeleine under-went a $10 million renovation in the early 1990s that included the addition of a 20-foot Gothic altar screen made of white oak. The repairs to the sanctuary gave new life to the delicate detail of its paintings and statuary after years of aging.

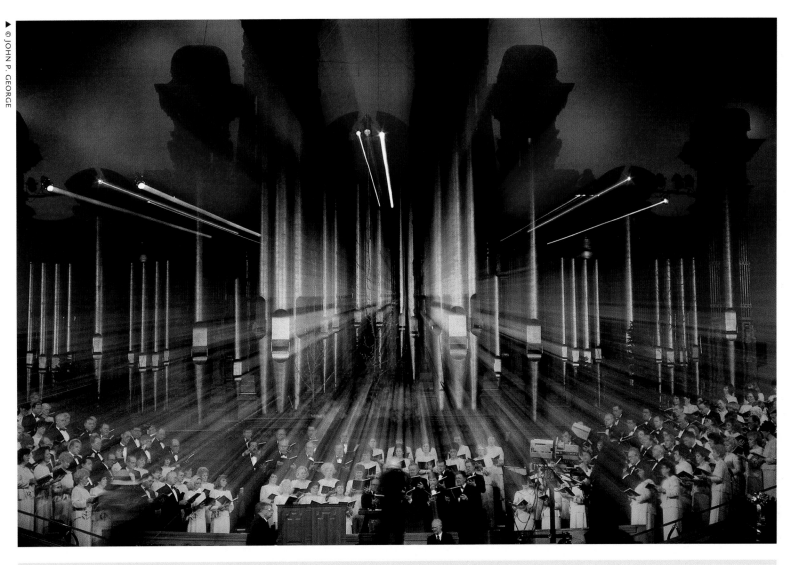

KNOWN THROUGHOUT THE world, the Mormon Tabernacle Choir is arguably Salt Lake City's most famous resident. Jerold Ottley conducts the 300-plus-member choir, whose Sunday morning broadcast, *Music and the Spoken Word,* is the longest continuously presented nationwide radio program in American history.

As organist for the Tabernacle, Clay Christiansen is likely the envy of musicians near and far who would welcome a chance just to sit behind the complex instrument he plays (PAGES 82 AND 83). Although the organ originally had 1,600 pipes, thanks to several improvements over the years, it now sports nearly 11,000, the smallest at three-eighths of an inch long and the largest at 32 feet.

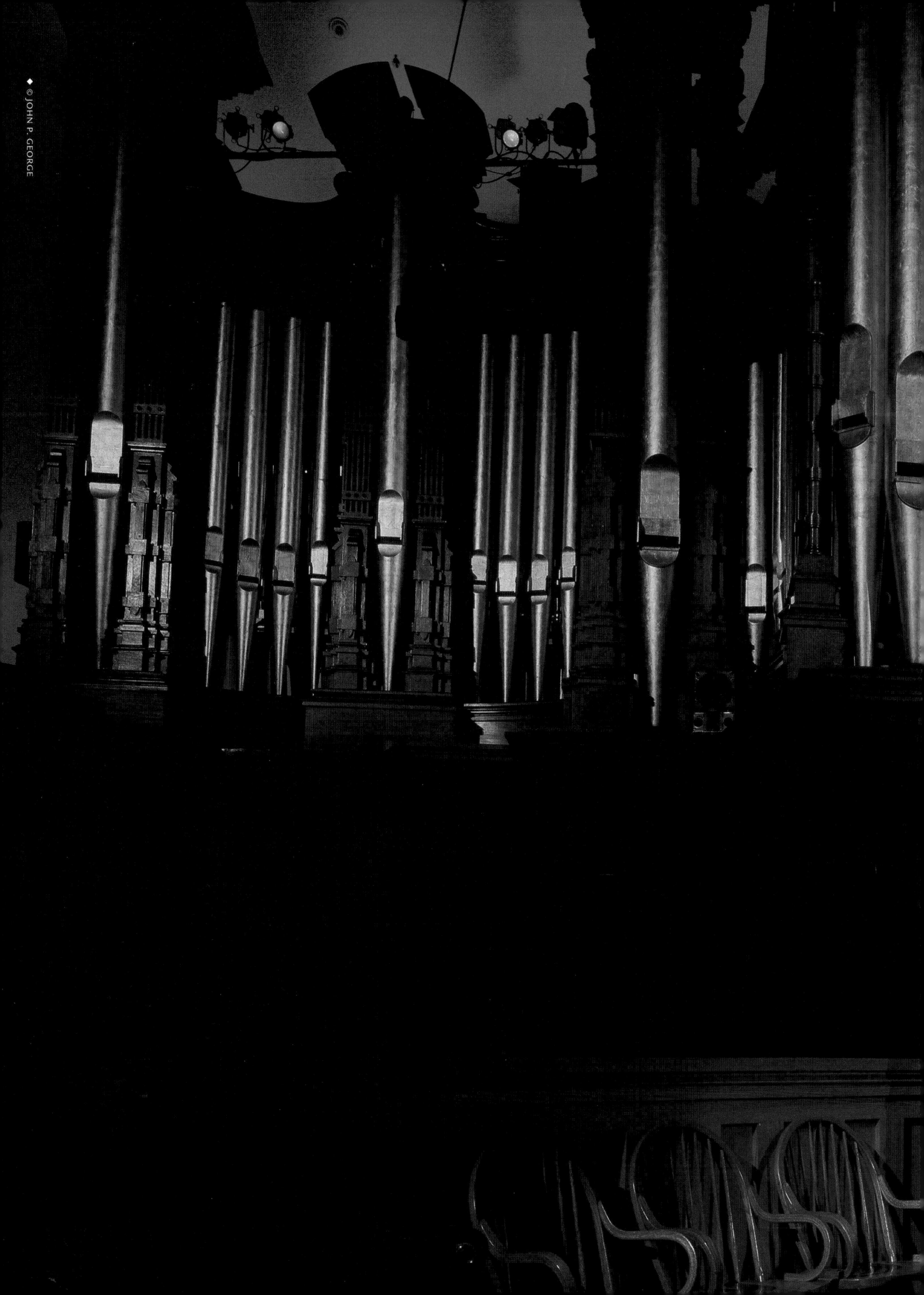

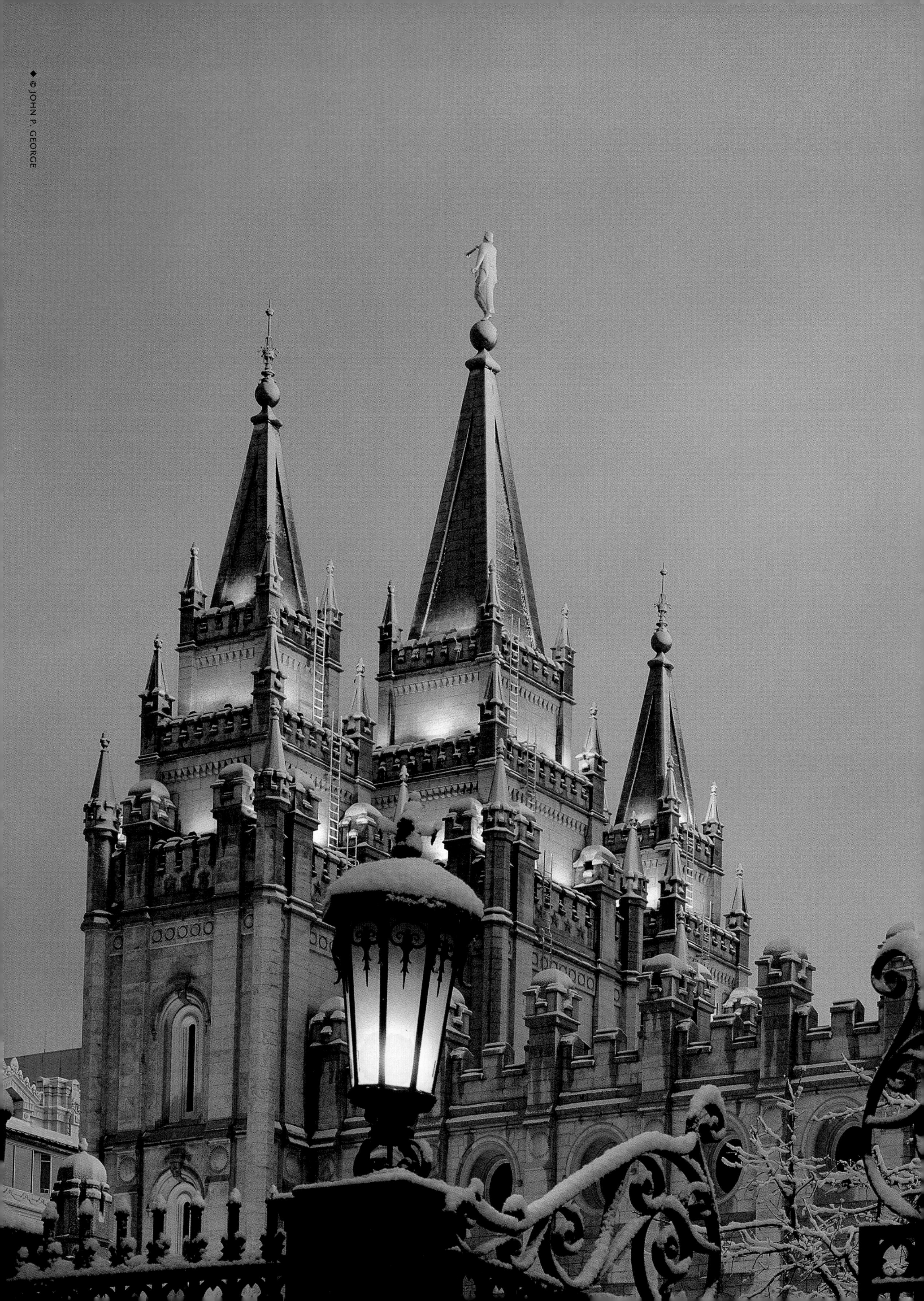

◆ © JOHN P. GEORGE

THE SIX SPIRES OF SALT LAKE'S magnificent Temple may be its signature feature, but the architectural gem offers much more (PAGES 84 AND 85). Built with granite quarried from Little Cottonwood Canyon, the Temple, which is open only to Mormons, took 40 years to complete.

A stunning example of Federal-Greek Revival architecture, Council Hall was erected downtown in 1866, but dismantled and moved in 1960 to its current spot on Capitol Hill (RIGHT). Once home to the Territorial Legislature and Salt Lake's city government, the hall now houses the Utah Travel Council and the Utah Tourism and Recreation Information Center.

IF THIS DOMED STRUCTURE LOOKS familiar, it's because the Utah State Capitol was designed to imitate its national counterpart in Washington, D.C. Constructed in 1915, the building is made of unpolished Utah granite and Georgia marble, and took three years to construct at a cost of nearly $3 million. With its stately dome covered in Utah copper, the capitol is considered one of the best examples of the Renaissance Revival style in the United States.

The interior of the Utah State Capitol includes a 165-foot-high rotunda decorated with WPA-era murals depicting key moments in Utah's early history. Above it all is a 6,000-pound chandelier, suspended on a 7,000-pound chain.

With the Wasatch Mountains as a backdrop, Salt Lake's grand City and County Building could easily be mistaken for a palace. Instead, the immense and elegant structure in Washington Square is home to several of the city's government offices and served as the capitol for the first 19 years of Utah's statehood.

ACK IN 1896, WHEN SHEER EFFI-
ciency was not as important
a consideration as it is today,
the City and County Building was
designed with high ceilings, ornate
tiled floors, and ornamental railings.
In 1989, seismic improvements were
made to the structure, resulting in a
new, rubberized foundation to safeguard the historic landmark during
earthquakes.

THE ZCMI CENTER MALL HAS its roots in Zion's Cooperative Mercantile Institution, a commercial enterprise founded by the Mormon Church in 1869 that lays claim to being the first-ever department store. After moving to its current location on Main Street, the mall became one of the first in town to get electricity—no doubt a big lure to shoppers—and later topped that feat by installing hydraulic elevators. Today's consumers are drawn by the variety of goods and services available in the center.

PPORTUNITIES ABOUND FOR higher education in the Salt Lake area. The John Park Building on the University of Utah campus honors the man who introduced the humanities and sciences to this one-time commercial academy (RIGHT). Founded in 1875, Westminster College is a prestigious, liberal arts school whose ornate architecture is evident in the turn-of-the-century Converse Hall (OPPOSITE BOTTOM). Some 50 miles down the valley in Provo, Brigham Young University is as well known for its role as the official educational institution of the Mormon Church as it is for its championship football team (OPPOSITE TOP).

WELCOMING THE WORLD

STATUARY IN AND AROUND Temple Square is further reflection of the city's deep Mormon roots. The lion, like the industrious bee, is a popular Mormon icon and was selected by architects to guard the former Hotel Utah (ABOVE). Known today as the Joseph Smith Memorial Building, the once world-famous luxury hotel on South Temple now houses part of the church's genealogical research program, as well as a rooftop restaurant with wonderful views of the city and the surrounding mountains. At the nearby Temple Visitor Center, the sturdy and stalwart bull—a reminder of the area's pioneering spirit—watches over a replica of a baptismal font (OPPOSITE).

W HAT CITY WOULD BE COMplete without a zoo? Located at the mouth of Emigration Canyon, Salt Lake's Hogle Zoo is home to a vast array of exotic animals. The facility's giraffe house even offers the luxury of a balcony so visitors can look the long-necked beauties right in the eye.

Second only to its religious heritage is the beauty of Salt Lake's natural surroundings. Outdoor enthusiasts and nature lovers revel in the area's wildlife, which includes, among other creatures, white pelicans (OPPOSITE TOP), the snowy egret (OPPOSITE BOTTOM), and the great blue heron (LEFT).

Whether man or fowl, local attractions know how to draw a crowd. It's always a feeding frenzy at the Tracy Aviary in Liberty Park, a veri- table bird paradise that lays claim to being the oldest public aviary in the United States. At the Sundance Film Festival, held each January in nearby Park City, food may be an element of the event, but it's the slate of re- nowned independent films that brings this flock together.

For a free movie about the history of the Mormon Church, the Joseph Smith Memorial Building is the destination of choice (OPPOSITE). If live perfor-mances are more your cup of tea, the fully renovated Capitol Theatre will fit the playbill (ABOVE). Built in 1925 and originally known as the Orpheum, the theater is home to touring Broadway shows as well as the Utah Opera Company, Ballet West, and the Ririe-Woodbury Dance Company.

Under the watchful eye of owner Art Proctor (OPPOSITE), the Avalon shows only classics and G- or PG-rated films. One of the few remaining independent movie houses in the country, the theater is keeping up with the times by also renting videos and camera equipment.

ARTISTIC INDEPENDENCE IS JUST a way of life in Utah. Despite the incursion of the usual chain bookstores, small independent booksellers still flourish. Among Salt Lake City's contributions to the genre are Patrick DeFreitas and his Walking Owl Books near the University of Utah (OPPOSITE) and Sam Weller's Zion Bookstore, where the owner dons white gloves to handle his rare books and manuscripts (LEFT).

WHETHER IT INVOLVES THE morning paper in Park City (OPPOSITE) or a good book at Cup of Joe in downtown Salt Lake (LEFT), coffee drinking and its attendant pleasures—reading, dreaming, people watching—are alive and well in Utah.

Cuisine Salt Lake style is a treat for the taste buds. Pierpont Cantina (TOP), featuring a festive Mexican setting and food to match, and Baci Trattoria (BOTTOM), with its Northern Italian fare, are just two of the city's downtown eateries. For more down-to-earth culinary delights, try Ruth's Diner (OPPOSITE). Opened in 1931 in a surplus city trolley car, Ruth's was hauled several miles up Emigration Canyon in 1949 and remoored beside the road. Although the current owners have expanded the restaurant, the original front dining section remains intact.

OTHING BEATS A SAINT Patrick's Day parade for a convenient excuse to gather in green and commune with the neighbors.

OSING FOR THE CROWDS AT A
Main Street shop is all in
a day's work for this live man-
nequin (LEFT), but it's not so easy for
a group of aspiring entertainers as
they anxiously await the judges' decision at the Utah State Fair Talent
Pageant (OPPOSITE).

THE WORK ETHIC RUNS DEEP IN Salt Lake City as seen in these portraits of area workmen by photographer Barbara Richards, and in a multicolored mural on a building in the Art Space community (PAGES 126 AND 127).

O NCE THE DOORS ARE OPENED, the hoofs and feathers are sure to fly. But for now, a certain calmness belies the untapped energy behind the scenes at the Utah State Fair, where locals return to their agrarian roots each September.

THE TRADITIONAL 10-GALLON hat still makes a fashion statement in modern-day Utah, whether worn by serious farmers and cowboys or by effete Easterners trying to look like the locals.

C ALF-ROPING AND OTHER TRADI-
tional rodeo contests are all
part of Utah's annual Days
of '47 celebration, commemorating
the entry of the Mormons into the
Salt Lake Valley (PAGES 132 AND 133).

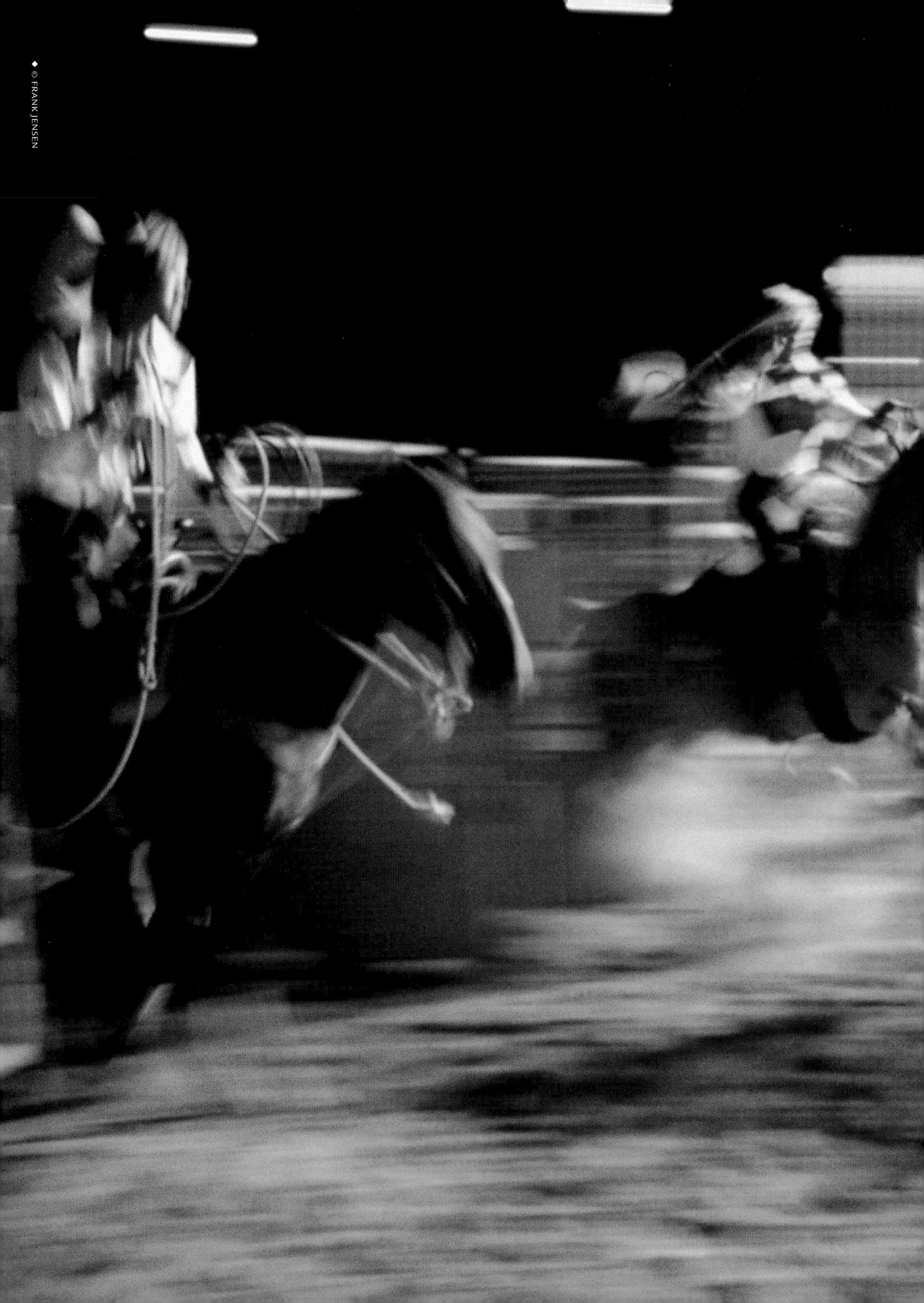

© FRANK JENSEN

THERE'S PLENTY OF ACTION FOR the younger set in Salt Lake, whether it's the gentle thrill of a kid-sized ride at the Utah State Fair (ABOVE) or a memorable turn on the ever popular merry-go-round at Liberty Park (OPPOSITE).

JUST NORTH OF THE CITY IN
Farmington, the magnificent
sunset that descends on the Great
Salt Lake in the distance meets its
man-made match in the Ferris wheel
at Lagoon Amusement Park (PAGES
136 AND 137).

Get your motor runnin'. . . Bikers everywhere live to ride, and in Utah, they enjoy the added bonus of wide-open spaces and incredible scenery.

But you don't need gasoline power to take in the sights (PAGES 140 AND 141). Bicycle racing has become a popular sport in this area known for its healthy, clean lifestyle.

WHETHER AMATEUR OR PROfessional, boxing enjoys a considerable following in the area. Venues such as the Salt Lake Boxing Center (RIGHT) and the Sorenson Multicultural Center (OPPOSITE BOTTOM), along with events like this tough man contest at the Utah State Fairpark, help fuel local enthusiasm for the sport (OPPOSITE TOP).

SALT LAKE CITY IS A SPORTING town, with four professional franchises and innumerable amateur leagues. Baseball fans at Franklin Quest Field are always ready to root for the Class AAA Salt Lake Buzz (ABOVE). No less loyal are those who flock to the area's softball games to cheer on the teams that play for the love of the sport (OPPOSITE).

THEY GROW 'EM TALL HERE IN Salt Lake, where a professional contract isn't required to perfect a classic slam dunk—as one high flier on a University of Utah playground proves (PAGES 146 AND 147).

S PURRED ON BY THEIR APPEARANCE in the 1998 NCAA Final Four, the University of Utah's Runnin' Utes are one of Salt Lake's main attractions (OPPOSITE). During the basketball drought of the summer months, the city turns to the WNBA and its Utah Starzz (ABOVE).

From THE VANTAGE POINT OF AN ultralight airplane powered by little more than a lawnmower engine (opposite) or a hang glider fueled by nothing but faith and gravity (ABOVE), soaring over the Salt Lake Valley is an intense experience.

SILHOUETTES—ONE IN BRONZE, one in flesh and bone—convey the essence of Utah. A monument to the past, located in This Is the Place State Park, pays tribute to the early Mormon settlers who established Salt Lake City at the mouth of Emigration Canyon (ABOVE). Today, the land they claimed offers unlimited natural wonders for the hardiest of outdoor enthusiasts (OPPOSITE).

THE GREAT SALT LAKE MAY BE vast, but it's also quite shallow (TOP). When John C. Fremont set out to explore the lake in 1843, his crew had to carry their rubber boat a long distance before they could even launch it. The lake's depth—or lack thereof—still requires a good bit of wading, leading to an equal amount of wear and tear on even the toughest equipment (BOTTOM).

THE ZEN-LIKE STILLNESS OF Green's Lake in Flaming Gorge's National Recreation Area provides an ideal setting for fly-fishing (TOP). The catch of the day doesn't come as easily, however, when Mother Nature's not on your side.

THE WASATCH RANGE IS THE site of outdoor activity year-round. On a sunny day, Emerald Lake provides an ideal spot for a little R and R atop Mount Timpanogos (ABOVE). If nonstop action is more your speed, there's always the Wasatch Front 100-mile Endurance Run, held each fall across mountain terrain that tests the mettle of even the most conditioned runner (OPPOSITE).

WHAT BETTER WAY TO TAKE in the awesome Utah panorama than from the basket of a hot-air balloon? America's Freedom Festival in Provo (LEFT) and the former Autumn Aloft Festival in Park City (OPPOSITE, PAGES 162 AND 163) draw hundreds of spectators and balloonists each year to admire and commandeer the colorful creations.

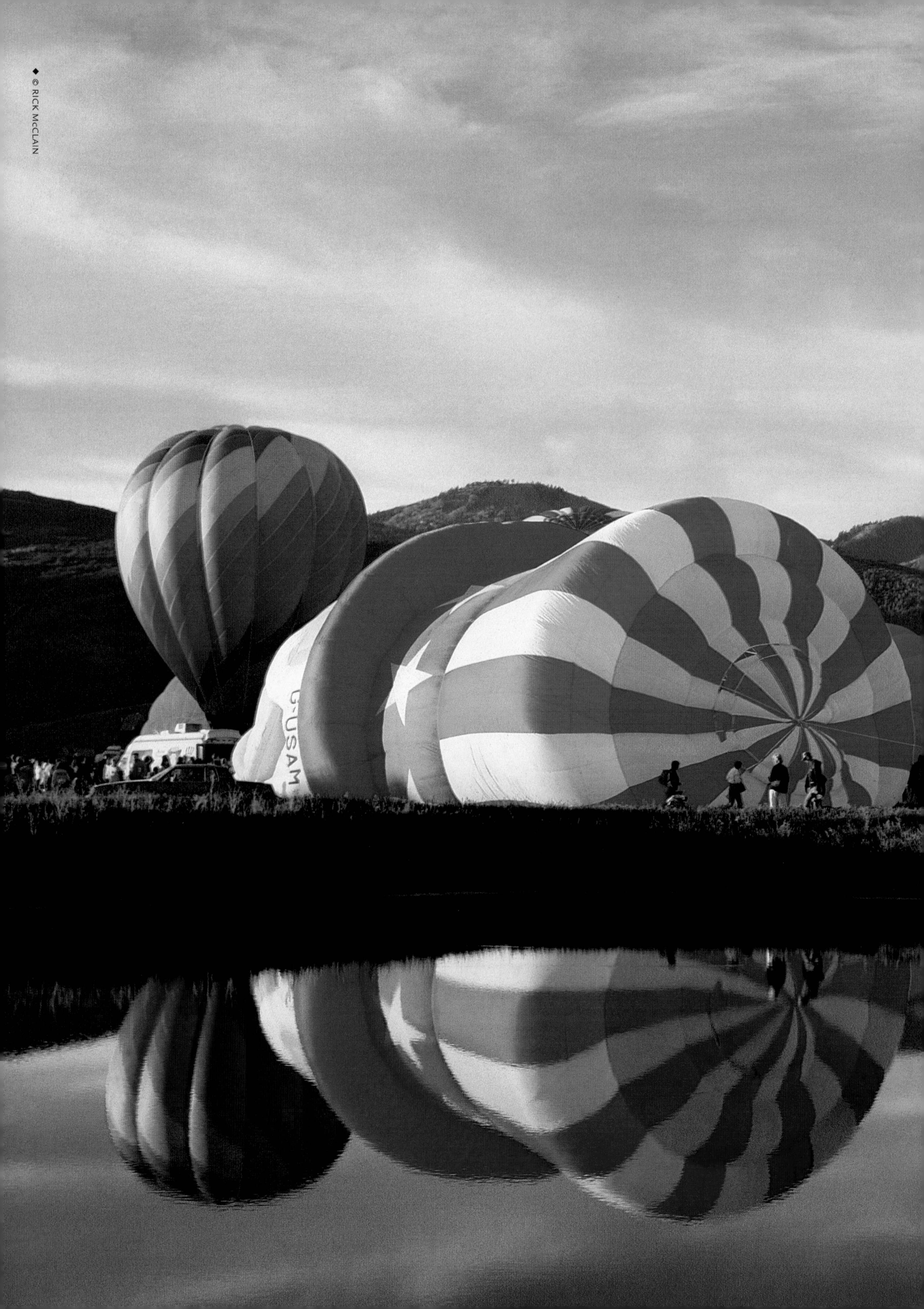
G-USAM

FANCY FOOTWORK IS REQUIRED on both the slopes and the streets of the Salt Lake area. Little Cottonwood Canyon is just one of many spots where skiers can enjoy their favorite wintertime sport (PAGES 164 AND 165, TOP). For those who prefer pavement to powder, a street race in the city's Liberty Park presents an ideal occasion (PAGES 164 AND 165, BOTTOM).

S WIMMING IN THE GREAT SALT Lake is something nearly every- body tries once, but it's the area's sailors who have the real fun.

Gliding along the briny water is truly delightful on a clear afternoon as the Oquirrh Mountains rise majestically in the background.

LEGEND HAS IT THAT A GIANT whirlpool in the middle of the Great Salt Lake once sucked unwary sailors to their doom. Today's boaters contend with less mysterious hazards, although the lake's average depth of 15 feet can prove quite treacherous when the winds and waves begin to rise.

WHETHER MAN-MADE OR natural, the sites around Salt Lake are often awe inspiring as they reflect the diverse elements that lie at the city's core— the icicles of its infamous, cold winters; the Temple spires of its religious foundation; and the sheer beauty of its lakes and mountains.

F OR ALL OF ITS NATURAL SPLEN-
dor, Salt Lake is still a city of
complex people leading active
lives (PAGES 172-173)

As downtown Main Street gives way to an early evening sky, another day of business as usual reaches its end (OPPOSITE). A few blocks west, a varied group of artists and businesses call the city's Art Space community home (LEFT). After years of decline, the area is making a comeback today thanks to the efforts of its dedicated occupants.

A LTHOUGH HORTICULTURISTS can find much to observe and admire in Utah (PAGES 178 AND 179), they probably won't be fooled by artist Dean Petaja's rusted-steel sunflower (OPPOSITE), especially with the real thing popping up all around (ABOVE).

FOR THOSE SEEKING RESPITE FROM a hectic day, havens abound in and around Salt Lake. Along the banks of the Jordan River, the 16-acre International Peace Gardens, begun in 1939 and dedicated in 1947, have expanded considerably over the years and are today maintained by the city (ABOVE). As part of the University of Utah's museum system, Red Butte Garden and Arboretum features 20 acres of gardens, four miles of trails, and 200 acres of undeveloped wilderness (OPPOSITE).

THE SCENIC JORDAN RIVER, namesake of the biblical body of water in the Holy Land, meanders along a north-south route through the city, connecting freshwater Utah Lake with the Great Salt Lake.

I F WINDMILLS ARE A STAPLE OF THE rural Western landscape, the city equivalent is the water tower. Modern systems may have rendered them obsolete, but these aging giants rise in silhouette against the Utah sky, a reminder of the still-precious commodity they once supplied across the great American desert.

NUMEROUS INDUSTRIES CALL the Salt Lake Valley home, but only Lehi Roller Mills can lay claim to one degree of Kevin Bacon. The local landmark south of the city was featured prominently in the 1984 movie *Footloose*, in which Bacon starred.

LESS FAMOUS, BUT NO LESS VITAL to the area's economy, a gasoline refinery north of Salt Lake stands tall and proud against the night sky.

Kennecott's Bingham Canyon Mine carves a gargantuan hole into the Oquirrh Mountains. As the world's largest open-pit copper mine, the site also functions as an area tourist attraction, with a visitors center and an observation deck.

UTAH'S MOUNT OLYMPUS, named for the home of the gods in Greek mythology, rears its twin peaks above the city, trailing storm clouds in a spectacular winter display.

T HE ARCHITECTURAL PEAKS AND valleys that form the heart of downtown Salt Lake range from the modern, glass facade of the Federal Building (OPPOSITE) to the delicate roofline ornamentation of one of the city's older structures.

T HE FALLING AUTUMN LEAVES reveal an otherwise secluded childhood getaway—a quiet place where worries are few and young imaginations run wild (OPPO- SITE). Adults find their own inspira- tion for fantasy, clinging to reminders of days gone by when technology was simpler and the Edsel was hot (ABOVE).

No Parking! Faded or not, the warnings come in all shapes and sizes—unless you're headed for Promised Valley Playhouse, where the cars are always welcome (OPPOSITE TOP).

THE EVAPORATION PONDS ON the shores of the Great Salt Lake become startlingly beautiful works of art in photographer Fred Wright's aerial abstracts (PAGES 198 AND 199).

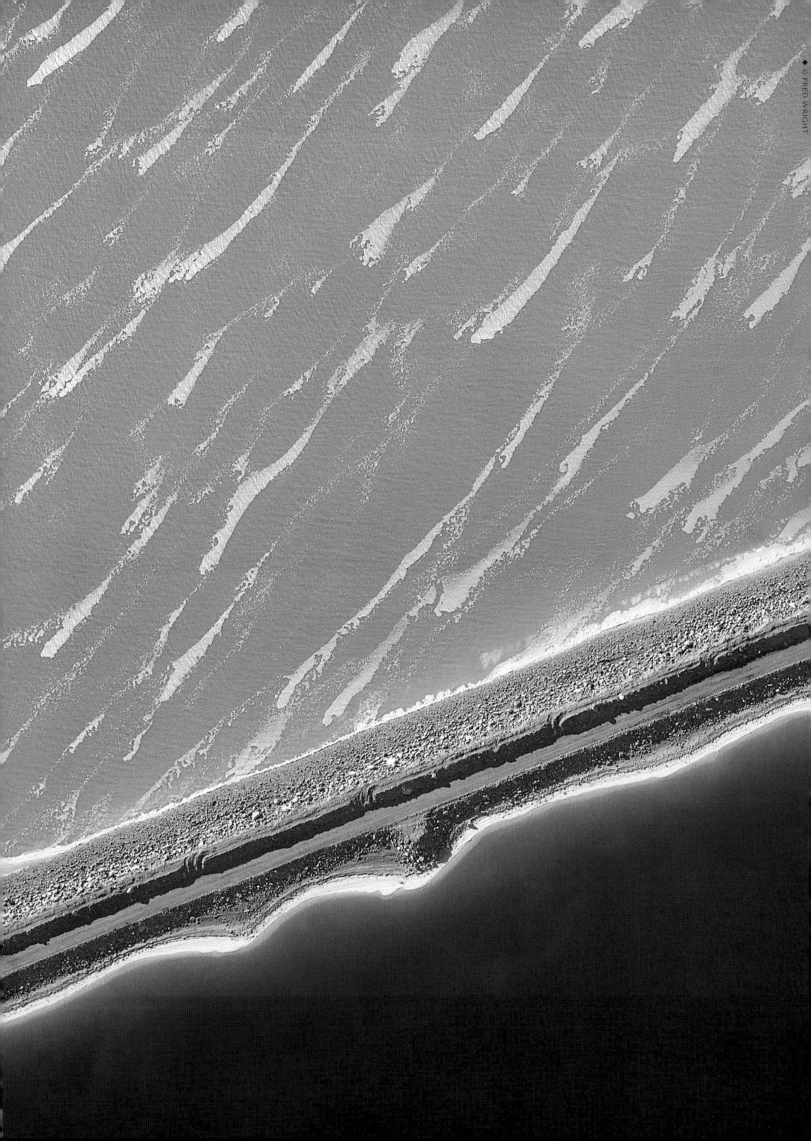

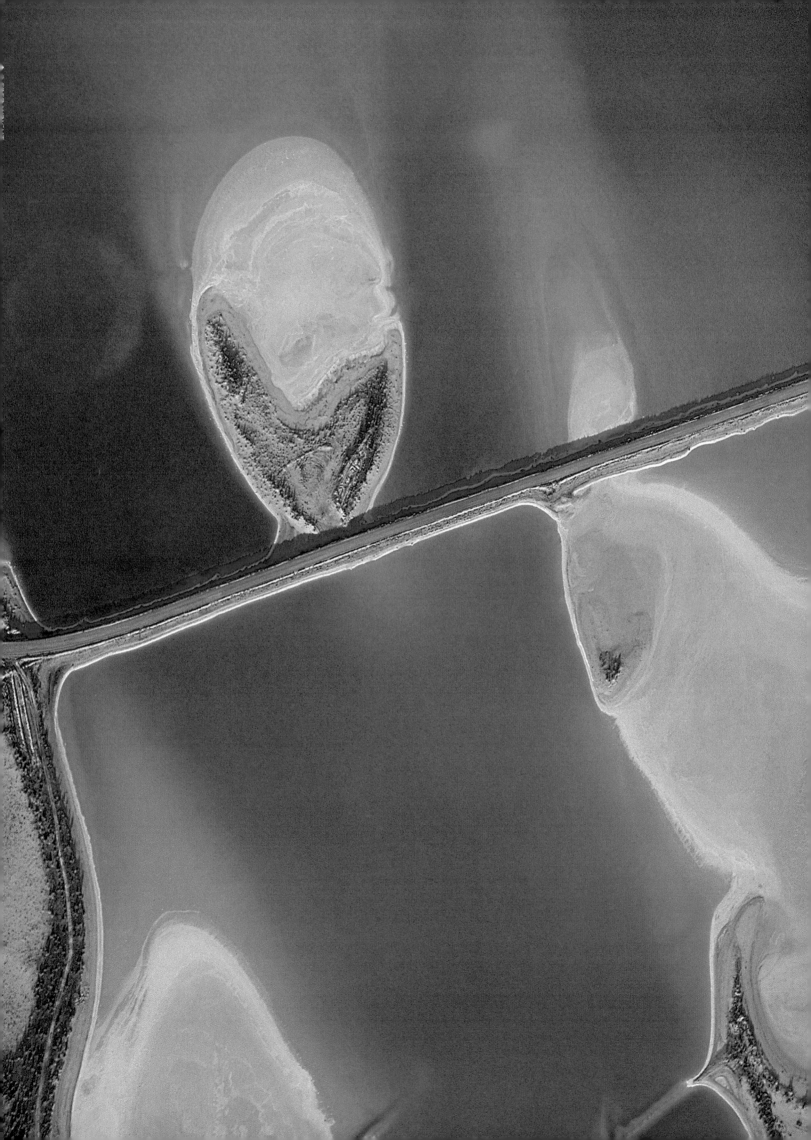

Native American petro- glyphs, on display at the Utah Museum of Natural History, depict a time in the state's history that predates the arrival of Europeans. Descendants of the area's prehistoric Native Americans include the Shoshone, Ute, Gosiute, and Paiute tribes.

THROUGHOUT THE AGES, GREAT art has taken inspiration from the human form. Frozen in time, a sculpture strikes an intriguing pose at the University of Utah (TOP), while the school's Department of Modern Dance offers a live version of its own (OPPOSITE TOP). Under the direction of faculty members Shirley Ririe and Joan Woodbury, the unusual antics of the Ririe-Woodbury Dance Company have been turning heads as a professional troupe since 1964 (BOTTOM AND OPPOSITE BOTTOM).

THE UTAH OPERA IS ONE OF Salt Lake City's most important cultural resources, presenting performances of such well-known pieces as *The Magic Flute* (ABOVE) and *Carmen* (OPPOSITE).

EVEN WITH ITS PERCH ON THE desert's edge, Salt Lake City receives some 59 inches of snow every winter. Offering a chilly serenity just before dawn, a fresh coat of white quickly gives way to the patterns of daily life.

Amid the area's many architectural gems, the new Salt Palace Convention Center stands out along the downtown skyline (OPPOSITE). Highlighted by a structurally complex tower, the center's facade is accented by windmill sculptures that rise above the nearby fountain. During the yuletide season, the tower provides a perfect spot for a giant Christmas tree, while Temple Square makes a strong showing of its own in the holiday decorating frenzy (LEFT).

THE BLUR OF LIGHTS IN MOTION signals activity along the streets of Provo, located some 50 miles south of Salt Lake, and home to Brigham Young University (ABOVE). Back in the city, things are always hoppin' at Trolley Square Mall, which makes its home inside the old City Trolley Barns, where streetcars once were housed and repaired prior to World War II (OPPOSITE).

FROM THE STATELY SPIRES OF the Temple (OPPOSITE) to the intimacy of the city's neighborhoods—including aptly named Christmas Street—Salt Lake comes to life for the holidays.

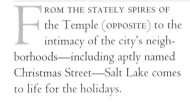

CRUISING DOWN THE CITY streets—whether in classic or contemporary fashion— remains a popular teenage pastime in Salt Lake, where the old and the new blend effortlessly as this community of tradition looks forward to welcoming the world.

STATE OF UTAH

Profiles in Excellence

A LOOK AT THE CORPORATIONS, BUSINESSES, PROFESSIONAL GROUPS, AND COMMUNITY SERVICE ORGANIZATIONS THAT HAVE MADE THIS BOOK POSSIBLE. THEIR STORIES—OFFERING AN INFORMAL CHRONICLE OF THE LOCAL BUSINESS COMMUNITY—ARE ARRANGED ACCORDING TO THE DATE THEY WERE ESTABLISHED IN SALT LAKE CITY.

Aero Tech Manufacturing, Inc. ▦ Affiliated Insurance Agency ▦ American Airlines ▦ American Express ▦ Ameritech Library Services ▦ Amoco Corporation ▦ Bank One Corporation ▦ Bettilyon Realty Company ▦ BNA Consulting Engineers II ▦ Bonneville International Corporation ▦ Catholic Diocese of Salt Lake City ▦ Colliers CRG (Consolidated Realty Group) ▦ Colvin Engineering Associates, Inc. ▦ Cordant Technologies ▦ Dames & Moore ▦ Doubletree Hotel ▦ EDO Corporation ▦ EDS ▦ The Episcopal Diocese of Utah ▦ Evans & Sutherland Computer Corporation ▦ Fairchild Semiconductor ▦ Fidelity Investments ▦ First Security Corporation ▦ First Utah Bank ▦ Fleming ▦ Harman Management Corporation ▦ Hogi Yogi Corporation ▦ Huntsman Corporation ▦ Intermountain Health Care ▦ L-3 Communications/Communications Systems-West ▦ Little America Hotel and Towers ▦ Macey's Inc. ▦ Mark Steel Corporation ▦ Martin Doors/Martin Freighting ▦ MegaDyne Medical Products, Inc. ▦ Merrill Lynch ▦ MHTN Architects ▦ Nightime Pediatrics Clinics, Inc. ▦ NPS Pharmaceuticals ▦ O.C. Tanner Company ▦ OEC Medical Systems, Inc. ▦ Olympus Tours & Travel ▦ Orbit Irrigation Products, Inc. ▦ Questar Corporation ▦ Reagan National Advertising, Inc. ▦ Residence Inn by Marriott-Trolley Square ▦ Salt Lake Area Chamber of Commerce ▦ Salt Lake City Corporation ▦ Salt Lake City Marriott ▦ Salt Lake Community College ▦ Salt Lake Convention & Visitors Bureau ▦ The Salt Lake Tribune ▦ Snow, Christensen & Martineau ▦ Summit Destinations ▦ TCI Cablevision of Utah, Inc. ▦ Utah Transit Authority ▦ Wasatch Advisors, Inc. ▦ Wasatch Crest Insurance Companies ▦ Workers Compensation Fund of Utah ▦

1851–1968

1851
Salt Lake City Corporation

1860
Martin Doors/Martin Freighting

1867
The Episcopal Diocese of Utah

1871
The Salt Lake Tribune

1878
Snow, Christensen & Martineau

1891
Catholic Diocese of Salt Lake City

1902
Salt Lake Area Chamber of Commerce

1908
Amoco Corporation

1909
Bettilyon Realty Company

1917
Workers Compensation Fund of Utah

1922
Bonneville International Corporation

1923
MHTN Architects

1927
O.C. Tanner Company

1928
First Security Corporation

1928
Questar Corporation

1946
OEC Medical Systems, Inc.

1947
Macey's Inc.

1948
Bank One Corporation

1948
Merrill Lynch

1948
Salt Lake Community College

1952
Harman Management Corporation

1953
Dames & Moore

1956
Cordant Technologies

1957
L-3 Communications/Communications
Systems-West

1958
EDO Corporation

1965
Reagan National Advertising, Inc.

1966
Little America Hotel and Towers

1967
Aero Tech Manufacturing, Inc.

1968
Evans & Sutherland Computer
Corporation

1968
Mark Steel Corporation

1968
TCI Cablevision of Utah, Inc.

Salt Lake City Corporation

ONE HUNDRED FIFTY YEARS AGO, A TOUGH BAND OF MORMON PIONEERS made its way into the valley of the Great Salt Lake, an empty, treeless semidesert ripe only with possibilities. Perhaps as a statement on the condition of the land, they named their encampment after the lake: Great Salt Lake City. ❖ Today, Salt Lake City has become the crossroads of the West, a bustling and burgeoning center of commerce and industry, a metropolis constantly rated by business magazines as one of the best places to locate, and a cosmopolitan community that is one of the fastest growing in the nation. Cranes seem as common in the downtown area as sunflowers in a cornfield.

New high-rise office buildings and hotels, a new state courthouse, new retail centers, and condo conversions are going up in seeming competition with one another. A new light-rail system is connecting downtown to the suburbs. An economy that varied from sleepy to moribund during the terrible eighties is alive, well, and sporting an attitude in the nineties.

But all this change notwithstanding, people in Salt Lake City cherish their roots and their traditions, Mormon and non-Mormon alike. And they can laugh together when a visitor asks, "Where can I see a Mormon?"—often asking it of a Mormon.

They can laugh together because the rich tradition of Salt Lake City is not solely a Mormon tradition. It is the tradition of the Greeks, Italians, Poles, Asians, Latinos, Native Americans, African-Americans—indeed, there was at least one African-American in Brigham Young's entourage on the Mormon trek west—and those of many other ethnic backgrounds whose forefathers were here before the turn of the century.

In 2002, Salt Lake City will host the Winter Olympics, and the world spotlight will focus on the city. Mayor Deedee Corradini sees the Olympics as pure opportunity: she plans to leverage the 2002 Games to assure Salt Lake City a bright future. "The Olympics can be the most important thing to happen to Salt Lake City in 150 years," she says.

Gateway Reclamation Project

Nothing defines the Salt Lake City of the late 1990s better than the Gateway reclamation project.

CLOCKWISE FROM TOP: THE SALT LAKE CITY TEMPLE OF THE CHURCH OF JESUS CHRIST OF LATTER-DAY SAINTS IS A DISTINCTIVE STRUCTURE ON THE SALT LAKE CITY SKYLINE.

TOURISTS BOARD A HANSOM CAB FOR A TOUR OF THE BUSY DOWNTOWN AREA.

SALT LAKE CITY HAS BECOME THE CROSSROADS OF THE WEST, A BUSTLING AND BURGEONING CENTER OF COMMERCE AND INDUSTRY, A METROPOLIS CONSTANTLY RATED BY BUSINESS MAGAZINES AS ONE OF THE BEST PLACES TO LOCATE, AND A COSMOPOLITAN COMMUNITY THAT IS ONE OF THE FASTEST GROWING IN THE NATION.

◄ UTAH TRAVEL COUNCIL, FRANK JENSEN

◄ ▲ UTAH TRAVEL COUNCIL, FRANK JENSEN

Just west of downtown Salt Lake City is an area of more than 700 acres of old railroad sidings, rundown warehouses, freeway overpasses, abandoned buildings, and withered fields. Through this blighted area runs I-15, above grade and connected to surface streets by a series of serpentine viaducts. For decades, they have separated east and west Salt Lake City like a Berlin Wall.

But today, the freeway is being rebuilt with shorter viaducts, the rails have begun to come up, property values in the Gateway area have shot up tenfold to downtown levels, and developers are lining up to become involved in the resurrection of Salt Lake City's west downtown area.

Thanks to an incredible number of pieces coming together, 20 miles of rail will be stripped from surface streets, with 66 grade cross-ings eliminated. Light will shine where it has not for 30 years, traffic will move freely, new businesses will be born, and new neighbor-hoods will emerge. It is the most exciting area in the city.

The world will be here in 2002, and Salt Lake City is happy to show off—no doubt about it. This place is urban and urbane. The population of the city itself is only 173,000, but the state capital is the geographic and cultural hub to a population of more than 1.5 million. The airport handled 21.3 million passengers last year, making it the 22nd busiest in the nation and the 36th busiest in the world. Many of those travelers were in hot pursuit of the "greatest snow on earth," found at seven ski re-sorts within an hour of the airport.

Come 2002, it will all be on display: the new roads, the light-rail, the sparkling Olympic facili-ties, the world-class snow, and the city at the foot of the towering Wasatch Mountains.

"This is our opportunity to tell the world what we are and who we are," says Corradini. "Salt Lake City has come a long way in 150 years, and we're just getting our second wind as we head into the 21st century." It is a given, she says, that the city will continue to grow. The challenge will be to direct and manage that growth so that what makes Salt Lake City unique does not get lost in the dust and commotion.

"We have something special here," says Corradini. "If we want to keep it, we have to remember the values and priorities that got us here. We can point to five-star hotels and fine restaurants and call that progress. But unless we can also point to safe streets, ad-equate housing, and a strong sense of community, we can't call it prosperity."

CLOCKWISE FROM TOP LEFT:
BUILT BETWEEN 1912 AND 1915, THE CAPITOL, CONSTRUCTED FROM UNPOL-ISHED UTAH GRANITE AND GEORGIA MARBLE, SITS ON A HILL IN A 40-ACRE PARK LANDSCAPED WITH TREES AND FLOWERS.

THE NBA'S UTAH JAZZ USUALLY PACKS THE HOUSE DURING GAMES AT THE DELTA CENTER.

VISITORS TO LIBERTY PARK ENJOY THE RELAXATION AS WELL AS THE RECRE-ATION THE PARK HAS TO OFFER.

MARTIN DOORS/MARTIN FREIGHTING IS A FAMILY-OWNED COMPANY with safety and quality in mind. Martin doors are professionally installed in more than 35 countries worldwide. ▪ In 1853, Robert Martin, at age 23, moved from Scotland to Utah. In 1860, he sold his butcher shop and provisions store located in the middle of 1st South and Main Street, Salt Lake City, and went into freighting. In its earliest beginnings, Martin Freighting serviced mining camps in Utah and Nevada. The company, now owned by Robert's grandson, Dave Martin, delivers Martin steel garage doors in the western United States.

In 1936, Leno Baird Martin, Dave Martin's brother, invented a one-piece overhead garage door. Health reasons caused Leno to sell the business in 1951 to Dave, who brought with him both an intellectual curiosity and a love of innovation that have marked the company's products ever since. In 1960, Martin Doors surpassed one-piece door designs with more fashionable aesthetics, and in 1976, it began roll-forming pre-painted galvanized steel into popular steel sectional garage doors.

Product development continued in the 1980s with the introduction of Martin's beautiful, raised panel steel doors, which have the look of wood and require low maintenance.

In the 1980s, Dave Martin began to appear on television. His famous "Stiff" commercial won several national advertising awards, including a Clio. It has also been broadcast worldwide on programs like *The World's Funniest Commercials* and Dick Clark's *TV's Bloopers & Practical Jokes*.

The popular commercial dramatically helped the company's profile along the Wasatch Front and beyond.

Martin Doors Now International

In 1987, Martin Doors began to distribute garage doors worldwide. As an example, Dave Martin points to a trip he took to Tel Aviv, Israel—location of Martin Doors' first international dealership. During his trip, Dave had the opportunity to visit a number of biblical sites, including Mt. Carmel, Jericho, Hebron, and Nazareth. Everywhere he went, he claims, there were Martin garage doors. "It got me right here," he says, patting his chest, "to see Martin garage doors in such a special historical location."

Now, Martin doors are being professionally installed by Martin dealers in more than 35 countries worldwide. Whether hanging on

IN 1987, MARTIN DOORS BEGAN TO DISTRIBUTE GARAGE DOORS WORLDWIDE.

SINCE FEBRUARY 17, 1996, ALL MANUFACTURED MARTIN DOORS UP TO NINE FEET HIGH COME EQUIPPED WITH NEW, SAFER HINGES AND FINGER SHIELD™, AN APPARATUS WHICH HELPS PREVENT USERS FROM SLIPPING THEIR FINGERS INTO THE DOOR SECTION JOINTS AS THE DOOR CLOSES.

beautiful, million-dollar homes in China or replacing a worn-out door on a home in the United States, Martin doors are quality garage doors, built to last a lifetime.

In 1994, Martin Doors received the President's "E" Award for excellence in exporting from Ron Brown, the late U.S. secretary of commerce. Based on a series of strict guidelines and sales-volume criteria, the "E" Award recognizes what thousands of consumers already know—Martin Doors is committed to continually improving the world's finest, safest doors.

But even with its worldwide success, Martin Doors remains very much a Utah-based enterprise, with manufacturing, main offices, and management decisions emanating from a 14-acre facility in South Salt Lake City.

THE FUTURE OF GARAGE DOORS

While its family-owned base has changed little in 10 years, the components that go into a Martin door continue to improve, setting a precedent that leads others to follow.

Safety and quality have always been at the top of the list for the Martin Doors team. Recently, federal government involvement has helped boost the urgency of Martin's safety improvement agenda. In 1995, the U.S. Consumer Product Safety Commission (CPSC) published data pointing out the risk of accidental injury associated with the largest moving item on the home—the garage door. Their report listed various injuries to children and adults, some being very serious. "I'm determined to improve the areas pointed out by the CPSC," affirmed Dave Martin in response to these reports.

Since February 17, 1996, all manufactured Martin doors up to nine feet high come equipped with new safer hinges and Finger Shield™, an apparatus which helps prevent users from slipping their fingers into the door section joints as the door closes.

SAFER FOR CHILDREN

Beginning May 1, 1998, Martin started equipping their doors with several new safety benefits. Roller shields, hemmed tracks, and track bracket shields help protect children from various roller/track related injuries. Many other safety features for both children and adults became standard at that time. The risk of injury increases with electrically operated doors. Dave Martin says, "Children are told never to play with an automatic door, but they do. Therefore, it is our responsibility to try to make the door safer."

Today, the Martin Doors team manufactures as many as 600 quality doors per day. Educational achievements include awards in manufacturing/resource/planning and just-in-time planning techniques. The company also will soon receive ISO certification.

Concludes Dave Martin, "I've been in the door business all my life, yet recently I've felt as though I'm just getting started. I don't think I'll want to retire for another 20 years. It's still exciting to me." And with his company's continued growth and commitment to quality, it is bound to be exciting for decades to come.

WHEN EPISCOPAL BISHOP DANIEL TUTTLE ARRIVED IN UTAH DURING the summer of 1867, his vast mission field included Idaho and Montana, as well as the entire state of Utah. And, according to one account, his first Salt Lake City service was held for a congregation of three women. ▨ Life in Utah has changed dramatically

since Tuttle and his fellow missionaries held services in a borrowed room, but many of Tuttle's early efforts to help establish a solid footing for the Episcopal Diocese of Utah are still evident today, according to Bishop Carolyn Tanner Irish. "Bishop Tuttle arrived in Salt Lake City when Protestant churches were in a missionary mode," she explains. "In that missionary spirit, we founded St. Mark's Hospital and the Cathedral Church

of St. Mark, which is the oldest church in Utah still in continuous use. Even though we're small in numbers, we've contributed a great deal to life in Utah."

COMMUNITY CONTRIBUTIONS

One of Tuttle's first acts upon arriving in Utah in the late 1860s was to pay a courtesy call on Mormon Church President Brigham Young and establish a

cordial relationship. Today, Utah's Episcopal Diocese is maintaining that tradition. "We've always been ecumenical, partly because of the places we are located in the world and partly because of the Catholic and Protestant traditions we draw on," says Irish. "It's sometimes said that we're not an either/or church, but a both/and church. It's important for us to have good relationships with all our neighbors, including the Latter-day Saints Church."

The diocese also contributes to the community by maintaining an outreach program, which includes a generous and wide-reaching grants program. In 1989, following the sale of St. Mark's Hospital, the diocese began offering grants to nonprofit social service agencies throughout Utah, specifically targeting domestic violence, indigent health care, youth programs, disabilities programs, and issues related to homelessness. In 1998, nearly $500,000 was distributed to approximately 68 agencies.

In the future, Irish predicts the Episcopal Church will work even more closely with members of Utah's other faiths to promote a spirit of cooperation. "On December 24, 1997, we began an organized Community of Churches in Utah to support each other and not compete with each other. I have high hopes we can sponsor services together during the Olympics and be involved in establishing other ecumenical activities," she says.

INTEGRATING RELIGION

As the Salt Lake City area continues to grow and take on an increasingly cosmopolitan cast, the Episcopal Church and its members recognize the need to embrace change. "For a lot of people, the church represents the unchangeable in their lives, but it's the nature of faith to stay in reality and adapt," Irish says.

CLOCKWISE FROM TOP LEFT: WHEN EPISCOPAL BISHOP DANIEL TUTTLE ARRIVED IN UTAH DURING THE SUMMER OF 1867, HIS VAST MISSION FIELD INCLUDED IDAHO AND MONTANA, AS WELL AS THE ENTIRE STATE OF UTAH. HIS MOTTO WAS, "WE HAVE A FAITH NOT AFRAID TO REASON AND REASON NOT ASHAMED TO ADORE."

THE CATHEDRAL CHURCH OF ST. MARK IN SALT LAKE CITY IS UTAH'S OLDEST CHURCH BUILDING IN CONTINUOUS USE.

A 1910 IMAGE OF ST. MARK'S HOSPITAL, UTAH'S FIRST HOSPITAL AND NURSING SCHOOL, APPEARS ON A POSTCARD.

JEFF SELLS

St. Mark's Hospital, Salt Lake City, Utah.

"Churches change as cultures change. In Bishop Tuttle's time, when people read the Bible, they thought they were reading literal history. But our understanding of reality has changed dramatically in the past 150 years with the arrival of Darwin, Marx, and Freud—people who changed the nature of reality. Today, we have to consider modern science, philosophy, and historiography."

Far from being threatened by today's expanded scientific understanding, Irish believes that people should embrace both the empirical and the spiritual in order to lead complete lives. "I sense incredible spiritual hunger in this culture that has taught us to value materialism, striving, and succeeding. More and more, I think people are looking for some kind of community, belief system, and way of life that liberates them from our cultural norms. I see religion as a force at the center of all a person's longing, yearnings, and understandings."

JOURNEY OF FAITH

Irish describes the Utah diocese's future direction as a journey of faith. "It's my nature to take not just the constructs of religion seri-

ously, but also the journey," she says. "I believe we can be discerning about change and move into it. I'm also tremendously excited about the possibilities in this diocese."

One thing that will never change is the diocese's active involvement in important local issues. "We feel it's vital for us to weigh in for struggles for justice and reconciliation in the larger culture," Irish explains. "For instance, nearly half of our grants in 1997 went to victims of violence across the state."

The Episcopal Church also works to protect the environment. "One of the ways we try to be active in the community of Utah is the protection of the environment," Irish says. "We are all creatures and we all benefit from clean air, soil, and water. I've participated in a number of panels exploring the connections between nature and religion. The areas of nature and the environment will always be part of what we serve."

As the number of churches grows with the state population, Utah's Episcopalians will continue to fill a need. "We're always looking for ways to be a greater presence in the communities than we are currently," Irish says. "We just called a priest to serve in Cedar City, and we're growing very rapidly in other parts of the state."

But more important than numbers is the good the church does and the role it fills in its members lives. "We have a very broad and inclusive philosophy," Irish says. "We tolerate ambiguity more than many traditions do. We don't sign people up and make them subscribe to one single philosophy." And with this philosophy, along with its years of service to the community, the Episcopal Church will continue to grow in Utah for years to come.

BUSATH PHOTOGRAPHY

*T*he *Salt Lake Tribune*, SALT LAKE CITY'S 127-YEAR-OLD NEWSPAPER, HAS not changed dramatically since the paper was purchased early in the century by politician/businessman Thomas Kearns. "Senator Kearns believed the paper's mission was to improve the social and economic situation of all Utahns," Dominic Welch, president and publisher of

The Tribune, says. "And we're sticking with that. We're a small company, but we're big in clout. Even in today's technological world, the newspaper writes the first draft of history every day. And that's a major responsibility for reporters and editors."

A HISTORY OF ENTERPRISE JOURNALISM

*T*he *Tribune* was founded in 1871 by a group of businessmen Welch describes as "dissident Mormons who disagreed with the church's economic and political positions." During its first year of existence, the paper was called *The Mormon Tribune*. A year later, the word "Mormon" was dropped and the paper became *The Salt Lake Daily Tribune and Utah Mining Gazette*. Soon after, the name was changed again to *The Salt Lake Tribune*.

In 1901, mining magnate and newly elected U.S. Senator Thomas Kearns and his business partner

David Keith bought the publication, but *The Tribune*'s financial struggles were far from over. According to one account, Kearns once confided to a friend, "It takes a great mine to run a newspaper."

In its earliest years, the paper was almost as well known for its antipolygamy stance and fiery, independent-minded editorials as for its reporting. Gradually, though, the paper toned down its rhetoric and began, in Welch's words, to "follow Thomas Kearns' interest in improving the lot of working Utahns." Soon, *The Tribune* began to grow in circulation and advertising revenues.

After Kearns' death in 1919, his family bought out the Keiths. Majority ownership of the paper remained in the Kearns family until 1997, when the paper was purchased by Tele-Communications, Inc., a cable television and multimedia operation. However, heirs to the senator hold an option to purchase *The Tribune*.

GROWING WITH THE COMMUNITY

*T*hroughout its history, *The Tribune* has been credited with shaping and developing the community it serves. John F.

Fitzpatrick, a former secretary to Kearns, assumed the role of publisher in 1924, and is credited for reconciling with former foes to enhance *The Tribune*'s increasingly prominent position in the community. "Next to the LDS [Latter-Day Saints] Church, *The Tribune* has had the greatest positive impact of any institution in the state since that time," Welch says. He believes Fitzpatrick "made *The Tribune* a newspaper as opposed to an advocacy publication," thereby laying a solid foundation that subsequent publishers John W. Gallivan (1960-1983), Jerry O'Brien (1983-1994), and Welch himself have followed.

In addition, *The Tribune* has attempted to cast light on community problems and seek solutions. "Since about 1970," Welch says, "our focus has been on social needs as opposed to, say, arts needs. Through our columns and fund-raising efforts, our goal has been to solve the problems of the people we consider most in need: the homeless, the poor, and minorities, for instance."

Although *The Tribune* has supported other institutions, such as the state's performing arts groups and nonprofit hospitals, Welch points out, "Our biggest contribution has been in our news pages. We try to help solve people's problems."

Tribune employees, too, are the beneficiaries of the company's generosity. "In addition to all the usual employee benefits, since 1977, employees have had a stock ownership plan," Welch says. "This was a family-held company, but the family thought employees should benefit from the company's success."

Despite the recent purchase of the paper by a large corporation, Welch is confident that its operations, autonomy, and editorial stances will remain unaffected. "We'll remain an independent voice," Welch says.

A Contract with Readers

With circulation figures of more than 130,000 for the daily editions and 160,000 on Sundays, *The Tribune* is far and away the leader in the Utah newspaper market. "We're the last of the mass media," Welch says. "As many people read the paper as watch all three local television news broadcasts."

But, Welch warns, the paper's continued viability is dependent on maintaining its bond with readers: "We have to be bright, informative, and hardworking. It is the quality of our product that will give us the trustworthiness to reach the public. Seven days a week, we present news and information and communicate to the community."

Part of maintaining this bond, Welch says, involves changing with advances in technology. "Newspapers will be around forever," he predicts. "The concept will be around forever. Newspapers themselves will change. Technology will have an impact on the advertising side and papers will get smaller, but the portability, the collectibility, the editing for accuracy and readability—all of that makes papers indispensable.

"There's an old saying: 'The only thing a dog doesn't bark at or sniff at is the newspaper on the porch,'" Welch says. "We've been around that long and we're going to be around a lot longer."

*A*LONG-STANDING MEMBER OF THE SALT LAKE CITY COMMUNITY, Snow, Christensen & Martineau traces its Utah roots back to 1878, when Samuel R. Thurman formed a partnership in Provo with George Sutherland, later a justice of the U.S. Supreme Court. Over the years, the firm has established itself as a cornerstone of

the state's legal community—a full-service professional law practice with a rich tradition of advocacy and commitment to the profession.

Historic is another way to describe Snow, Christensen & Martineau. Even the firm's headquarters hints at its stature. In 1981, its shareholders bought the Newhouse Building, which was constructed between 1908 and 1910. The Newhouse Building was one of Utah's first skyscrapers, a monument financed by mining magnate Samuel Newhouse, who hoped to build a western Wall Street on Exchange Place downtown. Listed on the state and national historic registers, the building's classical

design suits Snow, Christensen & Martineau's distinguished character.

In addition to Sutherland, the firm's list of outstanding alumni includes two state supreme court justices, a U.S. senator, a dean of the University of Utah law school, a U.S. attorney for the District of Utah who is now a U.S. district court judge, and two state court judges.

FOCUSED PRACTICE AREAS

*L*itigation has always been the cornerstone of the practice at Snow, Christensen & Martineau—in particular its representation

of the medical and insurance industries. The firm excels in liability law—including product, automobile, governmental, and toxic/hazardous waste matters, as well as medical, accounting, and engineering. In addition, the firm handles a variety of complex fraud, securities, antitrust, and intellectual property litigation. Its lawyers have extensive trial and appellate experience in state and federal courts.

In recent decades, Snow, Christensen & Martineau has broadened its scope to excel in corporate, business, commercial, and water law. Since the passage of the state's Governmental Immunities Act in 1965, the firm has been counsel to cities, counties, and statewide governmental agencies. Likewise, its real estate department has grown to keep pace with local development, which entails an expanded practice to take on issues surrounding natural resources, energy, and financing. The firm has also developed expertise in software and technology licensing.

SUPPORTING THE LEGAL PROFESSION

*S*now, Christensen & Martineau has made a concerted effort to invest in the legal profession. To that end, the firm takes great pride in supporting activities of the Utah State Bar. Three of its members have served as bar president. In addition, Snow, Christensen & Martineau was instrumental in founding and developing the nationally prominent Inns of the Courts program to train young lawyers.

The firm has been serving the business and litigation needs of the Intermountain West for more than a century. It will continue to develop its expertise to meet those needs well into the next century.

OVER THE YEARS, SNOW, CHRISTENSEN & MARTINEAU HAS ESTABLISHED ITSELF AS A CORNERSTONE OF THE STATE'S LEGAL COMMUNITY—A FULL-SERVICE PROFESSIONAL LAW PRACTICE WITH A RICH TRADITION OF ADVOCACY AND COMMITMENT TO THE PROFESSION (RIGHT).

IN 1981, THE FIRM'S SHAREHOLDERS BOUGHT THE NEWHOUSE BUILDING, WHICH WAS CONSTRUCTED BETWEEN 1908 AND 1910 AS ONE OF UTAH'S FIRST SKYSCRAPERS. LISTED ON THE STATE AND NATIONAL HISTORIC REGISTERS, THE BUILDING'S CLASSICAL DESIGN SUITS SNOW, CHRISTENSEN & MARTINEAU'S DISTINGUISHED CHARACTER (BELOW).

*A*S THE HEALTH CARE ECONOMY ENCOURAGES HOSPITALS TO CUT COSTS and shorten patient stays, minimally invasive surgery is naturally expanding and along with it the products of OEC Medical Systems. Real-time intraoperative imaging plays a vital role in minimally invasive surgery, helping surgeons visualize with fluoroscopy what

they would not otherwise be able to see. OEC is a world leader in the niche market for fluoroscopic surgical imaging systems. More surgeons use fluoroscopic imaging equipment from OEC, with its more than 7,500 C-arms and 900 urology table installations in some 54 countries, than from any other company.

Open procedures have given way to minimally invasive surgery, and the health and cost benefits are considerable. Orthopedic surgeons used to perform many open procedures that usually involved large incisions and usually longer surgical time. After the procedure, the surgeon would close the patient's wound and take him or her to X ray in another area of the hospital to verify the alignment. If the device was misaligned, the surgeon would reopen the incision and try again. Now, with OEC's intraoperative digital X-ray equipment, the surgeon can make a much smaller opening, perform the procedure, and verify the alignment or accuracy of the work during the surgery in real time on a video monitor. There is considerably less trauma to the patient, which results in less pain, faster recovery, and reduced costs for the hospital and the patient.

A HALF CENTURY OF LEADERSHIP

Since its founding as Orthopedic Equipment Company in 1946, OEC has developed into the U.S. market leader for surgical imaging, with more than 50 percent market share. The company installed its first mobile C-arm in an operating room in 1972. Since then, it has developed the broadest line of mobile X-ray products in the industry—ranging from its Mini C-arm for orthopedic extremity imaging to its full-size

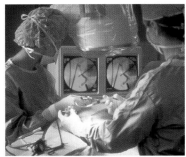

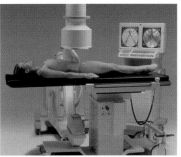

Series 9600 mobile C-arm, used in hospitals and surgery centers for everything from minimally invasive gall bladder removal to heart surgery.

Traded on the New York Stock Exchange under the trading symbol OXE, OEC has enjoyed a 104 percent increase in stock performance over the last two years. This success is the by-product of the company's strong operating performance. In 1997, OEC posted sales of $155 million and net income of $12.2 million. Although the company's international growth is a forward going, key factor, the bulk of these sales currently come from its U.S. market dominance. The increasing emphasis on managed care and health care cost containment will continue to move procedures in the direction of minimally invasive surgery, and

even out of the acute care hospital into outpatient surgery centers and physicians' offices. All of these trends continue to strengthen OEC's market in the United States.

OVERSEAS MARKET SHARE

OEC is also increasing its market share abroad. With a manufacturing facility in Germany, OEC also has its own distribution facilities in Switzerland, Germany, France, and Italy, and distributor relationships in Asia and Latin America. This international infrastructure positions OEC to leverage its U.S. leadership to the rest of the world, where the growth potential is considerable.

Strong market leadership, healthy industry trends, and a solid financial position show OEC poised for strong growth well into the next century.

CLOCKWISE FROM TOP:
SINCE ITS FOUNDING AS ORTHOPEDIC EQUIPMENT COMPANY IN 1946, OEC HAS DEVELOPED INTO THE U.S. MARKET LEADER FOR SURGICAL IMAGING, WITH MORE THAN 50 PERCENT MARKET SHARE.

OEC'S SERIES 9600 PRODUCT WITH A 12-INCH FIELD OF VIEW LEADS THE MARKET THROUGH IMPROVED TECHNOLOGY AND SUPERIOR IMAGING CAPABILITIES.

THIS LAPAROSCOPIC GALL BLADDER REMOVAL ILLUSTRATES HOW REAL-TIME IMAGING GUIDES SURGEONS TO IMPROVE OUTCOMES.

*T*N 1776, TWO FRANCISCAN FRIARS, FRANCISCO ATANAZIO DOMINGUEZ AND Silvestre Velez de Escalante, left Santa Fe in search of an overland route to the sea. The Dominguez-Escalante expedition was the first recorded crossing made by Europeans into what would become Utah, and the beginning of a long and distinguished Catholic presence. ▦ A procession

of missionaries, mountain men, hunters, and trappers extended the Catholic faith into mountains and deserts, etching the sign of the cross into the trail sides and red rock canyons to mark their passage. Even today, visitors to Fremont Island in the Great Salt Lake can brush their fingers along the outline of a cross etched in

stone in 1843 by Kit Carson, a Catholic frontiersman and Indian agent.

"In many aspects, we are still very much a missionary church," says Bishop George H. Niederauer, eighth bishop of the Catholic Diocese of Salt Lake City. "We are a growing, diverse, and vibrant community of believers."

Catholics are also a religious minority. In a state where the dominant religious majority constitutes two-thirds of the population, Roman Catholics are the second-largest denomination (close to 6 percent). "Yet," says Bishop Niederauer, "we are blessed with happy problems—growing pains."

When Lawrence Scanlan, who would become the diocese's first bishop, arrived in Utah in 1873, there were less than 100 Catholics. Now, there are more than 100,000, and the number is increasing rapidly. Some of that growth comes from settlement, as Utah continues to attract newcomers from other parts of the country. Most notable is the growth among the Hispanic population, the state's largest and fastest-growing minority group, which also is predominantly Catholic. The number of Hispanics has doubled since 1980.

To accommodate the population boom, the diocese has concentrated on strengthening the institutions necessary to support its members, and has sustained its social outreach in the community. This has been a two-fold endeavor.

BISHOP GEORGE NIEDERAUER OF THE DIOCESE OF SALT LAKE CITY SHARES A MOMENT WITH STUDENTS OF THE MADELEINE CHOIR SCHOOL. THE SCHOOL WAS THE SECOND OF ITS KIND TO OPEN IN THE UNITED STATES.

BARBARA STINSON LEE

BARBARA STINSON LEE

STAFF MEMBERS OF THE BISHOP WILLIAM K. WEIGAND RESOURCE CENTER IN SALT LAKE CITY GREET CLIENTS.

On the one hand, Catholics in Utah are spread throughout the state. In many less-populated areas, a parish priest may celebrate mass two or three times for different congregations, driving to far-flung missions—there are 19 altogether—where 20 or 30 parishioners await his arrival. The church is planning to open even more missions and parishes in the central, more remote part of the state.

On the other hand, along the Wasatch Front—from Ogden in the north to Provo in the south—where most of the state's population lives, the diocese is experiencing the sort of urban explosion unusual for parishes, even in America's largest cities. To meet this growth, more masses have been added to the weekend schedules, church facilities have been enlarged, and new churches planned. One of the diocese's priorities was to complete restoration of the Cathedral of the Madeleine, which area Catholics regard as the liturgical heart of the diocese. That project was culminated in 1993, under the supervision of former Bishop William K. Weigand.

The cathedral, located on South Temple just east of Temple Square, is listed on the National Register of Historic Places and the Utah State Register of Historic Sites. Inspired by the Romanesque and Spanish Gothic designs of the late Middle Ages, its high stained-glass windows are considered among the most beautiful in North America. The renovation cost $9.7 million, which included the refurbishing of the art, woodwork, and stained glass; the installation of a new organ; the rebuilding of the lower level; and the construction of the new cathedral plaza.

Other parishes have also adapted to meet the growing congregation. This has meant not only more services, but also sensitivity to the needs of many different cultures. In Salt Lake City alone, for example, there are liturgies, outreach programs, and youth ministries offered in Spanish at Our Lady of Guadalupe and Sacred Heart parishes; in Vietnamese at Our Lady of Perpetual Help; in Polish at St. Therese of the Child Jesus; as well as special masses

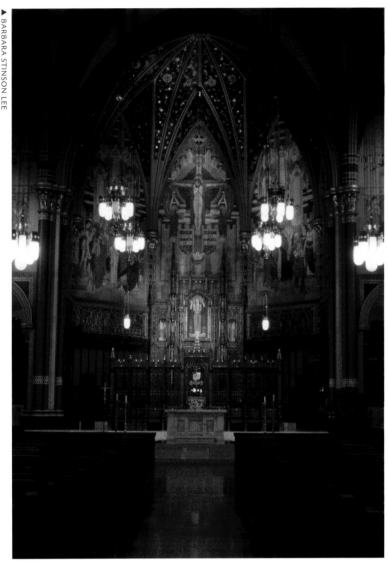

in Korean and Hmong, and for persons who are deaf.

EXPANDING MINISTRIES

The diocese is also expanding its school system. Recently, the diocese designated a plot of land—a donation from former American Stores Board Chairman Sam Skaggs, a Catholic convert—for a new parish (the diocese's 50th) and an elementary school named after St. John the Baptist. On the same site, the diocese is building a new high school named after Juan Diego, the Mexican peasant whom many Catholics believe was visited by the Virgin Mary near Mexico City in 1531. Juan Diego is the 14th Catholic school in a system that serves more than 4,000 students and is struggling to accommodate the increasing number on its waiting list.

Many newcomers to Salt Lake City also need help, in addition to schooling and liturgical needs.

Catholic Community Services of Utah helps many individuals and families become self-reliant. Most of the services, such as food banks and shelters, address homelessness and poverty. Other facilities and programs include substance-abuse treatment centers and refugee assistance, as well as helping immigrants adjust to their new life in Utah. The center also supports counseling, job placement, and children's day care.

With 70 priests, 40 deacons, 65 women in religious orders and several religious brothers, as well as an increasing number of the laity serving in ministries in the diocese, Bishop Niederauer says the church is prepared to face the challenges of the next century and of the new millennium. "We must do what the Catholic Church has always done," he says, "and that is to proclaim the gospel of Jesus Christ, to build up the kingdom of God in Utah."

BEGUN IN 1899 AND COMPLETED IN 1909, THE CATHEDRAL OF THE MADELEINE IN SALT LAKE CITY WAS REDEDICATED IN 1993.

OR NEARLY A CENTURY, THE SALT LAKE AREA CHAMBER OF COMMERCE has been the leading advocate for business and industry along the Wasatch Front. Founded in 1902, the chamber is Utah's most prominent business organization. Throughout its history, it has championed the community's vitality and economic growth. "The chamber is not just an organization," says Stanley B. Parrish, president and chief executive officer. "It's an institution. We are the voice of business in the community."

The chamber was born just after the turn of the century, when 100 charter members met to settle differences that had crippled the commercial business district. Today, the chamber's membership tops 1,800 firms, a group that represents a broad coalition of companies. A nine-member executive committee and 30-member board of governors recommend the chamber's policies and programs. A professional staff of 20 supervises more than 1,000 dedicated volunteers who serve on various committees.

Chamber members include the Salt Lake area's largest corporations, as well as mom-and-pop shops. They include virtually every industry segment—from health care and telecommunications to food service and construction. That breadth means power. With its collective muscle, the chamber has helped promote a variety of projects. Among the most notable were the creation of the international airport, the birth of a transit system, and the support of a downtown convention center.

WORKING TO SERVE THE BUSINESS COMMUNITY

Recent initiatives include the work of the Transportation Management Association, which plans solutions to transportation issues along the Wasatch Front. The reconstruction of Interstate 15 is expected to interrupt the flow of goods and people into the beginning of the next century. The association is addressing the concerns of employers, merchants, and truckers in moving employees, customers, and products. In the short term, the chamber will help ensure that businesses obtain the most up-to-date and accurate information about everything from ramp closings to alternate routes. In the longer term, the association is helping hammer out a strategy to manage the traffic demand and ease the impact of reconstruction on all the area's drivers.

For decades, one of the chamber's main purposes has been to create new businesses and jobs. In 1987, the chamber joined with public and private economic development agencies in Salt Lake County to form the Economic Development Corporation of Utah. This enables the agencies to leverage strength as a coalition, pursue opportunities in concert, and stay apprised of the most current research and demographic information.

The chamber provides information to thousands of newcomers and businesses interested in relocating to the Salt Lake area. In addition to distributing relevant

FOR NEARLY A CENTURY, THE SALT LAKE AREA CHAMBER OF COMMERCE HAS BEEN THE LEADING ADVOCATE FOR BUSINESS AND INDUSTRY ALONG THE WASATCH FRONT. FOUNDED IN 1902, THE CHAMBER IS UTAH'S MOST PROMINENT BUSINESS ORGANIZATION (TOP).

"THE CHAMBER IS NOT JUST AN ORGANIZATION," SAYS STANLEY B. PARRISH, PRESIDENT AND CHIEF EXECUTIVE OFFICER. "IT'S AN INSTITUTION. WE ARE THE VOICE OF BUSINESS IN THE COMMUNITY" (BOTTOM).

JERRY SINTZ

STEPHEN SMITH

facts, figures, and research, the chamber also provides exposure. It produces several publications, including *Life in the Valley* magazine and the *Business Focus* monthly newsletter, as well as the *Metro Business Report* radio program and the *Utah Business* television show.

SMALL BUSINESS PARTNER

While working to attract, retain, and promote major companies, the chamber has also championed the small-business sector. The Business Development Council serves as a resource for small-business owners. It also offers programs to assist business owners in running their companies. Through its Small Company Action Networks groups (SCAN), the council offers a support system to non-competing businesses that network and act as each other's informal board of directors. The council also offers programs directed by the Multi-Ethnic Business Committee, which promotes and develops opportunities for the area's multiethnic businesses.

Another program, sponsored in part by a matching grant by the U.S. Small Business Administration, is the Women's Business Center. In addition to housing a high-tech center with a variety of business software, the center helps women business owners with counseling, training, loan packaging, marketing, management, finance, and procurement.

Another program of the chamber is the Work Force Alliance program, which provides support services for people moving from welfare to gainful employment. The types of industries represented in the program include health care, hospitality, restaurant, and other service-related industries.

BENEFICIAL ADVANTAGES

Because of its size, the chamber has been able to secure quality benefits programs at lower rates. These include Blue Advantage, which provides small-business members with health insurance at a 5 percent discount; Member's Advantage, a workers' compensation insurance program that offers competitive rates; and a top-quality 401(k) program. "We provide value

STEVE GREENWOOD

STEVE GREENWOOD

THE CHAMBER PROVIDES INFORMATION TO THOUSANDS OF NEWCOMERS AND BUSINESSES INTERESTED IN RELOCATING TO THE SALT LAKE AREA. IN ADDITION TO DISTRIBUTING RELEVANT FACTS, FIGURES, AND RESEARCH, THE CHAMBER ALSO PROVIDES EXPOSURE. IT PRODUCES SEVERAL PUBLICATIONS, INCLUDING *Life in the Valley* MAGAZINE AND THE *Business Focus* MONTHLY NEWSLETTER, AS WELL AS THE *Metro Business Report* RADIO PROGRAM AND THE *Utah Business* TELEVISION SHOW.

for all our members," Parrish says. "We view them all as investors."

Six councils supervise the chamber's initiatives: the Business Development Council, Communications & Marketing Council, Government Relations Council, International Trade Council, Membership & Sales Council, and Special Projects Council. The Special Projects Council oversees the annual Business to Business Expo. The expo features more than 350 exhibits and is the largest trade show of its kind in the Intermountain West, attracting about 17,000 businesspeople annually. The council also sponsors educational seminars such as Leadership Utah, the Women & Business Conference, Utah Business Week, and other special functions.

The Membership & Sales Council has four full-time account executives to recruit new members. The Government Relations Council monitors bills at the state and federal levels, and provides members with updates on legislative issues that affect business. The Communications & Marketing Council keeps members abreast of chamber events and programs through publications and media relations efforts.

"We've represented our members well for nearly a century," Parrish says. "And we'll continue to work hard at that well into the century to come."

Amoco Corporation

As Amoco Corporation looks back over nearly a century of operations in the Salt Lake Valley, it recognizes that its success has come from a number of factors. Commitment to excellence in valuing its people's talents and diversity, protecting their health and safety, protecting the environment and the users of the company's products, and producing products of the highest quality are just some of the major factors. Amoco Corporation has multiple operations—a refinery, pipelines, over-the-road transportation, and retail gasoline stations and convenience stores—in the Salt Lake Valley.

Whether it's a consumer filling up his or her car with gasoline at one of the 100-plus Amoco/Rainbo stations in the state, or an elementary school student taking a bird-watching trip to one of the company's refinery sites, Public Affairs Advisor Patrice Thisler affirms that Amoco is dedicated to the communities in which the company operates. "The environment and safety are our number one concerns," she explains. "As we grow, we still continue to meet and maintain stringent health, safety, and environmental compliance requirements."

Amoco's Salt Lake City Operations

Chicago-based Amoco Corporation is one of the world's leading petroleum and chemical companies. Amoco's Salt Lake City Business Unit refines and markets both petroleum products for commercial and government clients and gasoline for retail customers.

Amoco's Salt Lake City refinery was originally constructed in 1908 as the Lubra Oils Manufacturing Company, and was the first refinery to be built in the Salt Lake City area. Incorporated in 1909 as the Utah Oil Refining Company, the predecessor to Amoco, known as Standard Oil of Indiana, assumed controlling interest in 1917.

The refinery was originally built to handle only seven barrels of Wyoming crude oil per day. It was expanded in 1944 to produce 16,000 barrels and again in 1958 to handle 35,000 barrels. In 1998, the Amoco Refinery's capacity was 53,000 barrels per day, making it the largest refinery in the Salt Lake Valley. This represents more than one-third of the refinery capacity for the region.

Amoco continues to expand its business in order to meet the ever increasing demand for petroleum products in the Salt Lake Valley.

Amoco believes that recognizing the value of its people is a major factor in its success. "People are our greatest asset and competitive edge. Technology and products are available to everyone, but the difference between company A and company B is commitment. Commitment to our employees and their commitment to Amoco. People do make all the difference, and we value them highly," says Thisler.

The company stresses environmental, health, and safety concerns for its employees. Amoco also offers all of its 250 local employees a company-matched savings plan, an educational assistance program, medical compensation, and outstanding retirement benefits. To increase cultural understanding and cooperation, the company sponsors an annual diversity conference. "We really believe you have to attract, develop, and retain the right people," Thisler says. "For Amoco, that means people that are diverse and global, and that act consistently with our values. Celebrating diversity is something we really stress."

Environmental Protection

Thisler believes that a commitment to environmental protection is a chief factor in Amoco's success. The company has won

Chicago-based Amoco Corporation is one of the world's leading petroleum and chemical companies. Amoco's Salt Lake City Business Unit refines and markets both petroleum products for commercial and government clients and gasoline for retail customers.

numerous national awards for its emphasis on protecting wildlife habitats and demonstrating that wildlife and industry can coexist. "We have as many as 70 species of birds on some of our sites," Thisler notes proudly. "Here in Salt Lake [City], there are golden eagles using our properties as part of their habitat."

In addition to welcoming wildlife, Amoco partners with student groups, Boy Scouts of America troops, and civic groups to sponsor public-education projects. Thisler says there are two reasons the company is eager to work on wildlife issues. "There are opportunities for science projects, and we can expose young people to wildlife in their own backyard. For the inner-city kids, this is a real opportunity, since some of them might seldom be exposed to wildlife. Plus, it shows that the environment and industry can happily coexist."

COMMUNITY INVOLVEMENT

Through its business units and the Amoco Foundation, Inc., Amoco believes in giving back to the communities in which it operates. In 1997, the Amoco Foundation contributed approximately $21 million to community and education organizations in 33 countries. On behalf of employees who volunteered 50 hours or more in 1997, Amoco donated some $726,000 in grants to more than 680 organizations worldwide. The company also donated $2.2 million in matching grants to educational institutions. In addition, AmoCARES (Concerned Amoco Retirees Engaged in Service) volunteered about $600,000 in volunteer services.

Locally, Amoco is involved in a number of projects, including Junior Achievement, Toys for Tots, the United Way, the Children's Museum of Utah, and the adoption of several schools.

As Amoco embraces growth, the company is determined to maintain its commitment to stringent health, safety, and environmental standards. "We're investing in the community so that we can meet the increasing demand in the Salt Lake Valley for petroleum products," says Thisler. It is this commitment that has guided Amoco in Salt Lake City for nearly 100 years, and that will lead the company into the next century.

V.A. Bettilyon founded his real estate company in 1909, and incorporated in 1911 with five stockholders and total capital of $5,200. Bettilyon's descendants describe him as "the original type A personality" and with reason: By 1916, the Bettilyon Home Builders Company was publishing its own newsletter, had assets of $300,000, boasted 1,500 investors, and was completing an average of one home a week.

V.A. and his wife, Janet, had three boys, Verden, Lue, and Kyle, and one daughter, Aline Ruth. Both Lue and Kyle joined their father's firm and learned the business from him. Bettilyon impressed upon his sons the importance of "doing the homework" and really getting to know a piece of property before becoming involved in a transaction. He also taught them the value of integrity, both in personal life and in business. Finally, he made them understand that change is a regular event in the real estate business, and that they should adapt in order to survive in the marketplace.

V.A.'s sons learned their lessons well; in the 1940s and 1950s, Bettilyon was one of the largest, if not the largest, residential real estate companies in Utah, with an immediately recognizable trademark in its fleet of 40 white Thunderbirds.

Since its founding in 1909 by V.A. Bettilyon, Bettilyon Realty Company has been an influential and innovating force in the growth and development of Salt Lake City.

EAST AND WEST SIDE STORIES

Kyle Bettilyon often recalled his early years as a balancing act between the city's east and west sides: "My dad told me to go west of Main Street and stay there and learn to develop and sell commercial property. But I had a family to feed, so I would work the east side and sell three or four homes and then return to the west side and work industrial properties until I ran out of money, then back to selling homes."

Perseverance paid off, though; Kyle and Lue eventually brought dozens of national companies to Utah, including the American Oil Company, Commercial Credit Corp., Litton Industries, DeVoe Reynolds, Electrolux, Otis Elevator Company, Trane Company, Ryder Truck Rental, Standard Oil, Franklin Quest, American Pad and Paper, and Morton Thiokol.

In 1950, the two brothers bought Bettilyon Realty and Construction from their father. And in 1965, they divided the company, with Kyle becoming president of Bettilyon Realty Company and Lue heading Bettilyon Construction and Mortgage Loan Company. They continued to work together on constructing some of the most distinctive and visible investment properties in the valley, including Decker Lake and Research Park. Kyle continued to work and golf

Much like Salt Lake City itself, Bettilyon Realty Company has undergone great growth and transition during its 90-year history. The Bettilyon building, built in downtown Salt Lake City in the early 1950s, is still the corporate office.

BETTILYON OWNS AND LEASES 42 COMMER-
CIAL AND INDUSTRIAL BUILDINGS—A TOTAL
OF 500,000 SQUARE FEET—THROUGH-
OUT THE SALT LAKE CITY AREA.

every day until his death in 1988. The company is now owned by his wife Lael and two daughters, Bonnie Barry and Vicki Merchant.

A GOOD DEAL FOR EVERYBODY

Bonnie Barry, current president and CEO of the company, even today marvels at her father's prescience and business sense: "For the past 10 years, as I've grown and learned with this job, one of the things that I've learned is how smart my dad was. He had foresight in terms of investments and where to put his resources.

"Another thing," she continues, "was his integrity. He said: 'There's no such thing as a good deal for one party. A good deal has to be good for everybody concerned.' He really believed that. People know they can trust Bettilyon. We try hard to follow his legacy and operate the company the same way he did."

INDUSTRY ACCOLADES

In 1963, Kyle was elected regional vice president of the Society of Industrial Realtors. A year later, he was one of six U.S. real estate agents selected by President Lyndon Johnson to serve on the U.S. Real Estate Trade Mission to Europe. In 1973, he was elected national

president of the Society of Industrial Realtors, and represented the United States at the world conference in Sydney, Australia. Following in her father's footsteps, Barry gave up a career in the travel industry and studied for her real estate and broker licenses. She was the first woman in Utah to earn a designation as a Certified Investment Manager, which she describes as the real estate equivalent of an MBA.

But like her father, Barry emphasizes that the real estate business must be fun and rewarding. She recalls her father saying, "If you can't have fun, don't do it. If you don't get a big wallop out of putting a real estate deal together, forget it; do something else. To me, putting a deal together is more fun than golf, and I love to golf."

Many of Bettilyon's former salespeople have followed Barry's father's creed—with great success. Among these leaders are Todd Eager, Mel and Bill Thayne, Del Nichols, Mike Farmer, and Arlene Dean. All have been involved as officers and committee members of the Salt Lake Board of Realtors, and have received local and national awards.

The genesis of sharing commercial/industrial information by competing brokerages during

IN 1950, A. KYLE AND B. LUE BETTILYON
BOUGHT BETTILYON REALTY AND CON-
STRUCTION FROM THEIR FATHER, V.A.

breakfast meetings was initiated by Kyle and attended by Keith Knight, Meeks Wirthlin, and Dan Simons, among others. These meetings led to a change in attitude and a cooperative spirit, and soon became weekly luncheons. Eventually the concept of sharing became integrated into the CCI and NAIOP programs.

Barry says her future goals are simple: "My family and I are excited to meet the challenges of the next century with enthusiasm, integrity, and flexibility. We still honestly feel as though we're following the tradition of V.A., Lue, and Kyle."

ORKERS COMPENSATION FUND (WCF) IS UTAH'S PREMIER WORKPLACE insurance company. WCF integrates quality claims, medical, and vocation rehabilitation management with vigorous and resourceful safety, fraud, and customer service departments to offer employers comprehensive coverage to meet their needs. ▨ "Our focus is on workplace safety and preventing accidents," says Senior Vice President Thomas E. Callanan. "But if an accident does occur, we see that people get high-quality health care and the best outcome possible, so that he or she can return to work quickly. We've built the largest, most professional staff in the state, and consider ourselves a leader in our business not just in Utah, but in the entire country."

Established in 1917 by the state of Utah, WCF was spun out as a quasi-private company in 1988. It is the oldest and largest company of its kind in Utah, insuring more than half of all Utah employers. Companies of all sizes and industries rely on WCF for workers' compensation insurance, including major construction firms, educational institutes, municipalities, recreation facilities, manufacturers, performing arts companies, health care facilities, and truckers.

PROMOTING SAFETY AND SUCCESS

WCF is proud of its partnerships with major trade associations, including the Associated General Contractors, the Utah Manufacturers Association, and the Utah Roofing Association. All three organizations endorse WCF as their preferred provider of workers' compensation. "We foster safer workplaces because we provide safety training classes, on-site safety consulting, medical case management, and even discounts to employers who are members of these trade associations," Callanan says.

Safety professionals present seminars covering both basic safety and industry-specific programs to more than 3,500 customers around the state. According to statistics, companies insured by WCF enjoyed a 28 percent decline in workplace injuries over the past five years.

And the company's concern with workplace safety and preventing injuries has paid off. WCF is a mutual insurance company, which means it is owned by its policyholders. The company has paid its policyholders more than $80 million in dividends in the past five years—twice the industry average. The company currently boasts $700 million in invested assets and $200 million surplus. WCF recently received an "excellent" rating of A- from the industry rating organization, A.M. Best Company—only the second one given to a company of its kind in the country.

WCF has been an instrumental player in advancing Utah as a competitive marketplace that offers companies an advantageous environment in which to do business. "WCF's efforts are good for Utah because we have helped drive down costs of doing business here," says Callanan. "In fact, our premiums are among the lowest in the country. With lower premiums and a commitment to taking care of our policyholders, we have helped to make Utah a great place to do business."

COMMUNITY SERVICE

Returning available resources and time to the community in which it has thrived is a high priority at WCF. "Our CEO, Lane Summerhays, is a big believer in good works," Callanan explains. "We support charitable causes

WORKERS COMPENSATION FUND OF UTAH HEADQUARTERS IS LOCATED IN SALT LAKE CITY, WITH BRANCH OFFICES IN OGDEN AND ST. GEORGE.

WCF'S EXECUTIVE STAFF MEMBERS ARE (FROM LEFT) LANE A. SUMMERHAYS, PRESIDENT AND CEO; SENIOR VICE PRESIDENTS RAY D. PICKUP; THOMAS E. CALLANAN; DENNIS V. LLOYD; AND ROBERT H. SHORT.

financially and create a culture where we're involved in helping others."

The company and its employees contribute to many causes, including Walk to Cure Diabetes and Change for Charity, in which employees donate at least a dollar to a selected charity on Fridays in exchange for dressing casually. Corporate officers are involved with the Economic Development Corporation of Utah, the Utah Symphony, the University of Utah, Valley Mental Health, and Prevent Blindness Utah.

However, it is the Legacy of Learning scholarships and its partnership with the Murray School District that makes WCF's community leadership stand out. The Legacy of Learning scholarships offer educational assistance to spouses and children of WCF-insured workers who lost their lives in industrial accidents. Since 1990, more than 200 scholarships have been awarded.

Its partnership with the Murray School District has offered many unique opportunities. Programs include allowing employees off-time to participate in mentoring programs at area schools; hiring high school interns who want to acquire and use computer skills; donating computers to area schools; and sponsoring a performance of Ririe-Woodbury Dance Company for an entire elementary school to attend.

FUTURE DIRECTIONS

With its commitment to Utah employers, WCF now insures Utah-based companies with operations and employees out of state. "We're a Utah company," Callanan says. "We serve 27,000 Utah employers and their employees. We were created by Utahns to serve Utahns."

In the coming years, WCF will continue to offer superior services, expanding to meet policyholders' needs with such new programs as unbundled risk management services and wrap-up plans for large construction programs. The company's commitment to Utah and its employers is a reflection of the high standards of quality, integrity, and scope of services that WCF strives to provide.

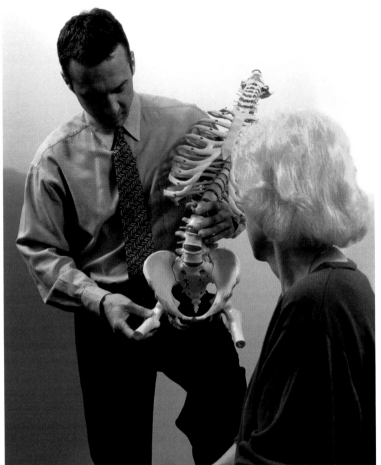

WHEN AN EMPLOYEE IS INJURED ON THE JOB, WCF IS THERE TO HELP. THROUGH ITS MEDICAL MANAGEMENT DEPARTMENT, WCF REVIEWS EVERY ASPECT OF AN INJURED PERSON'S CLAIM TO ENSURE THAT THEY GET THE BEST POSSIBLE TREATMENT.

PREVENTING WORKPLACE ACCIDENTS IS THE MAIN OBJECTIVE OF WCF'S SAFETY DEPARTMENT. ENGINEERS HELP EMPLOYERS IN ALL INDUSTRIES ESTABLISH AND MAINTAIN COMPREHENSIVE SAFETY PROGRAMS.

BONNEVILLE INTERNATIONAL CORPORATION (BIC) WAS FOUNDED IN 1964, BUT the company's roots stretch back to the 1920s. ▨ Bonneville grew out of KSL, one of Salt Lake City's earliest radio stations. KSL first went on the air in 1922. Such longevity separates KSL and BIC from the competition, according to Bruce Reese, president and CEO of Bonneville.

"We've had one owner for 75 years," Reese says. "Our people, our structure, and our programming may change, but our values remain pretty much the same. In such a dynamic industry, we draw strength from our historic stability. We call it Constancy Amid Change."

Bonneville is headquartered in Salt Lake City and employs almost 700 people locally. However, the company is very much a national and international concern, with six radio stations in Washington, D.C., three in Chicago, four in San Francisco, one in Los Angeles, and one in Salt Lake City; television stations in Salt Lake City and Cedar City, Utah; and a full-service advertising company, film production and distribution company, television production and audio/video mass duplication company, satellite company, full-time news bureau in Washington, D.C., and nationwide satellite radio network.

"We expect to make a positive difference in each of the communities where we operate," Reese says. "We provide our managers the resources, tools, and training necessary to run profitable operations, but we also provide resources and guidance to help them serve their communities. As far as we're concerned, the two go hand in hand. We can do good, and we can do well, at the same time."

A VALUES-DRIVEN COMPANY

Each year, Bonneville publishes its *Values Report*. It lists the company's mission and values, and it reports on how the corporation and its divisions are achieving those goals. The company's core values are integrity, excellence, service, profitability, leadership, and sensitivity.

"Our mission and values statements are not just words," Reese says. "We live by them. We encourage our associates to use those statements as guidelines when making business decisions. Broadcasting is different from other business enterprises because we have a community-wide voice. We provide a unique service to community leaders and organizations by helping them communicate their needs and tell about their service activities."

Off-air activities reflect the on-air commitment. Bonneville provides a broad range of benefits

CLOCKWISE FROM TOP: BONNEVILLE INTERNATIONAL IS HEADQUARTERED IN BROADCAST HOUSE, WHERE KSL RADIO CELEBRATED 75 YEARS OF SERVICE.

THE COMPANY'S ANNUAL *Values Report* IDENTIFIES COMMUNITY SERVICE ACTIVITIES.

BONNEVILLE FACILITIES IN LOS ANGELES, CHICAGO, SAN FRANCISCO, WASHINGTON, D.C., AND SALT LAKE CITY ARE AMONG THE FINEST IN THE NATION.

PAUL HARTMANN

and special projects. Video West also operates audio- and video-tape mass duplication facilities, which produce millions of tapes each year. For many years, Video West has been responsible for the production of the *Children's Miracle Network Telethon* from Disneyland or Disney World.

Bonneville LDS Radio Network is a 24-hour radio service designed for the special listening interests of LDS church members. It is broadcast by satellite, nationwide, and by FM subcarriers in selected cities.

to its associates, including retirement, health care, parking subsidy, and matching grants. Bonneville associates are active volunteers in their communities. The company provides paid time off for volunteer work. Associates are also active in industry and professional organizations, serving on boards and committees to strengthen the broadcast industry.

Whether raising $500,000 for Primary Children's Medical Center in Salt Lake City or organizing a volunteer fair in Chicago to help 2,000 eager volunteers find the volunteer job they want, Bonneville serves the community. In 1997, the company and its divisions provided more than $16 million worth of community service.

SALT LAKE CITY AND UTAH IMPACT

KSL Television and KSL Radio are broadcast leaders in Salt Lake City and the entire state of Utah. *KSL-TV News* has the highest audience rating of any local newscast in America. KSL Radio—with its 50,000 watts of power—is the source of radio news and information throughout Utah. KSL-TV is the only locally owned major commercial television station in the market, and KSL Radio is one of the few locally owned radio stations. They are the only stations in the market to broadcast regular editorial comments about local and national issues. They benefit from Bonneville's full-time news bureau in the nation's capital.

Bonneville Communications is a full-service advertising agency specializing in values-driven messages, which the company calls "heart-sell." Company clients include The Church of Jesus Christ of Latter-day Saints. The Homefront series of nondenominational, family-oriented public service announcements is the most widely broadcast public service series of all time, appearing on 600 television stations and 2,300 radio stations—and it has won more awards than any public service campaign in history.

Bonneville Worldwide Entertainment develops, produces, and distributes music products and movies for television, theaters, and the home market. The company concentrates on products designed for family entertainment.

Video West Productions handles television/radio production—sports, commercials, programs,

THE FUTURE

In the face of massive technological changes—including the imminent arrival of high-definition television (HDTV) and digital radio—Bonneville plans to continue emphasizing traditional values, even as the company embraces new technologies.

"We have survived plenty of ups and downs in business cycles," Reese says. "And we responded successfully to dramatic changes in the broadcast industry. The business environment may change around us, but our goals and values remain constant. They sustain us in hard times and drive us forward in good times. In another 50 years, I'm confident we'll still be here, we'll still be proud of a distinguished history, and we'll still be looking forward to a great future."

▶ PAUL HARTMANN

*H*AVING CELEBRATED ITS 75TH ANNIVERSARY, MHTN ARCHITECTS is in a unique position to assess how its own history of growth and development parallels the development of the state of Utah. Founded in 1923 by architects Raymond Ashton and Raymond Evans, the firm originally specialized in schools, office buildings, and medical facilities. Its earliest designs could be found on a number of public buildings including the Saltaire Resort, University of Utah Student Union/Library, Deseret News Building, and Payson Junior High School.

CURRENT OPERATIONS

Given MHTN's long history, it seems particularly appropriate that the company's 100 employees have been headquartered for the past seven years in the historic Newhouse Building. Although it also maintains an office in Tucson, company President Lynn Jones says that most of the firm's bread-and-butter work is conducted out of its Salt Lake City headquarters.

"Being big isn't necessarily important," Jones says. "We're among the two or three biggest architectural firms in the Intermountain area, but we're equally proud of our experience." MHTN is active in seven market segments: educational facilities, government facilities, commercial operations, health care facilities, interiors, landscaping, and research and development facilities.

"We're what you call a pure architectural firm," Jones explains, "in that we have no engineering services here. Although we do landscaping and master planning, architecture is our basis." The firm's current projects include the Salt Lake Courts Complex, Salt Lake City International Airport, Novell Corporate Headquarters, and Jordan District High Schools. Other recent projects include the Salt Lake County Government Center and the Utah and Weber County government centers.

"Additionally," Jones adds, "we've recently put a greater emphasis on architectural design, and we've won significant design recognition as a result." The firm has also received several corporate awards, including the 1996 Blue Chip Enterprise Initiative Award and the Salt Lake Area Chamber of Commerce award for 1995 as the Small Business of the Year.

A CHANGING INDUSTRY

"Ten years ago," Jones says, "I don't think we had a computer in this office. Now, we have a multimillion-dollar investment in high-tech computers. But in reality, the true designers are still pencil oriented."

The transition from paper to computer animation isn't the only change in the architecture industry. Jones, a third-generation partner in the business, has been in a position to watch the changes at MHTN and the industry in general. "For an architectural office, we're fairly sophisticated," he says. "We're far more departmentalized than we used to be. We now have dedicated design, interiors, specifications, marketing, business, and computer production departments.

"But the biggest change," Jones continues, "is the importance of human-resource philosophies. We now have a full-time person whose primary task is to make sure we hire and keep good employees. We have invested time and money in

MHTN AND HOK ARCHITECTS DESIGNED THE SCOTT M. MATHESON COURTHOUSE, WHICH HOUSES THE UTAH SUPREME COURT, UTAH COURT OF APPEALS, THIRD DISTRICT COURTS, THIRD DISTRICT JUVENILE COURTS, ADMINISTRATIVE OFFICE OF THE COURTS, AND STATE LAW LIBRARY.

NICK MERRICK, HEDRICH BLESSING PHOTOGRAPHERS

DOUGLAS KAHN

them. We strive to treat our employees like gold."

A SUPPORTIVE ENVIRONMENT

One part of the company's attempt to nurture employees, Jones says, is the creation of alliance groups. "All employees belong to an alliance group and every employee has a say in how the company is run," says Jones. "We have weekly staff meetings and a good internal communication system. Ten or 12 years ago, you wouldn't have thought of that and now it's the culture."

MHTN has been a consistent supporter of the University of Utah, making financial contributions to the architecture department, as well as sponsoring a standing scholarship fund. "That's paid off for us because we get a lot of really good graduates out of the school," says Jones.

MHTN is also committed to balancing historic preservation with responsible growth. "We're very involved in supporting the urban development of Salt Lake City: the upgrading of downtown, the Gateway District, and light-rail," Jones says. "We think the urban fabric has a lot of promise and there's a great opportunity to help it grow with distinctive buildings."

LOOKING TO THE FUTURE

Although Jones is confident that computers will play an increasingly important role in fu-

GREG HURSLEY

ture design, he says that competence and creativity are more important than methodology. "Raising the quality of our design is very, very important to us. Most of our designers have come from Michigan, California, Idaho, and elsewhere," he says. "Over half the staff, in fact, is from outside the state. That gives us a good cultural mix." While good design is important, client service in meeting the owner's program, budget, and schedule is the most important goal of the firm.

MHTN is working to expand its regional base to cover more work on large facilities such as hospitals and courthouses in other Intermountain states. "We're not focusing on the West Coast or anything east of Colorado," Jones says, "but we are interested in working more in Idaho, Wyoming, Nevada, Arizona, and Montana."

The firm is also constantly on the lookout for paradigm shifts. "We believe companies that don't do that are in trouble," Jones says. "One of the shifts we see is design-build construction, where we team with a general contractor and go after work together. We're increasingly active in design-build competitions where you're selected for a job on the basis of price and design. Contractors are our very best friends.

"The future for us involves continuing to do high-quality design that is program-compliant and reasonably priced. We plan to remain in our niche—working on large commercial and government facilities. It's a good niche if you can get there," Jones says. "To do that only took us 75 years. We are also ready to adapt to changes in the marketplace and go wherever our clients want us to go."

DOUGLAS KAHN

CLOCKWISE FROM TOP LEFT: ONE OF MHTN'S RECENT AWARD-WINNING EDUCATIONAL PROJECTS IS THE JORDAN HIGH SCHOOL IN SANDY.

MHTN COMPLETED THE FRANKLIN COVEY SALT LAKE CAMPUS IN 1996, INCLUDING OFFICES, EXECUTIVE SUITE, GYMNASIUM, CAFETERIA, AND OTHER OFFICE AMENITIES. MHTN IS CURRENTLY COMPLETING A REMODEL OF THE EXISTING TRAINING FACILITIES TO HOUSE THE UTAH JAZZ PRACTICE FACILITY.

WORKING CLOSELY WITH ZION'S SECURITIES CORPORATION, MHTN RECENTLY COMPLETED THE 18-STORY GATEWAY TOWER IN DOWNTOWN SALT LAKE CITY, ADJACENT TO THE SALT LAKE LDS TEMPLE.

MHTN COMPLETED THE SALT LAKE COMMUNITY COLLEGE SCIENCE & INDUSTRY BUILDING, WHICH HOUSES LABS, FACULTY OFFICES, AND CLASSROOMS, IN 1996.

O.C. TANNER COMPANY

Ask Salt Lake City residents about the O.C. Tanner Company, and chances are they'll tell you it's a respected jewelry retailer. Although that answer is true enough, the retail jewelry and high-end gift store on South Temple Street constitutes only a fraction of the company's business—about 2 percent. In fact, O.C. Tanner is much more global and complicated in scope than most people realize at first glance.

Founded in 1927 by philanthropist, arts patron, and businessman Obert C. Tanner, the company was originally known for its retail business in class rings. In the 1920s, Tanner was working as a schoolteacher in the town of Spanish Fork. Seeking to recognize the accomplishments of his students, he convinced his superior to buy lapel pins as a symbol of their achievements. Tanner made all of $12.50 on the transaction, but out of this humble beginning, the O.C. Tanner Company was born.

Even early on, as Tanner traveled across the state of Utah selling class rings and pins to high school students, he recognized the importance of beauty in jewelry design. In an attempt to improve the quality of available products, he began manufacturing rings in the basement of his mother's Salt Lake City home. Annual sales volume in his first year of manufacturing totaled about $5,000.

Gradually, as the company grew and the scope of the business expanded, Tanner and his nephew, Norman Tanner, who joined the business in 1937, began traveling around the United States meeting prospective customers. They realized that while jewelry was already important to high school graduates and fraternal organizations, its significance went largely unrecognized in American industry. As early as the 1930s, the Tanners began convincing companies that honoring longtime employees with items such as tie tacks, cuff links, bracelets, brooches, and rings was an ideal way to encourage loyalty and productivity. This solid marketing effort helped the O.C. Tanner Company become one of the first manufacturers and distributors of industrial service recognition emblems.

Kent Murdock serves as president and CEO of O.C. Tanner Company (left).

John Homer is the company's chief operating officer (right).

PIONEERS IN THE FIELD

As competitors began to spring up and increase the pressure on the fledgling company, O.C. Tanner gave up high school rings and pins to concentrate on corporate recognition awards. The company also grew increasingly sophisticated in its manufacturing techniques, moving from its original residential location to the basement of the Capitol Theatre downtown. But following complaints from neighbors and moviegoers about the noise associated with the manufacturing process, in 1956, O.C. Tanner constructed a modest building at the site of the current headquarters.

As the tools and jewelry-making processes became even more refined, so too did the company's marketing techniques. Tanner, a thoughtful and generous man, recognized that he was selling more than jewelry—he was also helping create memorable occasions where award recipients were recognized for their years of service. In one lecture, he reflected on this fact: "The O.C. Tanner Company's work, expressed in symbolic terms, is that of putting a drop of oil on the bearings of the free enterprise system. It helps companies run a little more smoothly, with a little less fric-

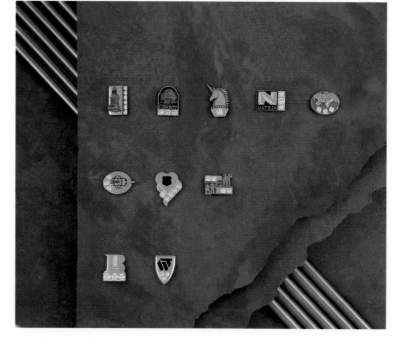

O.C. Tanner purchases more small diamonds than any other company in the world, and was honored in 1992 by the Manufacturing Jewelers and Silversmiths of America as the leader in the nation's service award industry. In the past decade, however, the company has developed and introduced new concepts in award selections, customizing its offerings to the needs of individual industries and furthering its competitive advantage.

tion, cultivating a more friendly environment where people work."

Tanner's approach proved successful: By the early 1980s, 2 million of the company's emblems were being awarded annually to employees of American industry. Boasting some 8,000 customers in all, O.C. Tanner today does business with 67 of *Fortune*'s top 100 companies and holds the corporate accounts for 33 of those organizations.

CURRENT HAPPENINGS

O.C. Tanner's annual sales volume of $240 million is roughly equivalent to the combined sales of its five largest competitors. Even so, the company continues to innovate in a variety of areas.

Traditionally, O.C. Tanner has emphasized the use of gold and diamonds in its recognition awards as a way to clearly communicate the importance companies place on the employees receiving them. Each award is, in effect, a physical expression of an employee's value. Because of Tanner's long-standing superior craftsmanship with gold and diamonds, the company's competitors "did everything in their power to convince their customers not to spend dollars on symbolic awards with gold and diamonds," explains CEO Kent Murdock. "That is our expertise; and the gap between us and our competition has grown ever larger."

O.C. Tanner still purchases more small diamonds than any other company in the world. It was also honored in 1992 by the Manufacturing Jewelers and Silver-smiths of America as the leader in the nation's service award industry. In the past decade, however, the company has developed and introduced new concepts in award selections, customizing its offerings to the needs of individual industries and furthering its competitive advantage. Currently, O.C. Tanner's 6,000 products range from heirloom-quality jewelry to home electronics, luggage, and outdoor accessories.

Another means of expansion has been the company's increasing emphasis on Internet or intranet employee recognition. For example, customers may now administer their award programs electronically, either partially or completely. Advantages of this approach include lower cost, superior aesthetics (award choices may be viewed in 3-D), and ease of accessibility. Customers also have the option of backing up O.C. Tanner's on-line programs with traditional print brochures if they so choose. Additionally, the company has introduced Outsourcing 360, a fully automated award-administration program that allows customers to stay in control of their chosen award through on-line communication, while O.C. Tanner handles

ordering, manufacturing, and delivery of awards.

Accounting for yet another source of growth, an increasingly large segment of the company's business is now international. "We put together all the logistics necessary to expand service awards to all employees, including expatriate employees," says John Homer, the company's chief operating officer. "We're the only company in our industry that can provide that service."

CORPORATE ENVIRONMENT

In the early years, O.C. Tanner's decision to remain headquartered in Salt Lake City may have proved a detriment. "Back then, no one thought you could do sophisticated business in Utah," Homer explains. "Everybody thought of Salt Lake as this place between Mississippi and San Francisco."

But two things have provoked a massive change in public opinion. The first is the company's efforts to bring in prospective clients, at Tanner's expense, to view the operation and the surrounding environs. Clients tour the factory, dine in the area's best restaurants, attend a symphony concert or ballet, and visit area

attractions. By the end of the tour, most are sold on the company and its hometown.

Secondly, modern-day Salt Lake City makes recruiting easy. The economy is thriving, cultural and recreational activities abound, the community is renowned for strong values, and it's relatively safe. "The greater package is appealing," Homer summarizes.

GENEROSITY INSIDE AND OUT

Befitting a company that specializes in corporate recognition programs, O.C. Tanner's employees enjoy a generous, open, comfortable work environment. The entire 350,000-square-foot headquarters facility is carpeted, including the factory. The founder's concern with aesthetics is evident everywhere, from the landscape paintings on the walls to the seven fountains strategically placed around the campus.

Complementing its attention to the physical work environment, O.C. Tanner also offers generous benefits for its employees. "We do things public companies probably don't do," Homer says proudly, offering a list that includes generous 401(k) and retirement plans, and the presentation to each employee of a $100 bill on Thanksgiving and $250 at Christmas, in addition to profit-sharing bonuses two times a year. Employees are also awarded turkeys, hams, and a Christmas buffet with prime rib during the holidays, and are periodically presented with Tanner shirts and pens, and gift certificates to ZCMI Department Store.

Showing Tanner's commitment to its people and an improved workplace, Kaye Jorgensen, its senior vice president of human resources, has received an award from the Professional and Business Women's organization for her human resource innovations at O.C. Tanner.

In the community, the company is no less beneficent. Following in the tradition established by its founder, the O.C. Tanner Company contributes to a broad range of arts and education organizations. Large donations are made to the Utah Symphony and Utah Opera, as well as the University

WORKERS AT O.C. TANNER POLISH EVERY GOLD EMBLEM AND SET EVERY DIAMOND AND GENUINE COLORED STONE BY HAND.

of Utah Humanities Center and Pioneer Memorial Theatre. Chair of the Board Carolyn Tanner Irish, who also serves as bishop of the Episcopal Diocese of Utah, has encouraged the company to donate to such causes as a local homeless shelter, the YWCA's programs for battered women, and a number of other charitable organizations.

According to Irish, most of this giving is done quietly, without concern for publicity: "It wasn't Obert's way to get public relations from giving. Gifts are from the heart." However, she adds, "It's absolutely part of our corporate ethic to take proceeds from the company and give back to the community. We all feel very strongly that a company has a much greater responsibility than employment of its people. It has a responsibility to see that some of its resources are used for the betterment of the community. That's one of the reasons people like it here, because the company is committed to that ethic."

IMPORTANT TRANSITIONS

Following the founder's death in 1993, the O.C. Tanner Company took time to reexamine its plans for the future. Although the transition was not easy, Murdock believes the outlook is positive. "We've never been more excited about the future," he maintains. "Prospects for growth are all around us."

The company's careful planning, Murdock believes, will continue to pay off in several areas. Even though O.C. Tanner currently commands between 10 and 15 percent of the available market in the

corporate recognition business, company planners believe that, with the application of careful marketing strategies, its share can be doubled or tripled.

Another potential source of growth for O.C. Tanner is multiple aligned businesses, such as executive gifts, performance awards, safety awards, and sales awards, among others—all of which are attractive to potential clients who understand the benefits of a comprehensive corporate recognition program but need assistance in establishing, organizing, and running one.

The company is also confident that its latest investment in Internet technology will improve customer service and create new products and services never available before. This will create additional competitive advantage in the marketplace for the O.C. Tanner Company.

As the O.C. Tanner Company faces the future, it remains well aware of its esteemed heritage as well as of its humble beginnings in the basement of a Salt Lake City home. "The Obert C. Tanner family has been extremely careful to invest in the future," Homer says. "We have a new management team and a strong board of directors. The new management, including myself, is committed to building on the legacy of the founders and shareholders of the company."

O.C. TANNER'S NEW, HIGH-TECH DISTRIBUTION CENTER IS LOCATED AT THE NORTH END OF THE CORPORATE HEADQUARTER'S 22-ACRE CAMPUS.

THE COMPANY FOUNDER'S CONCERN WITH AESTHETICS IS EVIDENT EVERYWHERE, FROM THE LANDSCAPE PAINTINGS ON THE WALLS TO THE SEVEN FOUNTAINS STRATEGICALLY PLACED AROUND THE CAMPUS.

CONCEIVED BY MARRINER S. ECCLES—FATHER OF THE MODERN FEDERAL Reserve and one of the architects of the New Deal—and founded in 1928 by him, his brother George, Marriner Browning, and E.G. Bennett, First Security Corporation is the oldest multistate bank holding company in the United States, and the largest banking organization headquartered

in the Intermountain West. Remarkably, in an era of bank consolidation, First Security still has an Eccles at the helm. Spencer F. Eccles, succeeding his uncles Marriner and George Eccles, was named chairman and chief executive officer in 1982.

The first thing customers notice when they walk into any First Security branch is the distinctive royal-burgundy-and-red signage. The second thing is likely the Currently Giving 110% motto prominently displayed in the lobby. This decade-old slogan has proved both durable and accurate, instilling confidence in investors, galvanizing employees' focus, and helping to differentiate First Security from its competition.

COMPANY ORIGINS

The roots of First Security extend back to Spencer Eccles' grandfather, David Eccles, a Scot who immigrated to the United States in 1863 and became a self-made millionaire in the timber, transportation, sugar, construction, and banking industries. His sons founded First Security in the late 1920s and began constructing today's company from a core group of 17 stand-alone banks in Utah, Idaho, and Wyoming.

According to Spencer Eccles, First Security has always emphasized two points: the safety of depositors' money (he proudly notes that even during the Great Depression, no customer lost a dime at First Security, and the bank actually came to the rescue of numerous insolvent institutions) and the ability to provide a return on stockholder investments.

"Our values haven't changed a bit," Eccles says. "We're an integral part of every community where we're located. We've been here through good and bad times, but we've always been here to help build each area we serve."

For a company with such a proud history, First Security has proved to be remarkably adaptable in the face of increasingly sophisticated technology and the globalization of the U.S. economy. Eccles attributes the bank's flexibility to one factor: "Competition—that's the reality of business. We've had to adjust and react to the changes in our industry and the economies in our region." As it looks to the future, First Security plans to stand firm at the forefront of the Utah banking industry by remaining alert to change.

COMMUNITY GOOD

It is impossible to separate First Security Bank from the half-dozen charitable foundations launched and maintained by the Eccles family. These long-lived organizations, which operate throughout the bank's trade area, have contributed inestimably to the Intermountain West in areas including sports, arts, medicine, and education. The Eccles family and First Security were also strong backers of Salt Lake City's bid to host the 2002 Winter Olympics. In Eccles' view, these diverse community-related activities are all contributors to Utah's quality of life: "We think the Olympics are important to Salt Lake City and the West as an opportunity to tell the Utah story correctly to the world. It will unify the people of Utah, just as it did in Lillehammer and Nagano."

And too, there's the economic impact of thousands of tourists and media representatives visiting the city. "It'll be the rising tide that lifts all ships," adds Eccles. "The Olympics will have a basic and long-lasting significance in Utah."

But even long after the Olympics have come and gone, First Security is confident it will remain a force in Salt Lake City and the West. Despite the consolidation frenzy that characterizes today's banking industry, First Security plans to

SPENCER F. ECCLES (LEFT), CHAIRMAN AND CEO OF FIRST SECURITY CORPORATION, AND MORGAN J. EVANS, PRESIDENT AND COO, REPRESENT THE COMPANY'S STRONG BACKING OF SALT LAKE CITY'S BID TO HOST THE 2002 WINTER OLYMPICS.

superior customer service, and produce high-performance results that will be represented in the company's stock price.

PIONEERING IN THE FUTURE

Throughout its history, First Security has boasted many firsts. After the Great Depression and World War II, it was the first bank to establish offices on military bases. In the 1950s, when the company relocated its headquarters from Ogden, it began construction of the first major office building in Salt Lake City since the 1920s. Things are no different today: First Security remains a leader in business, mortgage, and automobile financing; credit card services; and specialized banking for women-led and -owned businesses. With more than 9,500 shareholders and $18 billion in assets, the company is well positioned for whatever changes it may face.

"We're blessed to be in one of the strongest economic regions in the country right now," says Eccles. "It's a great time to be alive and in banking. First Security has been a brand name that has served us well in the past and will continue to serve us well into the future. I truly believe that the best is yet to come."

remain independently managed. Furthermore, the organization boasts a strong management team and a sound succession plan intended to assure the bank's prosperity in the next century. In fact, as a result of First Security's 1995 intensive restructuring effort—called Project VISION—the bank selected a new mission statement and identified a list of seven core

values by which all business decisions are now made.

But the company motto, Currently Giving 110%, remains the center of First Security Bank. Eccles describes it as "a battle cry, a way of life, and the single unifying factor within First Security's family." The motto, he insists, embodies the company's commitment to safeguard depositors' money, give

FIRST SECURITY REMAINS A LEADER IN BUSINESS, MORTGAGE, AND AUTOMOBILE FINANCING; CREDIT CARD SERVICES; AND SPECIALIZED BANKING FOR WOMEN-LED AND -OWNED BUSINESSES. WITH MORE THAN 9,500 SHAREHOLDERS AND $18 BILLION IN ASSETS, THE COMPANY IS WELL POSITIONED FOR WHATEVER CHANGES IT MAY FACE.

THE COMPANY MOTTO, CURRENTLY GIVING 110%, REMAINS THE CENTER OF FIRST SECURITY BANK. THE MOTTO EMBODIES THE COMPANY'S COMMITMENT TO SAFEGUARD DEPOSITORS' MONEY, GIVE SUPERIOR CUSTOMER SERVICE, AND PRODUCE HIGH-PERFORMANCE RESULTS THAT WILL BE REPRESENTED IN THE COMPANY'S STOCK PRICE.

QUESTAR CORPORATION

HEN MOUNTAIN FUEL SUPPLY COMPANY CHANGED ITS NAME TO Questar Gas Company at the beginning of 1998, some customers were alarmed. Had Mountain Fuel—a household name in northern Utah for more than 50 years—been acquired by some out-of-state conglomerate? ▧ The answer, of course, was no. The name change was made to align the gas-distribution utility with the expanding basket of products and services offered by its parent company, Questar Corporation. The change will allow Questar, in a deregulated energy market, to present a single name or brand that would come to represent its entire product spectrum.

Questar is an integrated energy resources and services company with $2 billion in assets distributed between regulated services, such as retail natural gas distribution and interstate gas transportation, and market resources, including gas and oil exploration, wholesale and retail energy marketing, gas gathering, and other field services. The company has 2,500 employees and the equivalent of about 850 billion cubic feet of natural gas reserves.

R.D. Cash, Questar chairman, president, and chief executive officer, explains that deregulation is allowing energy companies to venture into new lines of business. "On a wholesale level, a Questar company, Questar Energy Trading, has already started to market electricity," Cash notes. "And on a retail level, another of our companies, Questar Energy Services, is selling a range of products and services such as carbon monoxide monitors and home-security and appliance-maintenance programs. Yet another company, Questar InfoComm, markets information technology and telecommunications.

"Confusion among our customers is the last thing we want. Developing a simple strategy for linking Questar with the products and services all our companies offer is vital in preparing for a more competitive marketplace. When offered a choice of suppliers, customers will choose a name they know and trust," says Cash.

In some states, regulators already have started to encourage competition for retail customers. In Wyoming, at the urging of the state public service commission, Questar Gas invited its 22,000 customers to keep using the company for their full gas service or to buy gas from competing suppliers. The success of this effort in Wyoming may influence what happens in Utah in the coming years.

Although the names have changed, the Questar organization of 1998 is the direct descendant of the one established 70 years ago to bring natural gas to northern Utah from the fields of Wyoming and Colorado. The first pipeline has a unique place in company history. Started in the Wasatch Mountains in the dead of winter, the Pipeline of '29 pitted men and a few crude machines against the biggest obstacles Mother Nature could muster: heavy snow, bitter cold, paralyzing mud, and desert heat. But it delivered natural gas, on schedule, to the towns of north-

QUESTAR RECENTLY REMODELED ITS HEADQUARTERS BUILDING ON THE CORNER OF 100 SOUTH AND 200 EAST STREETS IN SALT LAKE CITY (TOP).

QUESTAR IS A PARTNER IN A GAS-MARKETING HUB—A PIPELINE INTERSECTION—AT MUDDY CREEK IN SOUTHWESTERN WYOMING THAT PROVIDES INTERCONNECTS BETWEEN FIVE MAJOR PIPELINE SYSTEMS (BOTTOM).

ern Utah by the fall of 1929. A writer for the *Deseret News* described it as "a construction task that has no western parallel."

That project set the tone for the following 70 years of company history. It spawned a generation of colorful, strong-willed, opinionated men and women who led the company for four decades. And their damn-the-torpedoes attitude remains a facet of the company character to this day.

In 1929, natural gas was considered a luxury. It was more expensive than coal and fuel oil, and customers were slow to embrace it. However, by the late 1940s, increases in the prices of competing fuels had made natural gas a hot commodity. In March 1950, people literally stood in line overnight to sign up for service.

At the end of World War II, Questar had about 45,000 customers. By 1998, it had 645,000. The 1950s and 1960s saw expansions into communities such as Logan, Brigham City, Tremonton, Heber, and Park City. The 1980s and 1990s saw the company extend its lines as far as St. George, in extreme southwestern Utah, and as far north as southern Idaho. Today, about 95 percent of Utah homes use natural gas. Even residents of coal-mining strongholds such as Price, Utah, and Rock Springs, Wyoming, have given up their old clinkers for the new fuel.

Natural gas has another attribute that makes it attractive, particu-

larly in urban areas: It burns more cleanly than any other fossil fuel. To clean up their emissions, industrial users and power plants have switched to natural gas. Today, companies such as Utah Power, Kennecott Copper, Geneva Steel, and Hercules are among Utah's largest consumers of natural gas.

Questar Pipeline Company has kept pace with increasing demand by enlarging capacity along its existing routes and expanding into new areas. The company is a partner in a large new line that will carry gas from northwest Colorado to existing interstate pipelines in northern New Mexico.

While exploration and production have always been primary Questar activities, they promise to take an even higher profile in the future of the corporation. Twelve years ago, practically all of Questar's exploration and production operations could be contained by a circle about 200 miles in diameter covering northeastern Utah, southwestern Wyoming, and northwestern Colorado. Today, Questar also has reserves and production in New Mexico, Texas, Arkansas, Louisiana, Oklahoma, Kansas, Alberta, and British Columbia. The exploration and production group hopes to double its oil and gas reserve base by 2002.

"By the year 2002, if we implement our strategies, we project net income from nonregulated businesses will represent 60 to 65 percent of corporate net income compared with approximately 47 percent at present," Cash says.

"Questar Corporation has a great future," says Cash. "It will probably change a great deal as competitive conditions in our industries change. But one thing that will not change is our heritage. Questar has a great heritage, thanks to the evolution of natural gas in the West, and the many people who have worked to get this great product to our customers over the years."

MACEY'S INC.

ORE THAN HALF A CENTURY AGO, WALDO L. MACEY AND HIS partner, Dale Jones, opened the Save a Nickel Market in Salt Lake City. That venture has grown into Macey's Inc., which operates eight full-time neighborhood supermarkets and prides itself on being Utah's homegrown market. ▣ "We're local grocers who have

grown up with Utah," says Ken Macey, the founder's son and president of Macey's Food and Drug Stores. "We stay in touch with our neighbors and try to be sensitive about their needs."

The first store, which opened its doors in 1947, was located downtown and had 3,000 square feet of floor space. The company expanded to four Save a Nickel Markets by 1963, and a year later, Ken Macey joined the business on a full-time basis, changing the company's trade name to Macey's Economy Store. Ken Macey became company president in 1980, and in 1986, founder Waldo L. Macey retired.

Today, Macey's supermarkets stretch along the length of the Wasatch Front, with stores located in Logan, South Ogden, Sandy, West Jordan, North and South Orem, Clearfield, and Spanish Fork. The stores range in size from 28,500 to 68,000 square feet.

Closed on Sundays, they are open 24 hours on the other days of the week.

Endeavoring to provide an alternative to conventional supermarkets, Macey's stores are designed to give busy customers the widest array of foods and services. Today, the stores are bigger than ever, with more selection and more conveniences. In 1947, Waldo Macey's store carried about 3,000 items. Today, some of the company's warehouse-type stores carry a range of 40,000 items. In addition, the stores place particular emphasis on maintaining a low-price image in the neighborhoods they serve.

A HOST OF PRODUCTS AND SERVICES

Each store carries a full complement of dry grocery products that range from most national brands to labels for the most budget-conscious consumers, including the Western Family private

label and Macey's private label products. "You'll see foodstuffs and staples piled pretty high in the center of each store," says Ken Macey.

At the same time, the stores provide customers with a wide selection of service departments to help consumers reduce the number of their shopping trips. Each store features a deli, bakery, meat and dairy section, pharmacy, automatic teller machine, and video-rental shop. Customers will also find ample, safe, and well-lighted parking conveniently located on store premises, and a clean, attractive, and friendly shopping environment inside.

Macey's also offers consumers the benefits of cost and inventory management using high technology. Unlike many warehouse stores and big chain supermarkets, Macey's stores keep track of their profit and loss on a weekly rather than a quarterly basis—no easy task for

"WE'RE LOCAL GROCERS WHO HAVE GROWN UP WITH UTAH," SAYS KEN MACEY, THE FOUNDER'S SON AND PRESIDENT OF MACEY'S FOOD AND DRUG STORES. "WE STAY IN TOUCH WITH OUR NEIGHBORS AND TRY TO BE SENSITIVE ABOUT THEIR NEEDS."

an independent, regional supermarket in competition with national outlets. "We need to know every week whether we're winning or losing," Macey says. "How else will we pass on savings and keep down prices?"

GIVING BACK TO THE COMMUNITY

What really distinguishes Macey's, however, is its relationship with the communities it serves. Macey's employs an average of 220 to 250 people in each of its stores. It is the company's policy to hire local residents and to promote from within. That policy not only creates jobs, but also ensures that each store is part of the fabric of its community and is tended by employees who have a stake in improving quality and service.

Over the years, Macey's employees have also given generously of their time, money, and talents to help make the Wasatch Front a better place to live. The majority of the company's efforts focus on children. "There are such great needs," Macey says. "We concentrate on kids because that way we're sure we can have an impact on our neighborhoods' future."

Macey's participates in fundraisers for Primary Children's Medical Center, in particular its

radiothons. The company is also active in programs for the Ronald McDonald House and KSL radio's Quarters for Kids project, which raises money to ensure that children have basic clothing items, such as shoes. Macey's has also teamed up with various community organizations to deliver tons of foodstuffs to food banks and soup kitchens in order to help ease the plight of the poor and homeless.

Most recently, the company's community-oriented projects have involved partnerships with local elementary and high schools. Macey's chooses three schools each quarter from applications sent from schools in its markets. The company urges the students and parents at the chosen schools to

save their Macey's shopping receipts. The schools then collect these receipts and return them to the stores. Macey's tallies the receipts and gives each school 1 percent of the total value in cash. In some cases, that has amounted to as much as $3,000 for participating schools. "That money is reinvested directly into the classroom," Macey says. "It goes straight to the kids."

Homegrown, convenient, and committed to Utah's Wasatch Front and its neighborhoods—Macey's Inc. identifies with Utah's local communities because it grew up with them. And Ken Macey wants to make sure it stays that way: "We want to be part of their future—our future."

*T*N 1948, A GROUP OF SALT LAKE CITY BUSINESSMEN WANTED TO CONDUCT their financial transactions at a convenient neighborhood institution. With some of them investing as little as $100, the group launched Valley State Bank at 2510 South State Street. In the years that followed, the bank grew, relocating its headquarters to downtown Salt Lake City and adding

branches and convenient customer service features such as drive-through banking.

In 1992, Valley Bank became part of the Columbus, Ohio-based Banc One Corporation, offering Salt Lake residents the advantages of big banking secured by the familiar feel of local roots. "Bank One is unique in national or large banking operations, in that we operate with decentralized authority," explains Brad Baldwin, president of Bank One, Utah. "It's still a partnership. We deliver goods and services in the local community through a national organization that brings sophisticated solutions for customers."

BALANCING LOCAL AND NATIONAL STRENGTHS

*T*oday, Bank One features 25 banking locations in Utah, and just as Valley State Bank was an early leader in services such as drive-through banking, Bank One has proved to be a leader in utilizing technical advances to simplify transactions.

"Banks need to be easy to do business with," Baldwin points out. "If we don't take care of our customers, someone else will. This is a highly competitive business and it's as simple as that."

As banking has changed, Bank One has changed with it, soon to become the country's fifth-largest bank holding company. Nationally, the corporation has managed assets of $140 billion. Locally, Bank One has 400 employees and Utah assets of nearly $2 billion.

Bank One offers a range of services and plans to fit the needs of any customer. In the area of commercial banking, for instance, the bank offers industrial revenue bonds, asset securitization, leasing, investment management, and public and private placement of debt. Many of Utah's largest developers, ski resorts, insurance companies, and manufacturers utilize Bank One's services.

Regular relationship reviews with customers enhance the company's appeal to some of Utah's most desirable business accounts. "We team with them to understand their needs and goals, and help them reach those goals. We want

CLOCKWISE FROM TOP RIGHT: BANK ONE HAS PROVED TO BE A LEADER IN UTILIZING TECHNOLOGICAL ADVANCES TO SIMPLIFY TRANSACTIONS.

SPECIAL GUEST STEIN ERIKSON, OLYMPIC GOLD MEDALIST, GIVES BANK ONE CORPORATE CLIENTS A FEW TIPS DURING THE BANK ONE-SPONSORED SKI DAY AT DEER VALLEY.

BRAD BALDWIN, PRESIDENT OF BANK ONE, UTAH; GIL WILLIAMS, PRESIDENT OF ROYAL STREET CORPORATION; AND STEIN ERIKSON, SKI AMBASSADOR FOR DEER VALLEY, ENJOY A RIDE UP THE MOUNTAIN.

Clockwise from top left: Brad Baldwin, president of Bank One, Utah, and Jim Jensen, executive director of the Boys and Girls Club of Greater Salt Lake, pose with a group of children at the Sugarhouse location of the Boys and Girls Club.

to be more than a service provider; we want to become a trusted adviser where we bring solutions and value-added services to the table," says Craig Zollinger, executive vice president.

Bank One is seeking to remain a leader in the retail banking industry by offering customers one-to-one financial solutions. These services include express banking locations inside retail establishments, Internet banking with Bank One On-line, loans by phone, and 24-hour-a-day call centers.

"But despite all the technological advances, service is still important and getting to know the customer is still important," Baldwin says. "This is still very much a relationship-oriented business. Banks must couple easy access with one-to-one service."

A People Business

Baldwin points with some pride to the fact that Bank One's Utah employees donate 3,000 hours annually to commu-

nity service, including Guadalupe Center, Traveler's Aid, Habitat for Humanity, Juvenile Diabetes, Walk America, and Utah Arts Festival. Most of the bank's local officers are simultaneously involved in several community organizations. "A commitment of time," Baldwin says, "is far more valuable than money. We try to choose community activities that make a difference in people's lives.

"Banking is a people business," Baldwin says. "More importantly, banking is a local business. Customers want to deal with banks that contribute to the vitality of the community. We recently adopted three schools in a partnership that involves financial support, tutoring, and teaching banking classes. We're also involved in the Millions of Pennies program in which high schools collect money for charity."

Whether it's helping to underwrite the Utah Arts Festival or lending money to low-income populations, Baldwin believes that community involvement falls squarely under the bank's mission statement. "Our motto is Bank One to One. I don't care how technical or sophisticated banking becomes," he says. "It's based on people and the relationship they establish with customers. Even though our name may be new, the people and their presence in this market date back 50 years."

"Despite all the technological advances, service and getting to know the customer are still important," explains Baldwin.

Bank One sponsors the Children's Art Yard, Planet Discovery, at the Utah Arts Festival. Bank One employees donate more than 3,000 hours annually to community service.

W ITH MORE THAN 100 YEARS OF EXPERIENCE, MERRILL LYNCH IS a leading global financial management and advisory company with a presence in 43 countries across six continents and approximately 54,200 employees worldwide. In Salt Lake City, Merrill Lynch has been in business since 1948. The downtown office,

located in the Eagle Gate Tower, is the headquarters for the state of Utah. The Salt Lake City office employs some 100 consultants and support staff, and also includes offices of Business Financial Services and Merrill Lynch Life Agency.

LONG HISTORY

Since its beginning, Merrill Lynch, founded by Charles E. Merrill, has operated on the belief that the opportunities of the markets should be accessible to everyone. It was Merrill's lifework to bring Wall Street to Main Street. Now, with total client assets of more than $1 trillion, Merrill Lynch is the leader in planning-based financial advice and management for individuals and small businesses.

As an investment bank, the company has been the top global underwriter of debt and equity

securities since 1991, and a leading strategic adviser to corporations, governments, institutions, and individuals worldwide. Through Merrill Lynch Asset Management,

the firm operates one of the world's largest mutual fund groups.

Another focus of Merrill Lynch that originated with its founder is putting the interests of the cus-

UTAH GOVERNOR MIKE LEAVITT SIGNS A PROCLAMATION DECLARING APRIL AS THE OFFICIAL SAVING MONTH FOR THE STATE OF UTAH. PICTURED (LEFT TO RIGHT): JESS SHACKELFORD, ADMINISTRATIVE MANAGER; EUGENE W. BANKS, SENIOR RESIDENT VICE PRESIDENT; LEAVITT; AND JOHN JACKSON, FINANCIAL CONSULTANT

MERRILL LYNCH MANAGERS AND EMPLOYEES POSE WITH THE TOURNAMENT CHAMPION AT A MERRILL LYNCH-SPONSORED SENIOR PGA TOUR EVENT AT PARK MEADOWS COUNTRY CLUB IN PARK CITY, UTAH. SPONSORSHIP OF THIS EVENT IS JUST ONE WAY IN WHICH MERRIL LYNCH IS INVOLVED IN THE COMMUNITY.

tomer first. Today, that customer-first philosophy is expressed in five principles that define the way Merrill Lynch does business: client focus, respect for the individual, teamwork, responsible citizenship, and integrity. These principles are the standards used by employees

of the firm to measure decisions made daily.

DEFINING FINANCIAL GOALS

Merrill Lynch's financial consultants stress planning that addresses a broad range of financial needs. The firm's consultants help clients define their financial goals, determine the amount of time they have to reach those goals, and establish their performance expectations.

A wide range of services work to tailor comprehensive strategies for managing clients' total portfolios, and Merrill Lynch continues to enhance and develop products to accommodate client needs. In 1977, the Cash Management Account was introduced, and this product has proved to be a powerful personal asset management tool for investing, saving, borrowing, and spending.

In 1977, Merrill Lynch On Line began providing a Web-based service that gives clients electronic access to account information, portfolio information, specialized research, and bill payment. In addition to financial consulting services, the client has access to specialists in areas such as mortgages, personal credit, insurance, estate planning, trusts, and small-business and employee benefit services.

Whether assisting with mergers and acquisitions for large corporations or consulting with a young couple just beginning a financial portfolio, Merrill Lynch leads the way in providing trusted advice based on financial expertise, global perspective, and long-term view. The principles of client commitment that originated with Charles Merrill himself are effectively guiding the firm toward a successful future.

MARTY MANNING, RESIDENT MANAGER OF THE OGDEN OFFICE, STRIVES TO UPHOLD THE FIVE PRINCIPLES THAT DEFINE THE WAY MERRILL LYNCH DOES BUSINESS: CLIENT FOCUS, RESPECT FOR THE INDIVIDUAL, TEAMWORK, RESPONSIBLE CITIZENSHIP, AND INTEGRITY.

WITH MORE THAN 100 YEARS OF EXPERIENCE, MERRILL LYNCH IS A LEADING GLOBAL FINANCIAL MANAGEMENT AND ADVISORY COMPANY WITH A PRESENCE IN 43 COUNTRIES ACROSS SIX CONTINENTS AND APPROXIMATELY 54,200 EMPLOYEES WORLDWIDE, INCLUDING APPROXIMATELY 40 EMPLOYEES IN ITS PROVO OFFICE.

WHEN THE PRECURSOR OF SALT LAKE COMMUNITY COLLEGE (SLCC) opened its doors for enrollment in September 1948, a total of 175 students signed up for the 14 classes offered. In September 1997, some 20,000 students enrolled in one of more than 84 programs of study comprising 2,000-plus class sections, which range from English composition and graphic design to environmental technology and welding.

BUILDING A SUCCESS STORY

Our growth has really been phenomenal," says Frank W. Budd, president of the two-year college since 1991. He credits much of this success to the massive population growth of the Salt Lake Valley and the concerted effort of the college to meet the current and future needs of the Wasatch Front's increasingly diverse population.

Budd also credits a decision of the Utah Board of Regents. "After I arrived here, the Board of Regents directed the University of Utah to increase admission standards and move more toward a research-level university," Budd recalls. "As part of that, the board wanted a greater difference in tuition costs between the university and SLCC. That's been partially responsible for our increase in enrollment."

But even with the difference in tuition, the two schools are closely connected. Because many of SLCC's students eventually go on to complete four-year degrees at the University of Utah, it was important that curriculum planners from the two institutions work together to ensure that Salt Lake Community College's credits be fully transferable to the university. This collaborative effort resulted in a more valuable educational experience for SLCC students. "Our philosophy," says Budd, "is to be responsive to student needs. That leads to success for everyone concerned."

Looking beyond curriculum issues, SLCC has traditionally enjoyed a reputation as an institution where students—many of them nontraditional—complete their general education requirements or enroll in vocational programs. But SLCC wanted to go beyond education. Encouraging a sense of community among students, the college reemphasized sports and theater programs, encouraged the formation of clubs and student associations, and—looking forward—promoted an ambitious expansion plan to create a multiple campus operation.

PLANNING FOR FUTURE NEEDS

Although the Salt Lake area has enjoyed a robust economy with virtually full employment throughout much of the 1990s, the college realized that its Taylorville campus was essentially operating at full capacity. If the state economy were to dip, causing a jump in enrollment, it was feared that the school's resources would be overwhelmed. Thus, SLCC began opening satellite locations around the

"OUR GOAL HERE IS TO BUILD A RESPONSIVE, TRUE COMMUNITY COLLEGE, NOT FORGETTING OUR TRADITIONAL MISSION TO PROVIDE AN OPEN-DOOR POLICY AND TO OFFER ASSOCIATE DEGREES AND VOCATIONAL EDUCATION, BUT TO EXPAND OUR MISSION TO INCLUDE APPLIED TECHNOLOGY AND OTHER PROGRAMS THAT WILL HELP OUR STUDENTS GO OUT INTO THE WORLD BETTER ABLE TO COMPETE," SAYS FRANK W. BUDD, PRESIDENT OF SALT LAKE COMMUNITY COLLEGE SINCE 1991 (TOP).

"OUR PHILOSOPHY," SAYS BUDD, "IS TO BE RESPONSIVE TO STUDENT NEEDS. THAT LEADS TO SUCCESS FOR EVERYONE CONCERNED" (BOTTOM).

AMONG MANY OTHER THINGS, SLCC IS UTAH'S ONLY PREMIER AUTODESK TRAINING CENTER, OPERATES THE AREA'S SMALL BUSINESS DEVELOPMENT CENTERS, IS A LARGE-SCALE TRAINING CENTER FOR THE UNION PACIFIC RAIL-ROAD, AND IS UTAH'S LARGEST PRO-VIDER OF APPRENTICESHIP TRAINING IN 22 AREAS OF SPECIALIZATION.

valley and a second campus to accommodate current and future needs.

These facilities include the former South High School, which opened as a second full-service campus of the college in September 1991 with 5,000 students. Satellite locations include a leased facility at the Sandy Mall capable of handling 2,000 students and the Millcreek Center in Holladay, which accommodates another 2,000 students. The college also has smaller facilities at Tooele, West Jordan, Riverside Center, Jordan Technical Center, the Utah State Prison, and the Salt Lake City International Airport.

With growth in the valley projected to move toward the southwest, in the mid-1990s, Salt Lake Community College acquired 114 acres at the junction of 9000 South and the Bangerter Highway. This site, named the Jordan Campus, is currently in the planning stages and will eventually accommodate students from the rapidly expanding communities of formerly rural southwest Salt Lake County.

CHALLENGES AND REWARDS

In the future, Budd is convinced that technology will play an increasing role in the classroom. "That will be another challenge,"

he predicts. "Dealing with rapid changes in technology and changes in societal circumstances can be uncomfortable for everyone. It brings pressure on us as educators. Most of us had not anticipated teaching in front of a camera or having students submit work via fax or computer."

But Budd, who himself attended a California community college, believes SLCC is uniquely situated to confront the twin challenges of growth and emerging technologies. "Our macro goals haven't changed very much," he says. "We want to build a responsive, true community college, expanding our mission to include new possibilities. We have to guard and protect our open-door policy. That's taking on new forms now, with the Western Governor University and distance education delivery. We have to devise means of providing education electronically without having a classroom and seat time. Technology is not cheap; in fact, it's almost a black hole."

Still, with challenges come rewards. "The real reward is knowing you've helped a person make a change in their lives for the better. If you'll work, we'll help make you successful. We don't care about how you did in high school or your ACT scores. We'll take you

as you are. Our goal here is to build a responsive, true community college, not forgetting our traditional mission to provide an open-door policy and to offer associate degrees and vocational education, but to expand our mission to include applied technology and other programs that will help our students go out into the world better able to compete."

A PRIMARY OBJECTIVE OF SLCC IS TO MEET THE SPECIFIC NEEDS OF BUSI-NESSES AND INDUSTRIES BY PROVIDING QUALITY, STATE-OF-THE-ART EDUCATION AND TRAINING BOTH ON-SITE AND/OR AT ONE OF THE COLLEGE'S 10 LOCA-TIONS. LAST YEAR, THE COLLEGE HAD TRAINING PARTNERSHIPS, WORKSHOPS, AND TRAINING FOR EMPLOYEES OF MORE THAN 700 DIFFERENT FIRMS.

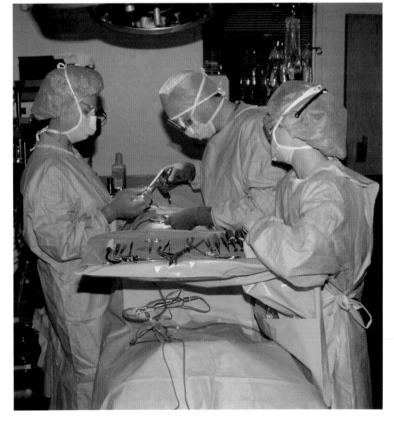

Harman Management Corporation

Leon W. "Pete" Harman may be the founder of the largest single domestic KFC franchise—with 266 restaurants spread throughout Colorado, Washington, California, and Utah—but he remembers 1952, when there was a single Kentucky Fried Chicken (as the chain was formerly named) restaurant in Salt Lake City at 3900 South

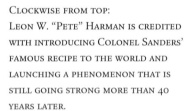

State Street. Harman ought to remember—his company, Harman Management Corporation, is credited with introducing Colonel Sanders' famous recipe to the world and launching a phenomenon that is still going strong more than 40 years later.

A native of Granger, Utah, Harman already had more than 15 years of restaurant experience in capacities ranging from dishwasher to owner when he met Colonel Harland Sanders at a National Restaurant Association convention in Chicago in 1951. The two men hit it off, but, as Harman recalls, "The colonel wasn't selling franchises at this point; he just showed me his recipe and his cooking process. He was showing me as a friend. But he knew food and was a great showman."

A History of Innovation

In 1952, Harman became the first franchisee for Colonel Sanders' Kentucky Fried Chicken. The concept was an immediate success, and by 1957, Harman owned three Kentucky Fried Chicken restaurants in Salt Lake City. Also in 1957, Harman created the bucket for easy-to-carry-out, take-home meals. Up until this time, Kentucky

Fried Chicken was only available at full-service restaurants or at a small take-home department within these restaurants.

The bucket concept was the key to creating enough volume at a take-home department to justify the take-home known today as an independent, quick-service restaurant. The bucket concept started selling meals for the entire family in an easy-to-carry-out container. For $3.50, customers got 14 pieces of chicken, 5 rolls, and a pint of gravy. The bucket remains an integral part of Harman's and the KFC system.

Harman's bucket innovation was an early example of his willingness to embrace change, a tendency that was to become a

hallmark of his company's management style. Early on, Harman Management Corporation initiated a profit-sharing plan, becoming one of the country's first companies to do so. All employees, regardless of position, receive an annual bonus based on their performance and company profits. In addition, restaurant general managers receive monthly bonuses, and all management personnel attend an annual, all-expense-paid training and incentive convention held at a different location each year.

Harman's commitment to free-enterprise principles and its generosity engender an unusual degree of loyalty among employees. Harman estimates that turnover among management hovers around 11 percent—a very low figure in the restaurant world. In fact, it's not unusual to find employees who have been with the company for more than 30 years.

One of those long-term employees is Jackie Trujillo. In 1953, fresh out of high school, she began working as a carhop for Harman's first restaurant. After stints as assistant manager, store manager, training manager, district manager, and division manager, she moved to California in 1983 to become executive vice president of operations for the company. In 1987, she was again promoted, this time to executive vice chairman. In 1995, she became chairman of the board.

"Most of the people in the company started at the bottom, just like me," Trujillo reflects. "Most of us didn't even think we wanted a career in this business. So many people stay with our company because they have an opportunity to grow."

Harman estimates that almost 500 couples of all ages are associates in his stores today because of the employee ownership plan he launched in the early 1960s. Under this plan, managers may own up to 40 percent of a store while Harman Management owns 46 percent. The balance is owned by others, including bookkeepers and district managers. "We've always been pretty good at motivating people," Harman allows. "The important thing is to see that it perpetuates itself, provides a living for the people who throw in with you. The ownership is key; it leads to higher satisfaction and lower turnover of management. We feel if we choose the right team member and treat them right, they'll be happy, and the customer is ultimately the winner."

Trujillo agrees. "We're always looking for ways to improve our management skills so we can be better employers," she says. "Our mission statement is to create a caring atmosphere for success and achieve 100 percent customer satisfaction."

COMMITTED TO UTAH

Although Harman currently makes his home in northern California, he maintains many ties

to Utah. In recent years, he has offered support to the Hale Theatre in West Valley City, to clean-up projects at the Taylorsville Cemetery, and to the restoration of his childhood home, which he opened as a senior citizen's center named the David and Grace Harman Home, in honor of his parents. "I'm proud of my Utah roots," Harman notes. "I'm glad to give something back there. You have a lot more fun giving things away than you do earning it. But I won't give anything away that won't do good for people."

Trujillo adds, "One of the reasons we're still here is because we're a company that's not afraid of change. You'll see a lot of changes to keep us looking good and new—to keep offering the same prod-

ucts and consistency but to keep the presentation and environment fresh and new."

Harman predicts his KFC franchises will continue to offer the products they are known for, while expanding to offer an even greater selection of low-fat offerings. He also believes delivery will occupy an increasingly large part of business. "People are busy today, and you have to offer convenience as well as quality. As long as it doesn't cannibalize your regular business," he concludes, "I'm all for it." And with these innovations, a history of business success, and a dedication to employee and customer satisfaction, Harman Management has made its mark in the Salt Lake City business community.

IN 1957, HARMAN (RIGHT) CREATED THE BUCKET AND THE TAKE-HOME CONCEPT.

LONG-TERM EMPLOYEE JACKIE TRUJILLO BEGAN WORK IN 1953, FRESH OUT OF HIGH SCHOOL, AS A CARHOP FOR HARMAN'S FIRST RESTAURANT. AFTER MOVING THROUGH THE COMPANY IN VARIOUS POSITIONS, SHE CURRENTLY SERVES AS CHAIRMAN OF THE BOARD (LEFT).

THE WORLD'S FIRST KENTUCKY FRIED CHICKEN (AS THE CHAIN WAS FORMERLY NAMED) OPENED IN SALT LAKE CITY AT 3900 SOUTH STATE STREET IN 1952 (RIGHT).

DAMES & MOORE IS ONE OF THE WEST'S MOST PROMINENT ENGINEERING and environmental consulting services firms. Today's Dames & Moore, part of the Dames & Moore Group, is a $650-million company with more than 5,500 employees and 130 offices throughout the world. The firm specializes in providing comprehensive,

integrated environmental, engineering, and construction management services that enhance the business, regulatory compliance, and technological commitments its clients must make on a global basis.

With more than half a century of international experience, the scope and quality of Dames & Moore's services, coupled with the firm's broad-based geographic operations, make the company unique among consulting companies.

LOCAL CAPABILITIES

Founded in Los Angeles in 1938, Dames & Moore opened its Salt Lake City office in 1953. With additional offices in Boise; Seattle; Spokane; Denver; Anchorage; Phoenix; Albuquerque; Portland, Oregon; and San Francisco, Dames & Moore has the capabilities to successfully manage complicated projects throughout the region.

From the 1940s through the 1980s, Dames & Moore was a consulting firm focused on geotechnical engineering and environmental and geologic sciences. In the early 1990s, the firm began expanding its technical capabilities to become a full-service engineering and consulting practice. During this period, the firm added to its capabilities by acquiring national firms such as Walk-Haydel, a process engineering company; DecisionQuest, which specializes in litigation consultation; BRW, which specializes in development planning and transportation; and O'Brien Kreitzberg, a leading construction-management firm. The acquisition of BRW and O'Brien Kreitzberg significantly increased Dames & Moore's capability to offer fully integrated services in public works and transportation projects.

Locally, Dames & Moore has worked on a number of transporta-

tion and infrastructure development projects, including the I-15 Northbound Expansion Study, the North-South Light Rail studies, waste resource and geotechnical issues at Kennecott, and remediation at Hill Air Force Base. The company been involved in hazardous waste management since its infancy in the late 1970s and early '80s. Since that market has matured, the company has strategically broadened and added diversified capabilities related to transportation, infrastructure, and mining services, including planning, GIS, waste management design, and construction management.

In addition, Dames & Moore offers a number of civil engineering and land-development engineering services, including preparation of construction drawings and specifications, construction inspection and observation, construction retrofits and corrections, cost esti-

LOCALLY, DAMES & MOORE HAS WORKED ON A NUMBER OF TRANSPORTATION AND INFRASTRUCTURE DEVELOPMENT PROJECTS, INCLUDING THE NORTH-SOUTH LIGHT RAIL STUDIES.

mation and construction reviews, fuel tank and pumping system design, geotechnical investigations and slope evaluations, quality control and quality assurance testing, and value engineering analysis of projects.

ENVIRONMENTAL AND COMMUNITY CONTRIBUTIONS

Since the 1980s, Dames & Moore has been heavily involved in environmental issues, in addition to the firm's traditional geotechnical practice. Dames & Moore prepared the first Environmental Impact Statement under the comprehensive federal law known as the National Environmental Policy Act. Today, the firm is actively working to promote sustainable development through its water resources work. One project that the firm describes as a keynote is a snowmelt model that is being used as a predictive tool for forecasting runoff, thus allowing the optimization of water resource management.

Since 1983, the firm has been involved in cultural resources work. A staff of 30 professionals works out of several of the firm's offices, including Salt Lake City, on issues including record searches, predictive modeling, sensitivity analysis, historic building inventories, drafting of agreements, archaeological testing, and data recovery.

Dames & Moore is also committed to volunteerism. It has been the firm's philosophy that it can't live in a community without being a part of it. The firm donates time and resources to the Utah Department of Transportation's Adopt-a-Highway plan, as well as to community causes such as Habitat for Humanity and food drives during the holidays.

DISTINGUISHED SERVICE

A key differentiator is a true commitment to client service. The staff listens to clients, identifies their needs, and comes up with creative solutions. In addition, Dames & Moore is experienced in

clearing regulatory hurdles in an economical way: The firm typically develops strategies that bring regulators and owners together to achieve a solution that appropriately regulates the project, as well as bringing it on-line affordably.

The company currently has approximately 600 clients in the Utah market, with contracts ranging in size from several hundred dollars to several million—and everything in between. Recent clients include the Utah Transit Authority, Boyer Company, the U.S. Army's Dugway Proving Ground, Summit Park Water District, Staker Paving Corporation, and Geneva Rock Products.

And in the future? The firm's principals feel that the future looks bright as new opportunities present themselves on a daily basis. Through Dames & Moore's corporate strategic vision, the goal is to continue to grow, expand service capabilities, meet clients' needs, and prosper as the firm approaches the beginning of the next millennium.

CORDANT TECHNOLOGIES, FORMERLY KNOWN AS THIOKOL CORPORATION, headquartered in Salt Lake City, is the parent company of three diverse, technology-based businesses that serve aerospace and industrial customers worldwide. Thiokol Propulsion is the world's largest producer of sophisticated solid fuel rocket motors for space and defense programs,

and commercial space launch applications. Huck International manufactures fastening systems for aircraft, heavy-duty trucks, railcars, and construction companies worldwide. Howmet International is a world leader in precision castings for jet aircraft and industrial gas turbine engines and cast aerospace structural components.

By design, Cordant is rapidly changing its business mix. "We are committed to the strategy of growing sales and earnings by broadening our business into attractive commercial and industrial markets," notes Chairman and Chief Executive Officer James R. Wilson.

THIOKOL PROPULSION

Thiokol Propulsion, the world's leading supplier of solid propulsion for space and defense systems, focuses on the nation's space program and defense industry, as well as on domestic and international commercial space markets.

Based in Utah, Thiokol Propulsion constitutes the original Thiokol Corporation, which until 1996 counted only the National Aeronautics and Space Administration (NASA) and the U.S. Department of Defense (DOD) as prime customers. In the years since its founding in 1929, Thiokol Propulsion has supplied reliable solid rocket propulsion for every human space flight program and every land-based U.S. solid rocket intercontinental ballistic missile system.

Notably, Thiokol Propulsion's reusable solid rocket motors have boosted every space shuttle since the first launch in 1981. For the last 30 years, Thiokol Propulsion has also provided rocket motors for the Minuteman land-based strategic missile, the cornerstone of the U.S. defense program. A U.S. Air Force contract that calls for the replacement of current potentially age-sensitive motors extends Thiokol Propulsion's Minuteman missile association beyond the year 2020.

Thiokol Propulsion also offers a broad range of propulsion systems for launching and positioning satellites for both military and commercial customers worldwide. These include STAR™ satellite placement motors, CASTOR® strap-on boosters, and the versatile CASTOR 120® motor designed for first-stage, second-stage, and strap-on applications.

HUCK INTERNATIONAL

Cordant acquired Huck International, Inc. in 1991 as part of its plan to diversify beyond the space and defense business. Huck provides proprietary engineered fastening solutions that deliver value to customers in the worldwide aircraft and industrial markets, including the heavy truck, railcar, and construction industries.

Huck's fastener components can be found on virtually every aircraft in the Western world. Revenues from commercial and military aircraft companies account for approximately half of Huck's annual sales. Huck provides sophisticated fasteners and fastening systems to Boeing, Airbus Industrie, Aerospatiale, British Aerospace, Daimler-Benz, Bell, Canadair, General Dynamics, Lockheed Martin, Northrup Grumman, Bombardier, and Raytheon.

Industrial markets provide the balance of Huck's annual revenues. Huck makes fasteners for use in

CLOCKWISE FROM TOP:
THE SPACE SHUTTLE IS THE LARGEST ROCKET MOTOR EVER FLOWN AND THE FIRST DESIGNED FOR REUSE. EACH LAUNCH REQUIRES THE BOOST OF TWO THIOKOL SOLID FUEL ROCKET MOTORS.

HUCK'S ALLIANCE WITH THE BOEING COMPANY IN DEVELOPING A CLOSE-TOLERANCE HEAD LGP18 LOCKBOLT TO SOLVE AIRCRAFT CUSTOMER COSMETIC ISSUES OF UNIFORM FASTENER HEAD FLUSHNESS IS NOW MOVING TOWARD AN INDUSTRYWIDE STANDARD.

THE LGP18 FASTENER, ALONG WITH OTHER HUCK PROPRIETARY FASTENERS, MAY BE FOUND FROM THE CABIN TO OTHER SECTIONS, INCLUDING THE WINGS, OF JETLINERS.

heavy-duty trucks, school buses, railroad cars, bridges, and commercial building construction. Customers include Ford Motor Company, Freightliner, and PACCAR.

Howmet International

Cordant owns the controlling interest in Howmet International, which is the largest manufacturer in the world of precision investment castings of superalloys and titanium alloys for jet aircraft and industrial gas turbine engines.

Precision investment casting is a more economical process for producing metal parts in complex shapes and in greater precision than forging or machining. These complex-shaped metal parts include state-of-the-art investment cast blades and vanes, large cast compressor turbine and rotor components, and high-quality aluminum components for aerospace and commercial applications.

Howmet's products are part of every aircraft turbine engine flying in the Western world. "When people fly in an airplane, most of them don't know that the jet engines are powered in part by our Howmet blades," says Wilson. "They probably don't know that the jet engine companies we work with are household names, including General Electric, Pratt & Whitney, and Rolls-Royce."

Similarly, Howmet has leveraged its decades of experience making large, complex metal parts to become the world's leading producer of high-tech industrial gas turbine components. High-quality, more durable turbine engine components allow energy providers to produce more power while enjoying lower gas turbine life cycle costs. Industrial gas turbine customers include global giants Asea Brown Boveri, General Electric, and Siemens.

Howmet's research and development facility is the only one of its kind in the investment casting industry. Howmet conducts extensive research and development of its material, product, and process technologies, and is expert in the most advanced single crystal and directional solidification casting techniques. Several new technolo-

gies from the research center are helping Howmet generate growth. Among these are gravity metal molding and vacuum die casting, which can replace forged or fabricated parts with lower-cost solutions in certain types of gas turbine and commercial applications.

Past and Future

Since its founding in 1929, Cordant has applied technology successfully for development of several landmark products, including the world's first synthetic rubber and the best solid propellant rocket fuel binder.

But since the end of the Cold War, this Salt Lake City company has doubled in size and evolved from a focus on propulsion-driven products in Utah to a diverse corporation that serves many blue-chip aerospace and industrial companies worldwide.

With 1998 sales exceeding $2 billion, a workforce totaling nearly 16,500, and a network of more than 30 operations throughout North America, Europe, and Asia, Cordant is a dynamic company. According to Wilson, "We continue to be a world leader in our solid rocket propulsion business, which remains an important part of the company. In 1956, we planted the seeds of the business in Utah where they have taken root firmly and now have spread worldwide.

"But we've grown beyond our propulsion business. Through acquisitions, Cordant has added our Huck high-technology fastener

From ignition to end of burn, the twin reusable solid rocket motors produce 6 million pounds of maximum thrust, or 71 percent of the power needed to propel the shuttle into orbit (left).

Each Thiokol solid rocket motor is 126 feet long and 12 feet in diameter. The entire booster, including nose cap, frustum, and forward and aft skirts, is approximately 149 feet long (right).

group, which serves a broad range of industrial and aerospace markets. We have also acquired a majority portion of Howmet, a producer of high-technology castings used in jet aircraft engines and in industrial gas turbine engines.

"Cordant today is a financially strong company with virtually no debt, a strong cash flow, and very good earnings potential. We are proud to call Utah our corporate home—a state whose motto, 'Industry,' bespeaks our satisfaction with the business climate here."

Blades like this evolve from cooperative efforts between customers and the Howmet Research Center, where more than 170 professionals and technicians focus on applied research and product support. Many of these blades help power jet engines.

L-3 COMMUNICATIONS
COMMUNICATION SYSTEMS-WEST

A SATELLITE PASSING HIGH ABOVE THE MIDDLE EAST COLLECTS information about troop movement in Iraq and beams the signal back to Earth. Aircraft carriers plying the waters of the Persian Gulf receive the message and relay exact coordinates to military fighters. The planes swoop low, sending high-resolution photographs back to intelligence officers in the field.

Much of this high-tech surveillance and reconnaissance—air to satellite, sea to air, and air to ground—takes place in part because of data links perfected by a Salt Lake City company: Communication Systems-West, or CS-West. CS-West is a division of L-3 Communications, and it is a leader in communication systems for intelligence collection, imagery processing, and satellite communications.

A HISTORY OF COMMUNICATIONS SYSTEMS

The parent company, L-3 Communications, headquartered in New York, employs about 6,000 people who are organized into 12 divisions. Its overall revenue in 1997 approached $1 billion. CS-West, with more than 40 years' experience building military communication systems, is the company's largest division, with more than 1,700 employees, including an engineer-ing staff of nearly 950. CS-West's products and support of military personnel in the field have contributed to a variety of covert operations—from the high-altitude missions of the U2 spy planes that took photographs of Cold War-era Soviet military installations, to the coordinated air and ground attacks in operations Desert Shield and Desert Storm in the early 1990s.

"We started with many large racks full of equipment used in early point-to-point communications," says Elaine Rebele, CS-West's director of communications. "That's changed. Now we're building data links that are smaller, lighter, faster, and packed with more capabilities," she says.

One of the airborne links, named Modular Interoperable Data Link, is a multichannel communications product that can transmit information at rates of 1.544 to 274 megabytes per second through a variety of frequency bands. These systems are so fast (instantaneous) and secure that the company has been the main supplier of such systems to the Department of Defense and several other U.S. government agencies, as well as some foreign customers.

In addition to its line of data links, CS-West also produces transportable satellite and interoperable surface terminals. These terminals are employed for a variety of military and commercial uses. Military uses range from manned and un-manned surveillance and recon-naissance aircraft to command and control for projects dating back to the Sargeant Missile pro-gram. In fact, an army contract for the integration and manufactur-ing of the Sargeant Missile was the company's first project for the Department of Defense in 1957, when the company was founded under the name of Sperry Utah Engineering Laboratories. The sat-ellite terminals, which were devel-oped and deployed extensively in the early 1990s, can be transported anywhere via a C-130 aircraft and can be set up within 12 hours.

"Many of the projects we've done in the past have been classi-fied," Rebele says. "Some are still sensitive, and many of our cus-

L-3 COMMUNICATIONS PRODUCES SATELLITE TRANSPORTABLE GROUND TERMINALS, WHICH ARE EMPLOYED FOR A VARIETY OF MILITARY AND COMMER-CIAL USES (LEFT).

THE RADIO BASED UNIT (RBU) USED IN THE FIXED WIRELESS LOOP SYSTEM IS BASED ON DIGITAL RADIO TECHNOL-OGY AND WAS DESIGNED FOR LOW-COST, HIGH-QUALITY WIRELESS PHONE AND DATA SERVICE (RIGHT).

tomers prefer that we safeguard their privacy."

A Transition to Commercial Applications

Airborne, surface, and satcom data links are CS-West's three main products. Since the end of the Cold War, however, the company has been developing commercial applications for its patented technology. "We have many patents on technology related to our communications products," Rebele adds. CS-West has established alliances with other telecommunications companies to test potential uses of its expertise for future wireless telephony.

Among the most promising commercial applications is a telephone system called fixed wireless loop, which is a system that combines some of the remote capabilities of a mobile phone and the reliability of a home phone that plugs into a jack. Instead of running wire lines from a house to a telephone pole, CS-West's technology would permit a wireless connection from a box on the side of a house to a fixed ground station or satellite. "When you lift up the receiver of one of these phones," Rebele says, "the sound quality is comparable to or better than a home phone. Voices do not break up or sound crackly as with mobile service." CS-West envisions that the phone will have a market in rural areas and in parts of Africa and South America,

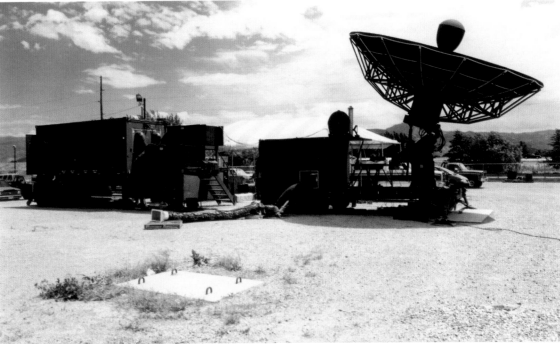

where it would be impossible to string or bury telephone cables.

Giving Back to Salt Lake

Though the company dominates a specific niche in defense electronics, it takes pride in being a good citizen of the Wasatch Front. CS-West employees take part in both the summer and winter Corporate Games. The company sponsors runners in most local charity competitions and takes part in the Utah Business Partnership Program to help schools with few resources. The company is a partner to Jackson Elementary School, and it sponsors the school's tutoring and fund-raising efforts, as well as donating surplus computers.

CS-West also works with the University of Utah's engineering clinic, conducting joint research projects. In 1994, the university presented CS-West with its Utah Minority Engineering Program's Corporate Award for support of minority engineering and computer science students.

As a partner to both commercial and governmental clients, CS-West maintains its dedication to applying the latest technological advances to a broad range of uses. With an equal commitment to partnership with the local community and to educational institutions, CS-West will continue to be a beacon for corporate leadership in the new millennium.

One of a family of three ground terminals, the Tri-Band Field Terminal (TFT) provides a single point tri-band satellite link for tactical field operations.

The Parabolic Antenna (left) and the Airborne Modem Assembly make up the heart of L-3 Com's airborne data link digital processing system. This small, light weight, and rugged technology has been developed for use on a variety of platforms.

EDO CORPORATION

*T*N 1925, EARL DODGE OSBORN, A WORLD WAR I VETERAN AND AVIATION pioneer, used his initials as the name of his fledgling enterprise, which built and tested seaplanes and aircraft floats in College Point, New York. Thus was born EDO Aircraft Corporation. ▨ For the next 15 years, the company's bread-and-butter product was aluminum pontoons for

seaplanes, which offered tremendous advantages over the cumbersome wooden floats then commonly in use on seaplanes. EDO floats were essential components in aircraft exploring the rugged, previously inaccessible back country of Canada and Alaska.

During World War II, EDO was selected by the U.S. Navy to develop a completely new seaplane. As an offshoot of the company's research efforts during the war, an electronics division was formed, staffed by experienced engineers who specialized in the design, development, and manufacture of underwater equipment. With this broadening scope of activity, the company changed its name to EDO Corporation in 1947. Unchanged, however, was EDO's industry-leading research. With the development of a deep-ocean depth sounder, the company moved to the forefront in the field of sonar.

GROWTH AND DIVERSIFICATION

In 1958, EDO Corporation acquired Electro-Ceramics of Salt Lake City, a manufacturer of piezoelectric crystals and ceramic elements used in the production of underwater acoustic electronic and other equipment. That company's name

was changed to EDO Western Corporation.

Eleven years later, in 1969, Fiber Science, Inc. of Salt Lake City became a wholly owned subsidiary of EDO. Fiber Science had developed techniques for fabricating composite parts using filament-wound glass and other reinforcing fibers. Initially, this innovation was applied to creating airborne fuel, water, and waste tanks. Later, though, the markets were expanded to apply more exotic, high-strength materials to aircraft structures, control surfaces, and specialized aircraft components. These suc-

cesses led to further diversification into large, composite fairings for offshore oil drilling; missile launch tubes; and stator cones for hydroelectric generators.

EDO TODAY

EDO's Salt Lake City operation consists of some 320 employees in two business units: Centrally located within the Salt Lake valley is Electro-Ceramic Products, which produces piezoelectric ceramic components for medical, aerospace, commercial, industrial, military, and geophysical applications; and located near the Salt Lake Inter-

national Airport is Fiber Science, a manufacturer of composite-wound water and waste tanks for commercial airliners, fiberglass turbine blades for wind power generators, and sonar domes for ships and submarines.

EDO Electro-Ceramic Products is North America's largest producer of specialty solid-state piezoelectric products, materials, shapes, and sizes commonly known as solid-state piezoelectric products. Its products enhance everyday life, but go virtually unnoticed by the average citizen. For example, Electro-Ceramic manufactures ultrasonic bubble detectors used in kidney dialysis equipment; safe, low-energy fuel level sensors for major commercial aircraft; active vibration control devices used in the photolithography industry; piezoelectric transducers for ultrasonic cleaners and fish finders; and underwater sensors used by geophysical oil exploration teams.

Electro-Ceramic General Manager Gary Springfield describes the company's current atmosphere as forward looking and enthusiastic. "What I see today is a much more diversified company focusing on core industries," he says. "The company is discovering what we do well and then searching other industries to develop applications for our strengths."

Meanwhile, the company's Fiber Science Business Unit is expanding into new realms requiring larger, lighter, stronger, corrosion-resistant composite structures and pressure vessels for use on spacecraft, railcars, trucks, and offshore oil platforms.

Mike Therson, EDO Fiber Science general manager, points out that the one thing tying all these widely varied applications together is the opportunity to significantly improve the performance of all these products by applying the skills of a diverse, yet well-trained workforce. "There's a lot of potential in both our current and new markets. We are constantly improving our workforce and product base to utilize our materials and process expertise where it is needed most," he says.

Employee Involvement

In addition, EDO is involved to an ever increasing extent in the affairs of the community. Demonstrating interest in doing more for each other and for the community—and not requiring the impetus of a management-mandated programs—the company's personnel engage in a wide variety of service projects. EDO employees are active in local church leadership and several youth activities, including scouting organizations. They also sup-

port Angel Trees and Shoes for Children, and have initiated a companywide wellness program.

EDO's diverse workforce is a key to the company's culture and future. The Salt Lake City facilities employ people originally from Vietnam, Thailand, China, Korea, South and Central America, Russia, and Bosnia, and their commitment and enthusiasm far outweigh any concerns about cultural differences. The company is looking for the best people for the job, as the technical work performed by both business units is highly process-oriented and requires many skills. EDO employees are committed to working together to take the company into exciting new realms.

THE EDO FLAT-PAK PASSIVE HYDRO-PHONE ARRAY MOUNTS ON THE SIDE OF A SUBMARINE LIKE A LARGE BILLBOARD.

AN EDO EMPLOYEE WORKS ON THE PRECISION LAYUP OF A 65-FOOT COMPOSITE WIND BLADE AT FIBER SCIENCE.

A RECENT PROMOTIONAL CAMPAIGN FOR REAGAN NATIONAL Advertising, Inc. emphasizes how much the community has changed since a young entrepreneur named William Reagan began selling outdoor advertising in Salt Lake City more than 30 years ago. Today, more than a million people read Reagan signs every day—a clear indicator of how much the community and the company have grown.

EARLY HISTORY

Reagan started his business in the mid-1960s after being inspired by a *Fortune* magazine article extolling the virtues of entrepreneurism. He already had experience selling outdoor advertising for other companies in Ohio and Utah, and reasoned that he could do equally well on his own. Reagan's hunch proved correct; since 1966, he has worked exclusively for the company he founded, Reagan National Advertising.

Reagan divides the company's history into several periods. He characterizes the 1965 to 1970 era as the developmental period; the years 1971 to 1981 as the internal growth years; and the 1980s and early 1990s as a leveraged-buyout era. During that period, Reagan National Advertising purchased Galaxy Outdoor Advertising to become what Reagan calls "one of the dominant outdoor advertising companies in the state." In 1988,

the company acquired Heritage Outdoor to create the current Reagan National Advertising.

In the early years, Reagan built the business himself, working part-time from an office in the Freeport Center while completing a banking and finance degree at Weber State College (now University). In 1968, he entered law school at the University of Utah, but managed to keep the business going even as he endured the grueling law school regimen. Although

Reagan left the practice of law in 1973, the education was invaluable.

In 1978, Reagan attended Harvard Business School. There, he learned about financing sources, and was able to further expand his company. In 1987, Reagan raised $100 million in outside equity to purchase Heritage, a billboard company with properties in nine national markets. Reagan continued to operate in those markets until 1991, when he divested of everything but the operations in Austin, Texas, and Utah. "The starting years were just more fun," he explains. "Later, I was just spending most of my time in administration."

Reagan is proud of the fact that his two sons, Daniel and Bill Jr., and daughter, Frances, are involved; Reagan describes this as the "family succession" era. "In the early 1990s," Reagan admits, "I fell into a midlife period in business where I wasn't as interested; if we hadn't had family members in the business, I might really have considered retiring. These days I'm having fun and we're growing."

THE ADVANTAGES OF REAGAN NATIONAL ADVERTISING

When you don't want to keep it a secret . . . advertise on Reagan National Advertising," says Frances Reagan. "Reagan

WILLIAM REAGAN (CENTER) IS PROUD OF THE FACT THAT HIS TWO SONS, DANIEL (LEFT) AND BILL JR. (RIGHT), AND DAUGHTER, FRANCES, ARE INVOLVED IN REAGAN NATIONAL ADVERTISING. HE DESCRIBES THIS AS THE "FAMILY SUCCESSION" ERA.

REAGAN NATIONAL ADVERTISING'S CONSTANT REPETITION ENSURES THAT POTENTIAL CUSTOMERS THINK OF THE ADVERTISER'S BUSINESS WHEN THEY EXPERIENCE A NEED FOR A PRODUCT OR SERVICE.

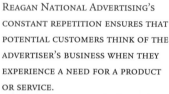

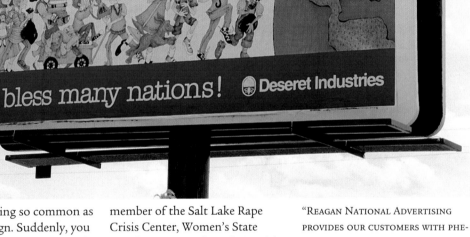

National Advertising provides our customers with phenomenal billboard locations, as well as statewide distribution. As the Wasatch Front has grown, so has our billboard location distribution. Reagan National Advertising supports a full-time staff of sales representatives, marketing professionals, construction workers, and skilled artists."

Most businesses, large and small, suffer from an identity crisis or lack of market population awareness of their products or services. Businesses that advertise on Reagan National Advertising repeatedly reach their potential customers. The company's constant repetition ensures that potential customers think of the advertiser's business when they experience a need for a product or service.

Reagan National Advertising offers three flexible ways to advertise. Bulletins, 14 feet by 48 feet, give a message a dramatic impact that customers won't forget. Posters give advertisers the ability to reach up to 100 percent of the market population the first day, and continue this level of saturation all month long. Thirty-sheet posters, 10 feet five inches by 22 feet eight inches, build instant awareness. Eight-sheet posters, five feet by 11 feet, affordably achieve high reach on frequency. Reagan National Advertising's repetition makes the message effective.

Over the past 30 years, William Reagan has seen phenomenal change in the billboard industry. He believes the most sweeping changes are yet to come, however: "In my lifetime, I see the electronic

billboard becoming so common as to be on every sign. Suddenly, you can have all the benefits of broadcasting radio messages via low-powered signals. I see the sign becoming a TV set and people listening to an audio message, if they want to. That's all coming. The most important thing for getting your message out, though, is going to remain distribution and location."

A RECORD OF COMMUNITY SERVICE

Reagan has been active in many community and industry organizations and has sat on the boards of Weber State University's National Advisory Board, the Utah Bicentennial Commission, and the Outdoor Advertising Association of America, among many others. His wife, Julia, has been a board

member of the Salt Lake Rape Crisis Center, Women's State Legislative Council, Utah Special Olympics, Children's Center, and United Way Appropriation Committee. Both William and Julia are members of the United Way Alexis de Tocqueville Society.

Reagan believes the future for outdoor advertising is promising. As he says, "There's a demand for the product because it's effective and simple. As long as people want to drive a car and go where they want to go, there'll always be outdoor advertising. We may not know the size, or where they'll be, but they'll be there somewhere." And Reagan National Advertising will also be there, adapting and changing with the times to remain a leader in the outdoor advertising industry.

"REAGAN NATIONAL ADVERTISING PROVIDES OUR CUSTOMERS WITH PHENOMENAL BILLBOARD LOCATIONS, AS WELL AS STATEWIDE DISTRIBUTION," STATES FRANCES REAGAN.

Aero Tech Manufacturing, Inc.

SINCE ITS FOUNDING MORE THAN THREE DECADES AGO, AERO TECH Manufacturing, Inc. has established itself as a leading producer of precision sheet metal components for the computer, electronic, medical, water treatment, gaming, and printing industries. In addition to supplying components as well as turnkey equipment to third-party customers,

Aero Tech builds and installs its own radiant, acoustic, and security ceiling products for customers nationwide. And according to Tim Riley, the company's president, Aero Tech attributes much of its competitive edge to being a homegrown company. "We recognize that our employees are the reason for our success and the foundation upon which we build in order to meet the expectations of our customers and shareholders," Riley says.

Aero Tech has been making a name for itself in the manufacturing of high-quality sheet metal products in North Salt Lake since 1967. After only a decade in business, Aero Tech was acquired by Toromont Industries Ltd., a Canadian public company based in Ontario with 2,200 employees across North America. It is an industry leader in refrigeration and heavy equipment. The refrigeration group includes recreational, industrial, process, and commercial refrigeration. The equipment group represents Caterpillar and other equipment lines, maintaining dealerships in Ontario, Newfoundland, and Labrador.

FROM UTAH TO THE WORLD

But even as a key division of an international company, Aero Tech continues to excel in the manufacture of custom precision sheet metal components and assemblies for third-party customers as its core business. Many customers have called on Aero Tech's expertise to provide engineering design and manufacturing services for complete product lines, including electrical/mechanical assembly and testing of equipment.

In the ceiling panel business, the company has completed installations worldwide. In Utah, these include the Novell headquarters in Provo, as well as Primary Children's Hospital, Utah state office building, Copper Hills and Jordan high schools, Sandy City Third District Court, Utah State Adult Psychiatric Facility, and University of Utah Bio Med Center in Salt Lake City.

High-profile projects nationally include custom acoustic ceiling jobs for the buildings that house Chem-Bank, Goldman Sachs, Merrill Lynch, Loews Theatres, Foley Square Federal Courthouse, Sacramento Federal Courthouse, and the 149th Street Station in New York City. Aero Tech's international assignments include custom work for the passenger boarding bridges at the new Hong Kong International Airport.

TRUE TO ITS SALT LAKE CITY ROOTS

Still, for all its national and international dealings, Aero Tech derives a competitive edge from its location in North Salt

ONE OF AERO TECH MANUFACTURING'S STRENGTHS HAS BEEN ITS ABILITY TO BLEND AUTOMATED TECHNOLOGY WITH A STABLE AND EXPERIENCED WORKFORCE.

AERO TECH IS VERY PROUD OF ITS EMPLOYEE TEAM. THEIR DEDICATION TO QUALITY AND CUSTOMER SERVICE HAS MADE THE FIRM SUCCESSFUL IN TODAY'S HIGHLY COMPETITIVE MANUFACTURING WORLD.

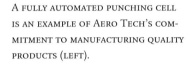

Lake. Only minutes from the Salt Lake International Airport, as well as major rail and other transportation centers, Aero Tech can distribute its goods anywhere in the world.

Aero Tech also helps to support the local economy. The company has eight local managers in its plant who have more than 140 years' experience with Aero Tech between them. In its 70,000-square-foot, state-of-the-art facility, the company employs a full-time staff of 125 skilled and dedicated craftsmen, most of them local hires. In addition, the fact that the company is owned by Toromont, a $500 million-plus-per-year corporation, means that Salt Lake City can count on Aero Tech's investment to continue. "As Salt Lake continues to grow," says Riley, "the company also gains more local customers and spends more on local suppliers."

PROVIDING AN ADVANTAGE

Aero Tech's local engineering team is one of the company's distinguishing strengths in a competitive market. The company employs six on-site engineering personnel. These specialists and support personnel are available to give assistance to architects, engineers, and contractors from beginning to end—from the design and detailing phase through the execution of the contract. "We're able to take jobs and see them through," Riley says, "from a thought to a piece of paper to a finished product."

In addition to its engineers, Aero Tech also has a ceiling installation division—Aero Tech Construction Services (ATCS). "We recognize that a ceiling system is no better than the installing contractor who installs it," Riley says. "So we have experienced crews to help local teams install projects nationwide." ATCS also provides expert advice on budget pricing and unusual construction details.

Aero Tech sells its ceiling products and services through a nationwide network of sales representatives in the heating,

ventilating, and air-conditioning industries. The sales reps call on specifying mechanical engineers while buildings are still in the design stages.

FOCUS ON QUALITY

Customer satisfaction through quality services and on-time delivery has always been and remains Aero Tech's ultimate goal. In order to maximize its ability to achieve this goal, providing employees with a challenging and rewarding work environment is essential. Providing these essential ingredients stimulates employee participation and team building, which in turn provide the customer with a quality product.

These goals and values have benefited the company and its customers for more than 30 years. By focusing on these core strengths and values, Aero Tech will continue its steady growth well into the next century.

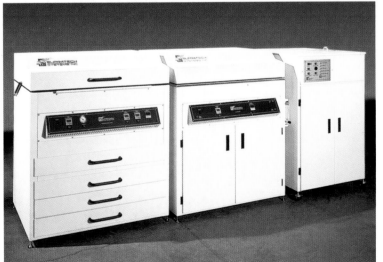

A FULLY AUTOMATED PUNCHING CELL IS AN EXAMPLE OF AERO TECH'S COMMITMENT TO MANUFACTURING QUALITY PRODUCTS (LEFT).

AERO TECH TAKES PRIDE IN THE FACT THAT IT CAN OFFER A WIDE VARIETY OF PRODUCTS, SUCH AS THE ALL-STAINLESS-STEEL FLEXSCOUR® UNDERDRAIN SYSTEM USED IN BOTH INDUSTRIAL AND MUNICIPAL APPLICATIONS FOR WATER FILTRATION (RIGHT).

THE HIGH-PRESSURE, ALL-STAINLESS-STEEL, POLYMER PLATE WASHOUT SYSTEM (ABOVE LEFT) AND THE PRINTING PLATE EXPOSURE/WASHER/DRYER SYSTEM ARE TWO EXAMPLES OF AERO TECH PRODUCTS THAT CAN BE TAILORED TO CUSTOMERS' NEEDS.

Evans & Sutherland Computer Corporation

WHEN EVANS & SUTHERLAND WAS FOUNDED IN THE LATE 1960S, THE computer graphics industry was in its infancy. In fact, the company, founded by David Evans, chairman of the computer sciences department at the University of Utah, and Ivan Sutherland, a professor in the department, was so far ahead of the market's understanding of using computers as simulators that it took five years to show a profit.

"They were really doing things on the leading edge," recounts current Senior Vice President/ Secretary Gary Meredith, who has been with the company almost since its inception. "They weren't sure who their customers were or how many might be out there."

FINDING FIRM FOOTING

With operating capital provided by the Rockefeller family, the company eventually found its niche. The industry began to catch up with the applications for the computer graphics technology Evans & Sutherland was pioneering.

"The original business plan was to use computer graphics for engineering," Meredith explains. "And a footnote to that was training applications such as pilot training. We shipped our first pilot training program in 1974; prior to that, we'd consulted on early pilot training simulators."

The company also explored a number of other avenues, creating one of the earliest page markup systems in 1971. A forerunner to today's desktop publishing systems, Evans & Sutherland's program was utilized by major newspapers, including the *Los Angeles Times* and the now defunct *Washington Star*.

But the company soon returned to its roots, concentrating on pilot training and computer graphics. "It's a very glamorous heritage we've spawned in terms of computer graphics," Meredith says proudly. He notes that the founders and/ or principals of many computer graphics firms—including Pixar, Adobe, and Silicon Graphics— were either University of Utah students, employees of Evans & Sutherland, or both.

EVANS & SUTHERLAND TODAY

While Evans & Sutherland has consolidated somewhat from a particularly adventurous period in the mid- and late 1980s, a healthy 15 percent of company profits are still invested in research and development of new products. The firm currently employs a staff of 800, including business operations, R&D, and manufacturing. Almost all company personnel work in the 400,000-square-foot, four-building facility located in Research Park.

Circumstances in Evans & Sutherland's primary markets— commercial airlines and the mili-

EVANS & SUTHERLAND WILL SOON BE EXPANDING AGAIN, ADDING A FIFTH BUILDING TO ITS HEADQUARTERS CAMPUS AT THE UNIVERSITY OF UTAH RESEARCH PARK (TOP).

EVERYTHING IN THIS TELEVISION STUDIO IS CREATED BY COMPUTER, EXCEPT FOR THE WOMAN. SHE IS ACTUALLY STANDING ON A 3-D BLUE SCREEN. EVANS & SUTHERLAND'S MINDSET VIRTUAL STUDIO SYSTEM CREATES THE "VIRTUAL SET" AROUND HER (BOTTOM).

tary—positioned the company well through the mid-1990s. The "do more with less" phenomenon swept through the military early in the decade, just as it did through the commercial sector. Computer-based training and simulation became increasingly important tools in helping armed services worldwide meet new operations and preparedness challenges. Also, sales of commercial airlines rebounded smartly during the decade, after a disastrous start; demand for training increased as well. The company successfully rode both trends and today has a commanding share of both markets.

Perhaps even more significant is Evans & Sutherland's commitment to drive its technology into new, high-growth markets. Evans & Sutherland decided early to ride the trend responsible for placing high-powered PCs into homes and businesses everywhere. Its high-performance 3-D graphics and simulation technology is now showing up in television, films, science centers, planetariums, and professional graphics workstations. "We supply the technology," Meredith says, "and others provide the content."

COMMUNITY INVOLVEMENT

Concerned with more than turning a profit, Evans & Sutherland has focused its community actions on several areas. "You cannot imagine how many worthy causes there are out there," Meredith says. "So we've tried to narrow our donations with the idea of giving fairly significantly to fewer causes." These causes include the University of Utah, Brigham Young University, United Way, Utah Opera Company, Utah Symphony, and Ballet West. Meredith also points out that Evans & Sutherland's executives donate significant amounts of time to professional and trade organizations, such as the Utah Information Technology Association and the governor's board on industry relations. "Plus," he adds, "we pay our employees well and all of them have stock options. As of this year, every employee is also on a personal incentive program."

ON THE HORIZON

In an industry given to shake-ups and left-field successes, Evans & Sutherland has thrived by looking for paradigm shifts and taking informed chances. But predicting the future is still a tough assignment, according to Meredith. "When we started shipping pilot training systems in the 1970s, the big military systems would be made up of as many as a dozen six-foot-tall storage systems; these were then the most advanced computers. While it still takes a lot of power to generate the pictures, a comparable system is now shipped in a box the size of a large suitcase."

According to Meredith, the computer industry has witnessed three paradigm shifts: from computers the size of a room to minicomputers to computer workstations. The industry is now in the midst of a fourth shift into the realm of Windows NT workstations. Evans & Sutherland has anticipated this shift and is aggressively driving new products that way. Meredith says, "The company is positioned to grow into Wintel; it's easier to deploy and cost effective. That's one of the high-growth areas we're aiming for."

But Meredith's predictions won't forsake Evans & Sutherland's sometimes lonely exploration of the frontier of computer graphics: "If you're trying to push the envelope all the time, you know some things will not work or will be more expensive than you'd planned. If you were to summarize the company's philosophy, it is to be fiscally conservative and technically aggressive."

THIS "OUT THE WINDOW" SCENE AND THE AVIONICS DISPLAYS IN THE COCKPIT OF THIS A320 FULL-FLIGHT SIMULATOR ARE TYPICAL OF REAL-TIME, COMPUTER-GENERATED VISUAL SYSTEMS CREATED BY EVANS & SUTHERLAND TO TRAIN COMMERCIAL AIRLINE PILOTS (TOP).

REAL OR SIMULATED? IT'S IMPORTANT THAT A PILOT IN A TRAINING SIMULATOR BE PRESENTED WITH THE MOST REALISTIC, OUT-THE-WINDOW VISUAL SCENE POSSIBLE FOR THE TRAINING EXPERIENCE TO HAVE MAXIMUM VALUE. EVANS & SUTHERLAND'S HARMONY IMAGE GENERATOR—THE MOST POWERFUL IN THE WORLD—CREATES REAL-TIME VISUALS OF SUPERIOR QUALITY (BOTTOM).

M ARK STEEL CORPORATION IS AS PROMINENT IN SALT LAKE CITY'S development as the buildings that define the city's skyline. And it's little wonder: The company fabricated the steel that makes many of these structures stand, from the Salt Lake Courts Complex and One Utah Center to the West Valley Events Center and Franklin Quest

Field, as well as the newly expanded Rice Stadium on the campus of the University of Utah.

Now in its fourth decade of operation, Mark Steel is the state's largest custom steel fabrication firm, maintaining two separate plant sites that together cover 17 acres of operating space. Each month, Mark Steel ships an average of 2 million pounds of fabricated steel. While the company markets aggressively throughout the United States and Canada, it ships the majority of its products to industrial and commercial sites in the western states.

BUILDING ON ITS FOUNDER'S SUCCESS

B ehind Mark Steel's success stands the figure of the company's founder, Abraham Markosian—businessman, philanthropist, and community pillar. Markosian died in 1998—three decades after setting up shop in 1968—but the legacy he left is as stout as the structural monuments his company erects.

The son of Armenian refugees who fled the Turkish massacres during World War I, Markosian was born in Murray in 1923. He graduated from Murray High School and joined the navy, where he served on a destroyer during World War II. Selected for officer train-

ing, he served as an officer in both World War II and the Korean War. He was trained at Harvard Business School and Tulane University, where he graduated with a degree in business administration.

In 1947, Markosian went to work at the Lang Company, Utah's first electric welding shop, where he quickly rose to the position of assistant plant manager. He left the company in 1960 to pursue other opportunities in the steel industry. Eight years later, he founded Mark Steel, setting out on a career that not only established a suc-

cessful business, but also shared that success with the community.

As a leader and philanthropist, Markosian focused on giving others what made it possible for him to succeed: reward for hard work and the occasion to take advantage of opportunity. He donated his time and money to Salt Lake Community College, where he served as a trustee, and took a special interest in the school's welding and other technical programs. His contributions and donations were acknowledged by the college, which awarded him an

DON BLAIR PHOTOGRAPHY

honorary doctorate and named the Markosian Library—located on the Redwood Road campus—after him.

Markosian was also a member of the Murray Rotary Club, and helped organize its annual projects to donate clothing, computers, and even school buses to poverty-stricken schools in Mexico. Markosian helped underwrite the airing of the documentary series *The American Experience* for the public television station KUED. He gave both his time and money to Salt Lake City's Olympic bid efforts, which culminated in the city's having been picked to host the 2002 Winter Games.

SUPPORTING SALT LAKE CITY'S LANDMARKS

Markosian's business legacy was also built to last. His company manufactured the girders, beams, and other elements used to build many of Salt Lake City's most striking structures: 1,056 tons of steel for Franklin Quest Field, home of the Salt Lake City Buzz triple-A baseball team; 3,159 tons for the Salt Lake Courts Complex; 4,150 tons for the 24-story One Utah Center in downtown Salt Lake City; and 3,883 tons for the West Valley Events Center, home of the Utah Grizzlies International Hockey League team and a future Olympic site.

Mark Steel also took part in the modernization of Kennecott Copper, providing more than 17,000 tons of fabricated steel. In addition, the company supplied the structural steel, platforms, and bleacher steel for the expansion of Rice Stadium, site of the opening and closing ceremonies for the 2002 Winter Olympics.

In southern Utah, at Hall's Crossing above the Glen Canyon Dam, the boat *John Atlantic Burr* ferries passengers across Lake Powell between Utah Highways U-276 and U-273. At the company's Jordan River plant, Mark Steel employees built and assembled the 245-ton vessel, which measures 44 by 100 feet and has the capacity to carry two buses, eight cars, and 150 passengers. After a dry-land inspection, the newly assembled vessel was taken apart, trucked

MARK STEEL MANUFACTURED THE GIRDERS, BEAMS, AND OTHER ELEMENTS FOR FRANKLIN QUEST FIELD.

IN SOUTHERN UTAH, AT HALL'S CROSSING ABOVE THE GLEN CANYON DAM, THE BOAT *John Atlantic Burr* FERRIES PASSENGERS ACROSS LAKE POWELL BETWEEN UTAH HIGHWAYS U-276 AND U-273. AT THE COMPANY'S JORDAN RIVER PLANT, MARK STEEL EMPLOYEES BUILT AND ASSEMBLED THE 245-TON VESSEL, WHICH MEASURES 44 BY 100 FEET AND HAS A CAPACITY TO CARRY TWO BUSES, EIGHT CARS, AND 150 PASSENGERS.

300 miles, reassembled for sea trials, and later certified suitable for service by the U.S. Coast Guard.

One of Markosian's final business initiatives was to retool the company's fabrication plant with an automated structural steel drill line, blasting machine, and paint facilities. The changes reduced labor costs and leveraged the company's economies of scale, enabling Mark Steel to improve its product and, in many instances, underbid its competitors.

As Salt Lake City's economy continues to thrive, Mark Steel finds itself well positioned to carry on the vision of its founder: "To establish a standard of excellence in the steel fabrication industry. . . and to do so with a firm commitment to human values."

TCI Cablevision of Utah, Inc.

TODAY, CABLE TELEVISION'S VARIETY OF PROGRAMMING CHOICES IS seemingly endless, but it hasn't always been this way. When the predecessor to today's Tele-Communications, Inc. (TCI) first began offering subscription television service to communities in rural Nevada and Montana in the late 1950s, viewers' choices were limited to the few broadcast stations in the area. Since then, TCI has been improving its service and offering entertainment and information to a constantly growing number of cable subscribers.

Founded in 1956 by Bob and Betsy Magness—who partnered in 1958 with Jack Gallivan, George Hatch, and Blaine Glasmann—the company began at a steady pace of growth by microwaving Salt Lake City-area television signals into remote communities. By the mid-1960s, the service boasted six systems and more than 12,000 customers. In 1965, TCI relocated to Denver to take advantage of the central location. In 1968, TCI began construction on a cable system in the Salt Lake Valley. Today, 3,500 miles of cable link 120,000 Salt Lake customers to viewing choices that range from HBO to MTV to the Discovery Channel to Animal Planet, among many others, making TCI the world's largest cable television operator.

As cable programming has become more sophisticated and diverse over time, so too has the company's technology. The earliest cable television systems consisted of two wires strung along a pole. Later systems were refined with then cutting-edge technologies such as coaxial cables, later followed by large tubes. Today, the majority of satellite transmissions are delivered via fiber optics and on digital compression systems developed by TCI.

USING TECHNOLOGY TO ENTERTAIN AND INFORM

In 1993, TCI opened the National Digital Television Center (NDTC) near Denver. NDTC converts analog signals to digital, allowing the distribution of digitally compressed programming to cable systems and home satellite systems across the nation. Carolyn Tschida, regional marketing director for TCI, believes the company will continue to engage in such groundbreaking investments: "We plan to be a very broad deliverer of entertainment from video to interactive services to Internet access. We're upgrading our networks now to handle services that will eventually allow our customers to work from their computers at home."

But, Tschida says, even as a new millennium approaches and technological advances arrive, the little company that began by offering a handful of channels to television-starved, small-town residents will remain an important part of the Salt Lake City community for a simple reason: "Cable will always remain one of the top entertain-

CLOCKWISE FROM TOP:
FROM THE TCI CUSTOMER SERVICE CENTER IN SALT LAKE CITY, TCI EMPLOYEES ARE AVAILABLE 24 HOURS A DAY TO ASSIST CUSTOMERS.

TCI EMPLOYEES AND McGRUFF® THE CRIME DOG VISIT A CITY CLASSROOM TO TEACH CHILDREN HOW TO COPE WITH THREATENING SITUATIONS THEY MAY ENCOUNTER.

TCI REACHES YOUNG MINDS THROUGH A VARIETY OF OUTREACH PROGRAMS, INCLUDING FREE CABLE HOOKUPS FOR CLASSROOMS, TEACHER TRAINING, LESSON OUTLINES TO HELP DEVELOP CURRICULUM FOR EDUCATIONAL PROGRAMS, AND THE ADOPTION OF SCHOOLS. LIBBIE EDWARDS ELEMENTARY SCHOOL IS ONE OF MANY TCI EDUCATIONAL PROJECTS.

ments. Quite simply, it's a worry-free system for the customer. We have people working 24 hours a day to keep it that way. Because of its variety of programming—entertainment, educational, and informational—it really can fit any lifestyle."

CARING FOR EMPLOYEES AND THE COMMUNITY

TCI also strives to care for its employees and the community. The company's 425 employees in the Wasatch Front enjoy a selection of programs and benefits, including educational reimbursement, a generous 401(k) plan, medical and dental insurance, a hot line for employees experiencing personal problems, and time off for those who choose to volunteer in the community. "We take care of our employees, so they'll take care of our customers," Tschida says.

And just as TCI stresses variety in its programming, so too does it promote variety in communities. "As diverse as America is, we want to mirror our communities inside our employee base," Tschida says. "We feel diversity is the key to our success. It's the core foundation needed for our communities to survive. And it makes a work environment that's enjoyable."

That philosophy extends to TCI's programming, as well. To encourage diverse, quality programming, TCI has made passive investments in a number of networks, including Black Entertainment Television, CNN, and The Discovery Channel.

TCI is also working to shape the leaders of tomorrow. "We have a strong commitment to the school systems in every community we serve," Tschida explains. "Cable TV is an ideal medium to reach young minds in a technological age." TCI does this through a variety of outreach programs, including free cable hookups for classrooms, teacher training, lesson outlines to help develop curriculum for educational programs, and the adoption of schools. In Utah, TCI has adopted Bates Elementary, Uintah Elementary, West Bountiful Elementary, Northridge High School, Roy High School, and Layton High School. And the company's support extends beyond Salt Lake City, as well. In nearby Provo, for instance, TCI has partnerships with Independence High School and the annual Freedom Festival.

Kent Pearce, general manager of TCI's Salt Lake Metro Area, says the company's educational efforts reach beyond the classroom. "We work with the Salt Lake Police Department to go into schools to demonstrate how children can ask for help if they are in a threatening situation. And we train all of our employees on how to help if a child approaches them," Pearce says.

TCI is also active in a myriad of community affairs, ranging from sponsoring a trip to the Sundance Children's Festival for physically or mentally challenged kids to participating in the Granite Foundation, which rewards excellent teachers. Pearce says, "We try to focus on children and education themes. Our programming gives parents choice and control over what's available for kids. By doing this—in addition to our quality service and community spirit—we try to be a responsible part of the Salt Lake City area."

LITTLE AMERICA HOTEL AND TOWERS

Salt Lake City's Little America Hotel and Towers, a landmark of style and excellent service since 1966, is part of a family of hotels that includes San Diego's Westgate Hotel; the Sun Valley Resort; and hotels in Flagstaff, Cheyenne, and Little America, Wyoming. Unlike patrons of chain hotels, guests at Little America feel they are truly pampered.

This ideal springs from the values of the hotel's owner, R.E. Holding. The company was built on the grassroots approach of taking care of the traveling public. Initially, people are surprised by details such as extra-large towels, oversize bathtubs, and top-of-the-line gift shops. That's the kind of pride Little America takes in attention to details.

LUXURIOUS ROOMS

Pride is evident in each and every one of Little America's 850 rooms: The Tower Suites are 650-square-foot units awash in luxurious appointments such as imported Italian marble, French oak or cherry furnishings, parlors, armoires, and posh seating areas. Similarly, the 300 Garden Suites offer vanities, a patio or balcony, and spacious views of the well-kept grounds. Guests can also take advantage of popular amenities such as the hotel's two swimming pools, Jacuzzi, sauna, and health club facility.

The hotel's elegant lobby frequently elicits admiring comments from first-time visitors. Appointed in Spanish marble, with French limestone around the fireplaces and British carpets on the floor, the lobby embodies the hotel's attention to fine detail. Just by setting foot in the lobby, guests can tell that Little America strives

to offer the most luxurious amenities available.

Less luxurious but equally popular is the hotel's famous coffee shop. The ambience is friendly and unpretentious, a great place for that first cup of coffee in the morning or a late-night stop after dinner and a play. Business travelers and local families alike enjoy the generous selection of specialties offered by the coffee shop, including a variety of daily specials and the famous breakfast buffet.

CONVENTION SPACE GALORE

Little America offers more than fabulous guest rooms and an excellent place to eat. The hotel boasts 22 meeting rooms for a total of 22,000 square feet of ballroom space. The Grand Ballroom alone can accommodate 1,000 people for a sit-down event, and the facility is frequently booked by nonprofit organizations, local trade groups, and wedding parties for special events. The hotel has state-of-the-art audiovisual equipment on-site for meetings and conventions, as well as complete catering service.

Perhaps the best feature of Little America, however, is its employees. From the doorman who

always greets customers with a smile, to the maître d' who remembers a customer's favorite table, to the eager-to-please bellmen who always wish patrons a pleasant stay, the staff at Little America wants every guest to feel like family.

With a wealth of amenities and second-to-none service, it is little surprise that Little America is continuing to grow. R.E. Holding is in the process of creating an additional magnificent, luxurious hotel with 350 guest rooms and 350 suites right across the street from the current Little America Hotel. To be called the Little America Grand Hotel, the new facility will also include 65,000 square feet of ballroom and banquet space. Klaus Kelterborn, the hotel's managing director, predicts that the addition will be a significant contribution to Salt Lake City's burgeoning reputation as a business destination as well as a vacation site. "It is going to establish Salt Lake City as a major location for the regional, national, and international traveler," Kelterborn says. "This is a big city, but it has a small-town feel with hardworking people, families, and an entrepreneurial spirit. You could not ask for more from a community, and Little America wants to be part of that community."

WITH A WEALTH OF AMENITIES AND SECOND-TO-NONE SERVICE, IT IS NO SURPRISE THAT LITTLE AMERICA HOTEL AND TOWERS IS CONTINUING TO GROW (TOP).

INITIALLY, PEOPLE ARE SURPRISED BY DETAILS SUCH AS EXTRA-LARGE TOWELS, OVERSIZE BATHTUBS, AND TOP-OF-THE-LINE GIFT SHOPS. BUT THAT'S THE KIND OF PRIDE LITTLE AMERICA TAKES IN ATTENTION TO DETAILS (BOTTOM).

1970-1998

1970 American Airlines	1983 Fleming
1970 BNA Consulting Engineers II	1983 Nightime Pediatrics Clinics, Inc.
1970 Utah Transit Authority	1983 Residence Inn by Marriott-Trolley Square
1971 Orbit Irrigation Products, Inc.	1983 Summit Destinations
1973 Huntsman Corporation	1984 Salt Lake Convention & Visitors Bureau
1974 Fairchild Semiconductor	1985 Colvin Engineering Associates, Inc.
1975 Intermountain Health Care	1985 MegaDyne Medical Products, Inc.
1975 Wasatch Advisors, Inc.	1986 Fidelity Investments
1976 Wasatch Crest Insurance Companies	1986 NPS Pharmaceuticals
1977 Affiliated Insurance Agency	1987 Colliers CRG (Consolidated Realty Group)
1978 First Utah Bank	1989 Hogi Yogi Corporation
1981 Olympus Tours & Travel	1992 EDS
1981 Salt Lake City Marriott	1997 Doubletree Hotel
1982 American Express	
1983 Ameritech Library Services	

A MERICAN AIRLINES OPERATES SEVEN DAILY FLIGHTS OUT OF THE Salt Lake City International Airport—three to Chicago's O'Hare and four to the Dallas/Fort Worth (DFW) International Airport—but the airline's presence in the market is much greater than those seven flights might suggest. Established in Utah's capital city in 1970,

American quickly made itself an important part of the community.

"What we're known for," explains Rob Britton, managing director of corporate communications for American Airlines, "is carrying people between Salt Lake City and locations east of Chicago you can't reach nonstop, such as Buffalo, Rochester, Syracuse, and Albany." American also offers more transatlantic flights out of Chicago than any other carrier. And out of DFW, American's headquarters, the airline offers transatlantic flights, as well as flights to a number of locations in Central and South America. "We're also a big carrier with missionaries for the LDS Church," Britton adds. In fact, American has a global marketing agreement with the Church of Jesus Christ of Latter-day Saints and carries close to 100 church members every week.

EARLY ON THE MORNING OF APRIL 15, 1926, CHARLES A. LINDBERGH TOOK OFF FROM CHICAGO FOR ST. LOUIS WITH A SINGLE BAG OF MAIL, THUS INAUGURATING THE FIRST REGULARLY SCHEDULED FLIGHT FOR WHAT WOULD LATER BECOME AMERICAN AIRLINES.

AN ILLUSTRIOUS HISTORY

Early on the morning of April 15, 1926, Charles A. Lindbergh took off from Chicago for St. Louis with a single bag of mail, thus inaugurating the first regularly scheduled flight for what would later become American Airlines. Lindbergh was the chief pilot for Robertson Aircraft Corporation of Missouri, one of nearly 80 companies that merged in 1934 to become American Airlines. In the decades since that merger, American has faced and met the challenges of an ever changing airline industry, becoming a global leader in air travel in the process.

Originally headquartered in New York City, American moved to the Dallas/Fort Worth area in 1979, and began developing its first hub at DFW International Airport two years later. Following the U.S. airline deregulation that

began in 1978, American expanded greatly, especially at DFW, its largest hub. Today, American and American Eagle offer more than 750 daily departures from DFW to 115 cities worldwide, including nonstop service to London, Tokyo, São Paulo, and 18 other international cities.

Throughout its years of service, American Airlines has consistently led the industry with its innovative ideas and programs. In 1934, the company originated an air traffic control system that was later adopted by all airlines and administered by the U.S. government. In 1953, American flew the first nonstop transcontinental routes with the Douglas DC-7, and six years later was the first to upgrade these same routes with the much faster Boeing 707. In 1959, American introduced SABRE, the world's first computer reservation system, which today is used by thousands of travelers in more than 70 countries. In 1981, American marked a revolutionary new way to attract and retain customers by developing the AAdvantage frequent flyer program, which has since been imitated by nearly every other airline. And in 1992, American opened the Alliance Maintenance and Engineering Base, which was the first state-of-the-art airline maintenance facility to be built in the United States in more than 20 years.

A PROMISING FUTURE

As American charts new courses in Internet technology, the company's tradition of pioneering ideas continues. In 1996, customers could book travel on-line via American's AAccess page, and by the following year, more than a million customers were receiving E-mail notices of discount fares through the NetSAAver program.

In addition, American is focusing on expanding the breadth and depth of its international network.

At the beginning of 1998, the airline added four new routes—to Tokyo from Chicago, New York-Kennedy, and Boston; and to Osaka from DFW—thereby strengthening the company's presence in the Pacific Rim. American also has announced, and in some cases finalized, several code-sharing partnerships with carriers across the globe that will considerably enhance the airline's international system.

A large part of American's long-range plans revolves around its 20-year partnership with Boeing. In 1998, American began acquiring several new 767s, with super-long-range 777s following soon thereafter. By 2002, American will have added more than 100 new aircraft to its system, ensuring that the airline continues to operate the youngest and most-advanced fleet in the industry.

From the days of Lindbergh's mail route to today's increasingly global and technologically driven industry, one trend is clear: American has been and will continue to be a leader in its field.

COMMUNITY INVOLVEMENT

One of American's strategies for remaining an industry leader is to take good care of its employees and customers. In Salt Lake City, the airline is involved in a wide range of charitable causes and corporate sponsorships, including the American Cancer Society, Snowbird Disabled Skier's Program, Boys & Girls Clubs, Make-A-Wish Foundation, Ballet West, the Utah Symphony, Senior PGA Championships, Smith's Balloon Festival, Dicken's Christmas Festival, and numerous other events. In addition, American provides flights for children and their families to the Park of DreAAms, a village American built near Walt Disney World for children with life-threatening illnesses.

"We try to be good, involved citizens and neighbors in every community we serve," Britton notes, proving once again that with American, there's *something special in the air*.

IN 1998, AMERICAN BEGAN ACQUIRING SEVERAL NEW 767S, WITH SUPER-LONG-RANGE 777S FOLLOWING SOON THERE-AFTER. BY 2002, AMERICAN WILL HAVE ADDED MORE THAN 100 NEW AIRCRAFT TO ITS SYSTEM, ENSURING THAT THE AIRLINE CONTINUES TO OPERATE THE YOUNGEST AND MOST-ADVANCED FLEET IN THE INDUSTRY (TOP).

THROUGHOUT ITS YEARS OF SERVICE, AMERICAN AIRLINES HAS CONSISTENTLY LED THE INDUSTRY WITH ITS INNOVA-TIVE IDEAS AND PROGRAMS (BOTTOM).

*T*N BNA CONSULTING ENGINEERS II'S EARLY YEARS, THE ELECTRICAL consulting industry was in its infancy. Planning for energy efficiency or lighting and telecommunication design were ideas just beginning to attract attention. ▨ "Our goal is to design a building that meets the requirements of the client who has become technically sophisticated. It

is our responsibility to understand this technology in order to provide lighting and electrical design suitable for the client and the community," says President Mark Bryant. "Our office is fully networked and has E-mail capabilities to strengthen communication between the engineers and our clients."

BNA's LIGHTING DESIGN AT THE SALT PALACE CONVENTION CENTER RECEIVED AN AWARD OF MERIT FROM THE INTERNATIONAL ILLUMINATION ENGINEERING SOCIETY OF NORTH AMERICA.

MEETING CUSTOMERS' NEEDS

*B*NA, which was founded in Pocatello, Idaho, in 1959 as Nielson Engineering and opened a branch office in Salt Lake City in 1970, specializes in electrical engineering for industrial, commercial, and institutional clients. Among the services the company offers are energy conservation, project management, lighting design, fire and security systems, and electrical master planning.

BNA currently boasts a burgeoning workload of 250 clients a year. Bryant attributes the firm's success to two factors: people and service. "Other companies might have some of the same capabilities as we do, but those two things set us apart," says Bryant. "We've been in a period of discovery where we've learned not to worry about competition, but about service. Our mistakes, frankly, have taught us a great deal in that if you give poor service, you run a risk of losing your client. We're a service organization; we always try to handle things as ethically and as professionally as possible."

BNA's recent projects include the electrical design, lighting, power, and security at Rice Stadium; the renovation and expansion of the Frank G. Moss Courthouse downtown; the historical renovation of the Egyptian Theater; the expansion of the University of Utah's Marriott Library; the construction of the Giovale Library at Westminster College; and the lighting design at the Salt Palace Convention Center, which received an award of merit from the International Illumination Engineering Society of North America.

EMPHASIZING PROFESSIONALISM

*B*NA seeks out employees who reflect the company's interest in developing and maintaining professional relationships with its clients. To do this, the company searches for people who are not just technically capable, but who also fit an ethical and professional mold. "We sensed a real need to find people who meet those criteria as a response to comments from clients who liked to work with a certain individual because

LANCE CLAYTON

of certain personalities," says Bryant. "We tried to evaluate those individuals and see if we couldn't fit them into our office structure. It's all in response to the growing sophistication of the community."

Another part of the firm's sophistication is evidenced by its willingness to embrace the available technology in the industry. "The advent of the computer has brought about the necessity for all of us to understand technical machines," Bryant explains. "We're here to meet challenges. As our clients have become more sophisticated, it's incumbent upon us to provide the most efficient and effective power and lighting design for their buildings."

BNA employees also make their presence known in Salt Lake City through a variety of charitable projects, including electrical design work for the Children's Museum of Utah and the Ronald McDonald House. In addition, BNA staff members donate their time to trade groups such as the Intermountain Electrical Association and the Illuminating Engineering Society.

ON THE HORIZON

Bryant believes that Salt Lake City's increasingly metropolitan atmosphere bodes well for BNA's future. BNA, he predicts, will continue to provide an eclectic selection of electrical engineering services, ranging from small remodeling jobs to massive, $100 million projects. "Salt Lake City now has all the attractions of a big city," Bryant says. "More and more people have landed here because of the workplace and natural environment. The people who come here for the quality of life still want to maintain all the facets of a large city."

And what part does BNA play in Salt Lake City? "One area of service is to meet the needs of the community and to have buildings with efficient energy delivery and a lighting design that highlights the architecture of a building," Bryant says. "It is easy to flood a building with light, but it takes a real vision to look at a building's design and help define the architecture with light."

▸ CAROL FELDMAN

▸ LANCE CLAYTON

BNA's recent projects include the historical renovation of the governor's mansion (top) and the Egyptian Theater (bottom).

UTAH TRANSIT AUTHORITY

URBAN GROWTH HAS ACCELERATED RAPIDLY THROUGHOUT UTAH in recent years, making it the sixth most urban populated state in the nation. Most of Utah's urban population lives along the booming Wasatch Front. In fact, population growth throughout the Beehive State is twice the national average. That increase, coupled with a

CLOCKWISE FROM TOP LEFT:
IN ADDITION TO SERVING DOWNTOWN COMMUTERS AND RESIDENTS, UTA CO-ORDINATES WITH LOCAL RESTAURANTS AND BUSINESSES FOR TRIPS TO AND FROM ENTERTAINMENT AND SPORTS ARENAS, SUCH AS THE DELTA CENTER.

MAKING DAILY TRIPS TO FIVE RESORTS, SKI BUS SERVICE IS ONE OF UTA'S MOST POPULAR SPECIAL SERVICES.

SALT LAKE CITY'S NEW TRAX LIGHT RAIL SYSTEM IS ONE OF THE MAJOR COM-PONENTS OF THE CITY'S INTERMODAL STRATEGY. UPON ITS EXPECTED COMPLE-TION IN EARLY 2000, TRAX WILL RUN NORTH AND SOUTH, LINKING DOWNTOWN SALT LAKE CITY TO SOUTH SALT LAKE, MURRAY, MIDVALE, AND SANDY.

robust economy, has made the Wasatch Front one of the most popular tourism and relocation areas in the western United States.

Since its founding in 1970, Utah Transit Authority (UTA) has experienced extraordinary growth of its own. In recent years, UTA has expanded the existing bus system for local commuters and has introduced specialty services, such as ski buses and old-time trolleys, geared toward visitors to Salt Lake City. Articulated buses, which carry 45 percent more passengers than regular-sized buses, are now used on express routes to meet the growing demands of commuters. Utah's heritage of phenomenal growth charts a path of steady expansion

anticipated well into the 21st century. UTA believes that mass transportation will continue to play a vital role in support of this growth.

FUELING A TRANSIT REVOLUTION

UTA is positioned as a key component in the transit revolution leading to the millennium. What started as a small, 80-bus operation with one garage serving only a portion of Salt Lake County has grown into a six-county regional transit system with more than 500 buses, 1,300 employees, and six state-of-the-art maintenance facilities—not to mention a newly designed light rail system. The area's booming population

growth, along with the upcoming 2002 Winter Olympic Games, presents enormous transportation challenges, and UTA plans to meet them with a number of creative transit options.

A major component of UTA's forward-looking strategy is its multimodal approach. This entails linking intercity express bus service, regular fixed-route transit, special services for the disabled, a shuttle feeder system linking passengers to intermodal centers and important regional hubs, and commuter rail service along the length of the Wasatch Front. These projects—combined with an emphasis on car pools and van pools, more bicycle routes, alternative

◀ KENT MILES

UTA XTRAX

BRW DMJM   RICHARD D CHONG AND ASSOCIATES   James Porter   Illustration

JAMES PORTER

work hours, and telecommuting—will help address the area's growing transportation demands.

UTA will also rely on Salt Lake City's new TRAX light rail system, one of the major components of the intermodal strategy. Upon its expected completion in early 2000, TRAX will run north and south, linking downtown Salt Lake City to South Salt Lake, Murray, Midvale, and Sandy. This 15-mile stretch of track will greatly enhance commuter travel in Salt Lake County. Commuters from Sandy will be able to reach downtown Salt Lake City in approximately 30 minutes, and a coordinated shuttle bus system will link passengers to east-west and other regional destinations in minutes. In addition, UTA will realign more of its bus routes to serve the south, southeast, and southwest portions of the Salt Lake Valley; increase east-west service in general; and add new express bus routes.

UTA is also developing intelligent transportation systems (ITS) that will revolutionize transit service for the general public and provide a safe and efficient alternative for worldwide visitors during the 2002 Winter Olympic Games. With the introduction of an automatic vehicle locating system, passengers will know exactly when to expect their bus at a particular stop. In addition, automated passenger counting capabilities will provide better information about the transit market for UTA. And new fare cards, which can be read efficiently by a payment machine rather than collected by the driver, will make it easier for passengers to pay for their transportation. UTA's Web page already offers a variety of information in several languages and user-friendly kiosks will offer important information, including real-time access to transit schedules, in a variety of languages and travel modes.

MEETING DIVERSE CHALLENGES

Beyond moving people efficiently from point A to point B, the region's multimodal revolution will enhance the quality of the environment by decreasing

KENT MILES

KENT MILES

congestion and air pollution in Salt Lake Valley and the surrounding region. Likewise, new approaches to fuel consumption—including the use of hydrogen, fuel cell systems, and hybrid electric-powered buses—can provide cleaner alternatives to traditional diesel options. Incorporating a modern fleet of both large and small buses will further augment energy conservation opportunities and provide more flexible service for area communities.

UTA's pollution reduction efforts go beyond the traditional role of a transit authority. Its regional Rideshare car pool and van pool program, for example, matches thousands of individuals across the Wasatch Front with riding partners and encourages a variety of conservation-oriented alternatives to driving alone. Partnering with local civic groups, schools, and businesses on issues such as car pooling, telecommuting, and urban planning is a progressive

approach to improving the community's quality of life.

Undoubtedly, the region's biggest transportation challenge will be the 2002 Winter Olympics. An efficient and effective transportation network for visitors is key to hosting a world-class event of that magnitude, and UTA and its partners will be at the forefront of this effort. To that end, UTA will rely on the advanced technologies of intelligent transportation systems, as well as specialized services designed to make each visitor's stay as hospitable and user friendly as possible.

The Utah Transit Authority's integrated approach presents an efficient and economical solution to the transportation demands facing the Wasatch Front. From high-technology innovations to on-the-street customer service, the people of UTA are improving the quality of the region's communities and moving forward to meet the challenges of the future.

CLOCKWISE FROM TOP LEFT: UTA'S OLD-TIME TROLLEYS PROVIDE A FUN WAY FOR VISITORS TO TOUR THE CITY DURING THE SPRING, SUMMER, AND FALL.

UTAH'S HERITAGE OF PHENOMENAL GROWTH CHARTS A PATH OF STEADY EXPANSION ANTICIPATED WELL INTO THE 21ST CENTURY. UTA BELIEVES THAT MASS TRANSPORTATION WILL CONTINUE TO PLAY A VITAL ROLE IN THAT GROWTH. CARRYING MORE THAN 40,000 PASSENGERS A DAY, UTA COVERS 1,400 SQUARE MILES THROUGHOUT SIX COUNTIES.

AS A PUBLIC AGENCY, UTA'S SERVICE AREA IS EXTENDED TO SOME 1.8 MILLION OF UTAH'S APPROXIMATELY 2 MILLION RESIDENTS.

Orbit Irrigation Products, Inc.

WHEN MAX ERICKSEN FOUNDED ORBIT IN 1971, HE DREW ON THE honesty and work ethic exemplified by his ancestors, who were early pioneer immigrants to Utah. It seems appropriate the company has grown and thrived in Utah, a state with a long history of harnessing water that dates back to the Mormon pioneers'

first arrival in the Salt Lake Valley. "The pioneers were really the first to manage water and water distribution. They depended on it for survival. Crops couldn't survive without water being distributed to them on a regular basis. At Orbit, we took that concept and combined it with technology," explains Executive Vice President—and Max's son—Mike Ericksen.

Being located in Utah has given Orbit an advantage. "We are able to test our products under real conditions—everything from the Wasatch Mountains to the blazing deserts down south, from the freezing cold winter nights to blistering summer days."

Originally, Max Ericksen started manufacturing because he was determined to make great products that target a valued customer. "Our goals haven't changed; we're still determined to manufacture high-quality, innovative products at a good value," Mike Ericksen points out.

Currently, Orbit offers more than 700 different lawn and garden products to customers worldwide. Its array of products includes Water-Master automatic controllers and valves, DripMaster micro-watering

products, and SunMate hose-end sprinklers. The company's flagship Orbit line includes gear-driven and stationary sprinkler heads, risers, valve boxes, tools, and other accessories. In addition, Orbit recently acquired Arizona Mist, a manufacturer of outdoor misting equipment. The misting systems can lower the temperature by as much as 20 degrees by add-

ing moisture into the air. Perfect for patios and pet kennels on a hot summer day.

Orbit's ability to oversee the entire production process allows it to offer superior products at an affordable price. Consistency is maintained by strictly controlling all phases of development, including design, molding, production, and packaging. In addition, Orbit's

CLOCKWISE FROM TOP:
THE ENVIRONMENT AT ORBIT IRRIGATION PRODUCTS, INC. PROMOTES TEAMWORK. "THE EMPLOYEES TAKE PRIDE IN THEIR WORK," MIKE ERICKSEN SAYS. "ORBIT HAS A CASUAL DRESS POLICY, SO PEOPLE FEEL COMFORTABLE HERE. THERE'S NO FEELING OF LAYERED MANAGEMENT. EVERYONE IS PART OF THE ORBIT TEAM."

ORBIT'S CORPORATE HEADQUARTERS IS LOCATED IN NORTH SALT LAKE CITY.

MAX ERICKSEN IS THE FOUNDER OF ORBIT.

advanced computer system ensures that orders are shipped accurately, quickly, and completely.

Orbit's dedicated customer approach to product development is exemplified by numerous Orbit products that have become industry standards. Orbit's WaterMaster timers use one programming method so they are simple to program and easy to use. Most recently, the company was the first to introduce a WaterMaster sprinkler timer with remote control to the retail market. The WaterMaster timer is the first ever that allows the convenience of controlling a sprinkler system from up to 200 feet away. It saves time and prevents the need for running back and forth to the timer when making adjustments or repairs.

The company was also the first to introduce retrofit micro-watering, often referred to as drip irrigation (derived from Orbit's micro-watering line, DripMaster). This type of watering system conserves water by taking it right where it needs to go, to the plant. It is most often used for watering individual plants, flowerpots, hanging baskets, and small, hard-to-water areas.

Orbit also manufactures an automatic yard watering system that combines a battery-powered electronic timer and valve. The system connects to a hose faucet and uses quick, snap-together wire connections that make installing the system simple. A wire remote accessory can be added to move the timer to a more convenient location, or for the ultimate in convenience, a wireless remote

control can be added that can operate up to 200 feet away from the timer. The system enables underground sprinklers, micro-watering, hose-end sprinklers, or patio mist cooling systems to be operated from a hose faucet.

The Voyager II pop-up gear drive head is a professional-quality sprinkler that is ideal for large-area coverage. The sprinkler spray pattern can be adjusted by using one of the 12 interchangeable nozzles. In 1998, the Saturn III head was introduced. The Saturn III is the most advanced medium-area, gear-driven head in the retail market. It fills the void between a spring-loaded pop-up and a standard gear drive or impact head. The Saturn III doesn't require a special tool to adjust sprinkler spray patterns, and adjustments can be made at the turn of a dial.

In the future, Orbit will continue to respond to the needs of its customers. "We want to be the first ones to come out with the most advanced technology available," Ericksen says. "And even as products become more technologically advanced, we want to be sure that they remain very easy to use. We're the pioneers of constantly creating something that's new and advanced—we'll always try to use less water to do more. The company slogan, Conservation through Innovation, signifies our commitment to developing innovative products that manage water. Water is a precious resource. The old-fashioned watering methods are being replaced by highly efficient water conservation systems."

The environment at Orbit promotes teamwork. "The employees take pride in their work," Ericksen says. "Orbit has a casual dress policy, so people feel comfortable here. There's no feeling of layered management. Everyone is part of the Orbit team." Furthermore, employees enjoy significant benefits, including an on-site exercise facility complete with treadmills, weights, stair climbers, and stationary bikes.

Orbit is also generous outside the confines of its facility, donating sprinkling systems to local schools, sponsoring community events, and contributing to charities, including food banks and Sub for Santa.

Orbit's conservation green earth approach in manufacturing and marketing one of the broadest, most innovative, and most reliable lines of irrigation products available is driven by the pioneer spirit and the technological advancements for which Utah is known.

*A*t Huntsman Corporation, it's impossible to separate business from philanthropy. And Jon M. Huntsman, founder of the family-owned company, wouldn't have it any other way. ▢ "Jon speaks of our associates not as employees, but as members of an extended family," explains Don Olsen, senior vice president of public affairs for the corporation. "It may sound surprising, but when he speaks at our company plants around the world, he doesn't talk about increasing productivity—he talks about the things that matter more, like kindness and personal relationships."

As a result, Huntsman Corporation enjoys extremely low turnover and high satisfaction among its 10,000 employees and full-time contractors. "Jon's philosophy is simple: If you treat your employees well, they'll treat you well," Olsen says.

A Lifetime of Giving

Huntsman is Utah's most prominent billionaire, but he grew up impoverished in Idaho and California, and today willingly shares stories of living in cramped student housing and helping to support his family by working three part-time jobs while his father completed a Ph.D. at Stanford University. Such experiences, Huntsman says, helped reinforce his philanthropic tendencies (he gave an estimated $43 million to various charities in 1997). "I started giving when I was making $220 a month," Huntsman recalls. "I think giving is innately part of someone's makeup. It's very difficult to teach somebody to be charitable. But we must never give up hope."

Huntsman's generosity is directed toward a worldwide array of educational, artistic, and health-related causes. In Utah, these include

Catholic Charities, the University of Utah, Primary Children's Hospital, LDS Hospital, Brigham Young University, Utah State University, and Southern Utah University.

But it is the Huntsman Cancer Institute at the University of Utah that has benefited most from its namesake's remarkable generosity. In 1995, Huntsman gave $100 million to the institute, which was established two years earlier with a $10 million gift from the Huntsman family. Olsen explains, "There's not a family in this country that cancer hasn't touched. Huntsman, who himself has had two bouts with cancer, knows so many people who have been impacted that his most enduring goal is to help find a cure for the disease."

Philanthropy through Business Strategy

Huntsman's business acumen, though, is as indisputable as his generosity. After graduating from the Wharton School of the University of Pennsylvania and

JON M. AND KAREN H. HUNTSMAN LEAD HUNTSMAN CORPORATION, THE NATION'S LARGEST PRIVATELY HELD CHEMICAL COMPANY.

ALTHOUGH THE COMPANY'S PRODUCTION FACILITIES ARE SPREAD THROUGHOUT THE WORLD, HUNTSMAN'S CORPORATE HEADQUARTERS HAS BEEN LOCATED IN SALT LAKE CITY FOR 25 YEARS.

serving in the Navy, he went to work for an egg company in the 1960s and helped develop the plastic egg carton as a more efficient alternative to cardboard packaging.

After launching his own small company in 1970, he followed his egg carton innovations with a remarkable string of successful products, including clamshell-style hamburger boxes for the fast-food industry, and plastic accoutrements for hospitals and cafeterias. From this relatively modest beginning has evolved Huntsman Corporation, the nation's largest privately held chemical company, whose operating companies manufacture 20.5 billion pounds per year of basic products for the chemical, plastics, detergent, personal care, rubber, and packaging industries. Huntsman-held companies today have annual revenues in excess of $5 billion from multiple locations worldwide.

Olsen identifies three company strategies that have contributed to its great success: The first is to pay down debt. The second is to invest in safe, efficient facilities. The final strategy is to give to the relief of human suffering, to contribute to the good of the community, and to encourage others to do likewise.

A COMPANYWIDE COMMITMENT TO GIVING

Huntsman's gifts may come in the form of a high-profile check-signing ceremony or a donation quietly slipped under a door. But the impulse remains the same, according to Huntsman: "We're probably the largest private, family-owned business in America. One reason we've stayed private is because we can operate more effectively if we can do things quietly, and to some extent, behind the scenes."

Similarly, many of the company's employees have also become involved in charitable causes. "Giving money is one thing," Olsen points out. "But giving time and giving of yourself is equally important. Our people are heavily involved in causes from the United Way to volunteering in their schools to working in their churches. There's just a real spirit of charity through-

THE ETHYLENE FURNACES AT HUNTSMAN'S PORT ARTHUR, TEXAS, FACILITY HELP TO MANUFACTURE 20.5 BILLION POUNDS PER YEAR OF BASIC PRODUCTS FOR THE CHEMICAL, PLASTICS, DETERGENT, PERSONAL CARE, RUBBER, AND PACKAGING INDUSTRIES.

IN 1995, HUNTSMAN GAVE $100 MILLION TO THE HUNTSMAN CANCER INSTITUTE, WHICH WAS ESTABLISHED TWO YEARS EARLIER WITH A $10 MILLION GIFT FROM THE HUNTSMAN FAMILY.

out this company," Olsen says. "That commitment to giving comes from the top down."

AT HOME IN SALT LAKE CITY

Although the company's production facilities are spread throughout the world, Huntsman's corporate headquarters has been located in Salt Lake City for 25 years. Olsen explains, "We're headquartered here because this is where our chairman chooses to

live. Salt Lake City's quality of life and the work ethic of its people make it an ideal place for us to call home."

Huntsman elaborates, "Before we moved our corporate headquarters here, everyone said we had to be located in L.A. or New York to be successful. When we moved, we were doing about $25 million a year in sales. Today, we're doing about $5.2 billion in sales. Salt Lake City has obviously been good to us."

W IDELY RECOGNIZED IN THE HIGH-TECH INDUSTRY AS A PIONEER IN the founding of northern California's Silicon Valley, Fairchild Semiconductor is in a unique position to assess the increasingly large role semiconductors play in all our lives. In today's global marketplace, Fairchild remains committed, in the words of its

president and CEO, Kirk Pond, "to be nothing less than the best multi-market semiconductor supplier in the world. Innovative products, competitive costs, and superior customer services are the cornerstones of our strategy for success."

TECHNOLOGICAL TRAILBLAZER

In 1947, the invention of the transistor sparked a revolution in the electronics industry. But researchers struggled to develop a manufacturing process that would satisfy the stringent requirements of more demanding transistor users. In the late 1950s, industrialist/scientist Sherman Mills Fairchild—who, throughout a long career, invented a series of aerial camera, aviation, and engine equipment—put up $3,500 in seed money to sponsor a group of young scientists in California striving to develop a new process for manufacturing transistors. The goal of Fairchild's

SHERMAN MILLS FAIRCHILD (CENTER, WITH HANDS IN VEST POCKETS), FOUNDER OF FAIRCHILD SEMICONDUCTOR, WAS ON HAND TO OPEN ONE OF THE COMPANY'S ORIGINAL FACILITIES IN 1963 (TOP).

INTEGRATED CIRCUIT MANUFACTURING REMAINS AN INTEGRAL PART OF THE ELECTRONICS INDUSTRY TODAY (BOTTOM).

scientists was to develop, mass-produce, and market semiconductor components that would meet the new industry's demanding specifications, thus laying the groundwork for a new company.

In 1959, Fairchild researchers attained their goal with the introduction of the Planar process.

Planar technology was soon the standard for producing transistors and integrated circuits, and remains today one of the most significant achievements in semiconductor technology.

Having established a benchmark in the semiconductor industry, Fairchild became a part of National Semiconductor in 1987. The company reemerged in March 1997, when a group of private investors purchased the company and spun it off as an independent entity.

THE SALT LAKE CITY OPERATION

Fairchild's sprawling Salt Lake City operation, part of the company's Discrete Power and Signal Technologies Group, is dedicated to the standard-products chip business, manufacturing semiconductors for a variety of markets, including the telecommunications, automotive, broadcast, and consumer industries. The factory produces discrete, memory, and analog devices in a world-class six-inch silicon wafer fabrication facility on-site.

Communications Specialist Yvette Englert says, "Our main focus is the building blocks of semiconductor products. Fairchild's products are used in a variety of

DIETZ ASSOCIATES INC.

applications: cellular phones, personal computers, entertainment systems, automotive applications, and other devices. In fact, we're the only company in the industry that focuses solely on multi-market products."

Englert explains that when National Semiconductor opened the facility in Salt Lake City in 1974, its emphasis was on consumer products, such as calculators and watches. With the advent of the personal computer paving the way, however, integrated circuits were soon being utilized in a variety of applications, from sewing machines to CD players to automotive assembly lines. Fairchild's facilities offer high-volume and low-unit-cost manufacturing capabilities, a key component in the company's drive for increased market share.

Englert cites the area of discrete devices as one example of how Fairchild has changed the technological landscape of our world. Discrete, integrated circuits are utilized for power management in a variety of devices, and the company leads its competition in the area of new product development and production processes.

COMPANY AND COMMUNITY BENEFITS

With an employee turnover rate of approximately 3 percent in 1997, Fairchild provides a rewarding work environment for its 600 employees. "Our leadership is top-notch in supporting the people and what they do every day," Englert reflects. "Because the industry is competitive, it's very important to attract and keep good people." Benefits include an on-site wellness center and cafeteria, competitive wages, and several programs rewarding employee productivity.

The company's humanitarian concerns go beyond the walls of its 300,000-square-foot facility, according to Englert: "One of our major focuses in the past few years has been partnering with high school teachers and students who may do monthlong internships to learn more about our industry." Fairchild also contributes to the community through the United

DIETZ ASSOCIATES INC.

IN TODAY'S GLOBAL MARKETPLACE, FAIRCHILD REMAINS COMMITTED, IN THE WORDS OF ITS PRESIDENT AND CEO, KIRK POND, "TO BE NOTHING LESS THAN THE BEST MULTI-MARKET SEMICONDUCTOR SUPPLIER IN THE WORLD."

Way, a holiday season fund-raising drive for the homeless, and Sub for Santa, among other programs.

STRATEGIC IMPERATIVES

Echoing the words of Pond, Englert describes the company's three strategic imperatives for the 1990s and beyond: innovative new products, cost competitiveness, and superior customer service. "We want to partner with customers to help them with their new products and supply them with high-quality integrated circuits," says Englert. Fairchild has a proud heritage of high-performance, state-of-the-art products. Customers can buy a wide range of products with Fairchild as a single source supplier, rather than going to several companies. The company's service programs make it easy for customers to do business, because they have access to the people with the answers to their questions.

As part of its growth strategy, Fairchild recently acquired Raytheon Electronic Semiconductor, an acquisition that will give the company additional expertise in analog and mixed-signal technologies. "Fairchild Semiconductor has grown in leaps and bounds with the technology and the markets we supply. We intend to remain at the forefront of our industry," Englert says.

FAIRCHILD'S SPRAWLING SALT LAKE CITY OPERATION, PART OF THE COMPANY'S DISCRETE POWER AND SIGNAL TECHNOLOGIES GROUP, IS DEDICATED TO THE STANDARD-PRODUCTS CHIP BUSINESS, MANUFACTURING SEMICONDUCTORS FOR A VARIETY OF MARKETS, INCLUDING THE TELECOMMUNICATIONS, AUTOMOTIVE, BROADCAST, AND CONSUMER INDUSTRIES.

T HE HEALTH CARE SYSTEM THAT IS NOW INTERMOUNTAIN HEALTH CARE (IHC) was originally created by The Church of Jesus Christ of Latter-day Saints. In 1975, the LDS Church decided to donate the 15 hospitals in its system to the communities they served. A charitable, nonprofit, nondenominational organization called Intermountain Health Care

was organized to steward that public trust.

From this starting point, IHC has developed into an integrated health system of doctors, hospitals, and health plans working together for the good of the patient. Now, 23 hospitals, 400 physician partners, and a broad range of health plans back up the IHC mission of commitment to the communities it serves.

QUALITY HEALTH CARE

A s an innovator in clinical quality improvement, IHC has received the nation's highest honors in recognition of health care quality: The Healthcare Forum/ Witt Award (1991) and the National Committee for Quality Health Care Quality Health Care Award (1996).

These awards are the result of hundreds of quality improvement initiatives, which have earned IHC an international reputation for quality health care. One study recently published in the *New England Journal of Medicine* demonstrates the impact of IHC's improvements. The study, performed at IHC's LDS Hospital, showed that physician use of a highly networked bedside computer system helped patients suffer fewer complications and show quicker recoveries—and

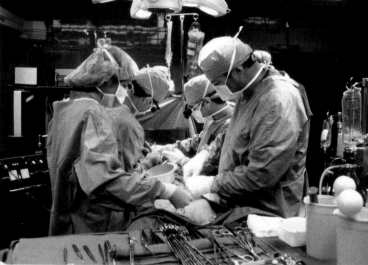

CLOCKWISE FROM TOP RIGHT:
AS AN INNOVATOR IN CLINICAL QUALITY IMPROVEMENT, IHC HAS RECEIVED THE NATION'S HIGHEST HONORS IN RECOGNITION OF HEALTH CARE QUALITY.

WHILE REDEFINING STATE-OF-THE-ART MEDICAL CARE, IHC STAYS TRUE TO ITS COMMUNITY ROOTS.

IHC HAS DEVELOPED INTO AN INTEGRATED HEALTH SYSTEM OF DOCTORS, HOSPITALS, AND HEALTH PLANS WORKING TOGETHER FOR THE GOOD OF THE PATIENT. NOW 23 HOSPITALS (INCLUDING LDS HOSPITAL SHOWN BELOW), 400 PHYSICIAN PARTNERS, AND A BROAD RANGE OF HEALTH PLANS BACK UP THE IHC MISSION OF COMMITMENT TO THE COMMUNITIES IT SERVES.

reduced the cost of treating each patient by nearly $10,000.

AFFORDABLE PATIENT CARE

I HC's clinical improvement efforts continually show that quality care costs less. IHC's average patient charges are 15 percent below the state average and 30 percent below the national average. Low hospital charges have also helped IHC keep its health plan premiums competitive. Keeping charges low is another example of IHC's service to residents in its service region of Utah, Idaho, and Wyoming.

◀ COMMITMENT TO COMMUNITY

C ommunities in the Intermountain West are as diverse as the landscape. IHC remains committed to individual communities through its more than 500 volunteer trustees. These volunteer community representatives serve on hospital governing boards and charitable foundation boards to keep IHC in tune with its mission and in line with the needs of the local communities.

IHC's mission of community service includes a commitment to provide quality medical care to persons with a medical need,

regardless of ability to pay. IHC hospitals and associated clinics provide more than $27 million in charitable assistance each year.

In addition to treating all those in need who enter its hospitals and physicians clinics, IHC reaches out to treat and prevent problems for low-income and underinsured populations. Numerous IHC foundations provide financial assistance to health clinics and preventive health efforts throughout the Intermountain area. IHC also joins forces with other community organizations and businesses to promote health and safety through Healthy Community initiatives. Indeed, while redefining state-of-the-art medical care, IHC stays true to its community roots.

*A*FFILIATED INSURANCE AGENCY PROVIDES BUSINESS INSURANCE for a number of manufacturing and mining companies, as well as shopping centers and the Snowbird Ski Resort. But President and CEO James Dickson never wants his company to forget the importance of forging a personal relationship with its clients.

"When we write an account, we do it on a long-term basis," Dickson says. "I want the client to look at our company on the same level as his attorney and CPA. Our goal is to build a solid, lasting relationship."

This philosophy has proved successful; the company has provided continuous coverage for many of its clients since 1977, when Affiliated was founded under its current name. However, the current agency was born of several mergers and can trace its lineage to the Tracy Insurance Agency, which was founded in 1889.

Today, Affiliated is one of the five largest insurance agencies in Utah. Some of that growth can be attributed to the company's policy of plainspoken honesty. For instance, Dickson has a simple answer when a client company asks him how much money it should spend on insurance. "I tell them that the most expensive insurance has the cheapest premium and doesn't adequately cover their exposure," Dickson says. "That's my philosophy in a nutshell."

TECHNOLOGICALLY ADVANCED

In keeping with the 1990s trend of accomplishing more with less, Affiliated has become increasingly automated. In 1977, the agency began with 24 employees and wrote $8 million a year in property and casualty premiums. To accomplish a threefold increase in just over 20 years, Affiliated has come to rely heavily on technology, including cutting-edge computers and software. In fact, all Affiliated customer service representatives have PC workstations with fax capability and E-mail, making the company highly flexible to changing trends.

Affiliated is also cognizant of the importance of maintaining a competent and pleasant customer service staff. "We're conscious of our reputation," says Dickson. "We want our image to be squeaky clean as far as what we do. We want to have the best employees and pay the top salaries. I'd rather have three exceptional employees than five average ones. Our people are very knowledgeable and have high

integrity. If we can't improve a customer's coverage, we'll tell him so. If we can't improve it, we don't deserve the business."

COMMUNITY INVOLVEMENT

Concerned with more than selling insurance, many Affiliated employees give back to the community in which they live. Dickson is heavily involved in community and trade organizations, and encourages his associates to do the same. "Salt Lake is a real diamond in the rough," Dickson says. "With the recreation, the University of Utah, and the family values, it's the best place to live in the world. There's no place like Salt Lake City."

In the future, Dickson projects a slow but steady expansion for Affiliated Insurance Agency. "At one point, I wanted to be the biggest agency; now, I want to be the best," Dickson says. "Growth takes care of itself. Growth for its own sake isn't the right policy. Our goal is to give our customers the best service possible."

"AT ONE POINT, I WANTED TO BE THE BIGGEST AGENCY; NOW, I WANT TO BE THE BEST," SAYS JAMES DICKSON, PRESIDENT AND CEO OF AFFILIATED INSURANCE AGENCY. "GROWTH TAKES CARE OF ITSELF. GROWTH FOR ITS OWN SAKE ISN'T THE RIGHT POLICY. OUR GOAL IS TO GIVE OUR CUSTOMERS THE BEST SERVICE POSSIBLE."

IN THE FIRST 23 YEARS OF ITS HISTORY, WASATCH ADVISORS, INC. was located in two historic downtown buildings. The bedrock values exemplified by the old buildings—stability, integrity, and experience—have come to represent Wasatch as well. In 1998, Wasatch moved to new corporate headquarters in Salt Lake City. The move reflected the

dynamic growth and success of what is now one of the country's most recognized money management firms.

When Sam Stewart, a professor of finance at the University of Utah, and a group of colleagues founded Wasatch in 1975, the idea of identifying and investing in small, undiscovered companies was not yet in vogue. In fact, Wasatch is considered by many in the financial industry to be a pioneer in small company growth stock investing. From this solid foundation, Wasatch grew, and now manages more than $1 billion in assets. Wasatch clients include individuals, pension and profit-sharing plans, retirement funds, foundations, endowments, and trusts. The firm also manages the assets of Wasatch Funds, Inc., Utah's first family of no-load mutual funds.

Nearly half the assets managed by Wasatch are in individual and institutional accounts. Investments

in Wasatch Funds make up the other 50 percent. Wasatch created its family of no-load funds in 1986 to mirror the investment strategies it had structured for larger, institutional clients. Wasatch realized that individuals with smaller amounts to invest could benefit from the firm's investment management expertise. Today, Wasatch offers one fixed-income fund, four growth-oriented equity funds, and a value-oriented equity fund. All the Wasatch Funds are designed for long-term investors. The Mid-Cap Fund invests primarily in fast-growing technology companies. The Growth Fund invests in stable companies growing at a steady pace. The company's flagship fund, the Aggressive Equity Fund, invests in growing small companies, and the Micro-Cap Fund invests in relatively tiny companies with outstanding growth prospects. The Wasatch Micro-Cap Value Fund also invests in very small companies, but with an eye on the value of a company's underlying assets relative to its stock price. The Wasatch-Hoisington U.S. Treasury Fund invests in U.S. Treasury Securities, which are considered to be the highest-quality fixed-income investment.

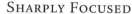

TOM SMART

SHARPLY FOCUSED

In spite of its growth and success, Wasatch has not lost sight of its goal to provide clients with superior portfolio performance and service. The company's in-house securities analysts focus on locating small companies with the potential to increase earnings two to three times faster than typical large companies. The company cautions that its portfolios are best suited for patient investors with a time horizon of at least five years because the stock prices of small companies are subject to wide fluctuations. A few of the

small, unknown companies that Wasatch has invested in during the past 23 years that have now grown to become leaders in their markets include Subaru of America, Inc., Cisco Systems, Inc., United States Surgical Corporation, Compaq Computer Corp., 3Com Corp., and St. Jude Medical. Wasatch has also made successful investments in many Utah-based companies. These include American Stores, Franklin Covey Co., NuSkin Asia Pacific, Inc., Novell, Inc., and Research Industries Corp.

Wasatch Advisors' success has not gone unnoticed. In 1996, Gov-

CLOCKWISE FROM TOP:
THIS HISTORIC BROWNSTONE, BUILT IN 1890, WAS HOME TO WASATCH ADVISORS FROM 1975 TO 1983.

BUILT IN 1908, THE MCINTYRE BUILDING LOCATED ON SALT LAKE CITY'S HISTORIC MAIN STREET WAS HOME TO WASATCH ADVISORS AND WASATCH FUNDS FROM 1983 TO 1998.

WASATCH'S NEW CORPORATE HEADQUARTERS AT SOCIAL HALL PLAZA MARKS THE BEGINNING OF A NEW ERA FOR THE FIRM.

Street, you think of giant corporations like GM and IBM. We look for up-and-coming companies, those destined to be the next Microsoft or Worldcom."

Employees show their involvement in Salt Lake City in a number of ways. Because Wasatch is small, any employee can propose an idea for community involvement and quickly find support from the company. Over the years, Wasatch and its employees have been active participants in numerous community projects, including Habitat for Humanity, Ronald McDonald House, Letters for Literacy, and numerous projects supporting education and the arts. The company has also taken an active role in providing financial scholarships, internships, and general financial support to the University of Utah.

As Wasatch looks to the future, its focus will remain on offering cutting-edge investment products, as well as maintaining a strong commitment to its investment discipline and strategy. As Jespersen puts it, "We seek to provide our clients with the kind of long-term investment performance that really helps their assets grow. We'll continue to add new products and enhance our services to meet our clients' needs."

fund. And, in 1998, *Money* magazine named the Wasatch Micro-Cap Fund in the top 10 of all U.S. stock funds for outstanding one-year returns.

NATIONAL REACH, LOCAL ROOTS

Despite having a national reach and clients all over the country, we're still very much a Utah company," says Wasatch Director and Portfolio Manager Roy Jespersen. "When you invest your money with Wasatch, you invest it with people whose families and roots are here." Furthermore, he says, with the significant population growth in the West, Wasatch invests in a number of companies located in its own back-yard, although he is quick to add that in-house analysts scout the entire United States and beyond for outstanding investment opportunities. Jespersen says, "Investing in small companies is gratifying because we provide entrepreneurs with business capital and that, ultimately, provides jobs."

Wasatch Advisors is owned by its employees. Consequently, teamwork, dedication, and motivation are essential assets. When the company started, most investment firms were located in large financial centers such as New York City. "Being away from there," says Jespersen, "gives you a unique perspective on what business is doing. When you think of Wall

ernor Michael Leavitt recognized Wasatch as the eighth-fastest-growing business at the annual awards ceremony honoring the top 100 companies in Utah. Over the years, Wasatch has been featured in numerous articles in prominent national publications, including *Forbes, Newsweek, Money, Fortune,* and the *Wall Street Journal.* The Wasatch Funds have also received national recognition. In 1990, Lipper Analytical Services, Inc., an organization that tracks the performance of mutual funds, named the Wasatch Growth Fund the number one small company growth fund. In 1994, *Worth* magazine named the Wasatch Aggressive Equity Fund the best small-cap growth fund in the country. In 1995, *Kiplinger's* named the Wasatch Mid-Cap Fund the year's top-performing long-term growth

CLOCKWISE FROM TOP: WASATCH ADVISORS' DIRECTORS ARE (BACK ROW, FROM LEFT) JIM K. MILLIGAN, MARK E. BAILEY, ROY S. JESPERSEN, ROBERT T. GARDINER, (FRONT ROW, FROM LEFT) JEFF S. CARDON, SAMUEL S. STEWART, JR., AND KAREY BARKER.

WASATCH RESEARCH ANALYSTS FOCUS ON FINDING SMALL COMPANIES WITH OUTSTANDING INVESTMENT POTENTIAL THROUGH A HANDS-ON PROCESS OF BOTTOM-UP, FUNDAMENTAL SECURITIES ANALYSIS.

DIRECTOR MARK E. BAILEY (LEFT) ACCEPTS AN AWARD HONORING WASATCH AS THE EIGHTH-FASTEST-GROWING BUSINESS IN UTAH FROM GOVERNOR MICHAEL O. LEAVITT.

Wasatch Crest Insurance Companies

WASATCH CREST INSURANCE COMPANIES IS ONE OF UTAH'S LARGEST carriers of workers' compensation insurance and has been recognized as one of the state's fastest-growing companies. The various companies were born and bred in the Salt Lake Valley and trace some of their roots back more than a century to 1886.

Early History

Wasatch Crest Insurance Companies consists of six entities: Wasatch Crest Mutual Insurance Co., organized in 1976; Wasatch Crest Group, Inc., organized in 1997; Wasatch Crest Insurance Company, organized in 1886 and acquired in 1998; Wasatch Crest Casualty Insurance Company, organized in 1964 and acquired in 1997; First Continental Life & Accident Insurance Company, organized in 1979 and acquired in 1993; and Electric Mutual Benefit Association, organized in 1966 and acquired in 1973.

Before 1993, Energy Mutual and Electric Mutual, as the companies were originally known, provided insurance products to Utah Power/Pacificorp. In 1993, Energy Mutual broke away from the utility, changed its name to Wasatch Crest in 1994, and began writing insurance broadly in the commercial marketplace.

The management team that broke away from the utility in 1993 included Orrin T. Colby Jr., who helped found Wasatch Crest in 1973 and is chairman and CEO;

Gordon B. Boyle, president and COO, who joined the companies in 1975 and was a major influence in the architecture of the insurance products and enterprise; and William J. Worlsey, vice president-finance and secretary. A certified public accountant, Worlsey joined the companies in 1979 and has helped build the financial and accounting systems from scratch.

In 1993, the companies acquired First Continental Life. Four years later, the companies acquired Wasatch Crest Casualty Insurance Company, formerly Transunion Casualty Company, of Cedar Rapids, Iowa; and Wasatch Crest Insurance Company, presently being formed out of one of the oldest insurance entities in the state.

The companies' products include group life, accidental death and dismemberment, disability, accident and health (medical), dental, vision, workers' compensation, auto, home owners, home appliance warranty, and travel accident. In 1993, when Wasatch Crest began pulling its six entities together, there were nine employees. Today, the companies provide employment

for some 130 families, largely in the Salt Lake City area.

This growth has not gone without notice. In 1996, the companies were recognized as some of the 100 fastest-growing companies in the state of Utah, and in 1997 were recognized as some of the 25 fastest-growing. This growth came about as a result of acquisitions and an overwhelming response on the part of the employers of Utah who want to do business with a local Utah insurance company offering quality service and competitive products.

But this growth has not been limited to Wasatch Crest's home state. In addition to Utah, the companies have an office in Portland, Oregon. In fact, the companies will offer life and medical insurance products in 42 states and property and casualty products in 24 states.

Community Service

"It's important to give of yourself and not just open your pocketbook," Colby affirms. "I had a CEO once who told me a person in my position should devote one-third

WASATCH CREST INSURANCE COMPANIES IS ONE OF UTAH'S LARGEST NON-STATE FUND CARRIERS OF WORKERS' COMPENSATION INSURANCE AND HAS BEEN RECOGNIZED AS ONE OF THE STATE'S FASTEST-GROWING COMPANIES.

ANDRÉ RAMJOUÉ

of their time to business, one-third to the community, and one-third to thinking. I try to apply that." Colby has served on the boards of numerous organizations, including the Association of Youth Councils, Utah Transit Authority, Utah Health Cost Management Foundation, Utah Health Data Authority, and Boys and Girls Clubs.

Furthermore, Colby's interest in helping others is reiterated by the companies' philanthropies. Wasatch Crest has been an active supporter of the Utah Food Bank, the United Way, children's athletic programs, the Boy Scouts of America, college and university committees, and local law enforcement programs.

The company believes it is important to give something back to the communities it serves: "We've been proactive in trying to provide things of value to Utah employers—not just profits for us. After all, we're locally owned and operated. We're part of the community. As with all worthwhile human endeavors, the management of the companies believes our mission is the betterment of human life and well-being," says Colby.

And the firm's attitude is expressed in actions, not just words. As an example, the officers point to the companies' efforts in promoting workplace safety. Wasatch Crest presents an annual award recognizing a Utah company that has taken a proactive approach toward managing a safe workplace with exceptional safety and health standards. In 1997, the recipient of the award was a coal-mining company in eastern Utah. "Where else in the world are you going to find a coal mine as the safest workplace? That's a far cry from the Willburg mining disaster," Colby says. "Many of the finalists were construction companies. That's because we concentrate on safety and prevention."

GROWTH PROSPECTS

In a time of massive growth and economic expansion, Boyle is understandably optimistic about the companies' prospects. "In our business, you either grow or die.

If you can't grow on your own, you'll get swallowed up. We want to grow to a size where we can be self-sustaining.

"Our product lines probably won't change much, other than providing more value for the dollar," Boyle continues. "Where you will see change is with volume and the territory. Small employers, for instance, will remain one of our niche markets; both our experience and our product lines are well suited to them. We'll also continue to work with professional

associations that strive to assist their members in securing competitive, value-added products and services."

As far as territory, Wasatch Crest will continue to grow rapidly throughout the Intermountain West, the Pacific Northwest, and the Midwest. The companies plan to continue expanding in rural areas, which management believes are often undeserved by insurance companies.

The origin of the name and logo of the companies is emblematic of the Salt Lake City area, Colby believes. "Wasatch" is a Native American word meaning a low pass in a high mountain range. And, he explains, the "crest" represents the peak or pinnacle and is a symbol of honor and strength. Colby believes these two symbols represent his firm's desire to help the members of the communities it serves, and its quest to hold itself to higher and higher standards of excellence. Working by these values, Wasatch Crest Insurance Companies will continue to be a mainstay in the state of Utah for decades to come.

BECAUSE OF WASATCH CREST'S DEDI-CATION TO WORKPLACE SAFTEY, UTAH HAS SEEN A DRASTIC DECREASE IN CATAS-TROPHES SUCH AS THE WILLBURG MINING DISASTER (TOP AND BOTTOM).

ALTHOUGH PERSONAL CUSTOMER SERVICE IS A POPULAR BUZZWORD IN the business vernacular of the 1990s, few institutions work harder to demonstrate a strong commitment to their customers than First Utah Bank. Even in the fiercely competitive banking industry, First Utah Bank constantly strives to meet the needs of each individual customer. And judging from the bank's impressive annual growth, averaging 35 percent over each of the past seven years, customers are responding in large numbers.

Today, First Utah Bank has grown impressively to $58 million in total assets (up from $8.5 million in 1992). The bank's 49 employees deal with 4,500 depositors, divided almost equally between commercial and individual accounts.

PUTTING CUSTOMERS FIRST

We worked hard from the beginning to prove our slogan Putting Customers First," explains President and CEO John R. Hanson, "and our strategy really hasn't changed. We're always trying to find a creative way to connect with customers through flexible payment plans suited to their particular needs, expanded hours, and business and personal checking accounts designed to simplify customers' lives. We have added the convenience of banking by phone 24 hours a day, staffed to have no waiting at our teller lines, and don't believe in voice mail. Whatever makes sense for the customers becomes an option."

Realizing an overhaul was imperative, the board hired Hanson in September 1991. The transforma-

FROM THE BEGINNING, FIRST UTAH BANK EMPHASIZED A PERSONAL APPROACH, THANKS TO THE EFFORTS OF BOARD MEMBERS (FROM LEFT) JOHN R. HANSON, JOHN S. WORMDAHL, SHIRRELL W. HUGHES, PAUL "HAP" GREEN, EDWARD "TED" JENKINS, M.D., AND CHAIRMAN SCOTT M. BROWNING, M.D.

tion included a new name and a new attitude. Growing from a single branch in Holladay in 1992, First Utah Bank currently operates six branches across the valley. From the very beginning, thanks to a courageous board led by Chairman Scott M. Browning, M.D., the bank emphasized a personal approach. Loan committees don't exist, and decisions are made face-to-face by officers Hanson describes as "experienced, bright, and empowered." John S. Wormdahl, the bank's executive vice president, "is remarkable, a lender with a real feel for the market, and he cares deeply about customers," says Hanson.

In building a staff, First Utah Bank kept the public's wishes in mind. "Most of the people who have come to work here did so because they recognized the valuable opportunity to think of ways to solve problems and to deal with customers. We are complemented by the high level of quality and experience our employees bring to First Utah Bank, and the customers can tell the difference," says Hanson.

The strong customer service attitude is exemplified in one of the bank's guiding principles: "The customer won't care how much you know, until they know how much you care." First Utah Bank individually tailors its loan plans to the needs of each customer. That's one reason, Hanson believes, that the bank's delinquency rate remains at 20 percent of its peer group. If a customer experiences temporary financial problems, the bank's officers are willing to work with him or her.

MEMBERS OF THE COMMUNITY

As First Utah Bank has become more established, it has sought opportunities to further integrate itself in the Salt Lake community. For example, it established locations in areas that were traditionally underserved, including West Valley City, Midvale, and the central city.

First Utah Bank is also a major sponsor of the Utah Grizzlies hockey team, children's charities, and Ronald McDonald House. And the bank has established a computer lab at the Faith Temple Church in order to provide underprivileged children and latch-key kids with after-school learning opportunities.

Finally, the bank sponsors a series of broad-based scholarships designed to honor students who might otherwise go unrecognized. "A lot of attention gets directed at higher-profile students," Hanson says, "but we want to focus on students who have prompted positive change in their community of students. In schools as well as our branches, we want to recognize and emphasize what's best in the community."

WHAT'S NEXT?

For the coming years, First Utah Bank has outlined an ambitious plan for dealing with its seemingly inevitable growth. First, the bank has established a data-processing subsidiary to more efficiently handle its back-room operation functions and those of other client institutions. Second, Hanson says the bank will add a network of ATMs and several new branch locations valley-wide. Third, by the end of 1998, the bank plans to launch its Internet banking service. And, as if all that weren't enough, First Utah Bank will also create a mortgage department and a small-business loan department. "These opportunities are going to keep us busy for the next few years," Hanson says.

"DEAR JOHN" CARDS

All the while, the bank will continue to seek its depositors' opinions. "Dear John" cards, displayed in the lobbies, allow customers to submit comments, compliments, and suggestions directly to the CEO. "In six years," Hanson notes, "I've gotten dozens and dozens that have been positive and praised our employees and services. I'm pleased they have written.

"I'll tell you what really makes us feel good," Hanson concludes. "We know our customers drive by other banks and credit unions in order to deal with us. As we talk to our customers, we find the vast majority want to do business with somebody who can deal with their individual situations and answer their questions. That's what we strive to do."

EXCEPTIONAL CUSTOMER SERVICE MEANS PROVIDING LOCAL DECISIONS TO LOCAL ISSUES. THIS BELIEF GUIDES FIRST UTAH BANK PRINCIPALS (CLOCKWISE FROM TOP LEFT) JOHN R. HANSON, SCOTT M. BROWNING, AND JOHN S. WORMDAHL.

Olympus Tours & Travel

I**N ITS NEARLY TWO DECADES AS ONE OF UTAH'S PREMIER TRAVEL** agencies, Olympus Tours & Travel in downtown Salt Lake City has gone on something of a journey itself. What once was a small agency serving almost an exclusively corporate clientele is now a full-service agency that also serves a growing cruise, leisure, and family market. ▨ "We strive to give our customers a total package of helpful information, gracious service, and individual attention," says Peter Billman, Olympus president and chief executive officer. "Whether for business or leisure travel, our clients find professional service with a personal touch."

Olympus Tours & Travel was organized in 1981. "It was sort of a one-man band back then," says Billman. "It was a good little company, small with a good reputation, but it hadn't blossomed yet."

Under Billman's leadership, Olympus has grown. He began by attracting corporate clients who seek a high level of quality service. Today, the Olympus client list reads like a who's who of elite businesses along the Wasatch Front.

Changing with the Times

In recent years, the airlines began making changes that have impacted travel agencies and all air travelers. "Airline commission caps and commission cuts," says Billman, "have forced several travel agencies out of business—the survivors have had to change."

Billman and his partner, Michael Galieti—once one of Olympus' corporate clients himself—have responded to this challenge. While they continue to offer top-notch service to a growing number of corporate clients, Olympus is now a quality cruise and leisure center as well.

The quality comes, in part, from sheer experience: the combined travel industry experience of the staff at Olympus exceeds 125 years. Most of the staff at Olympus, including Billman, have extensive experience working for the airlines before coming to work at Olympus.

The travel preferences of people in Utah are as diverse as Utah's growing population. This presents additional challenges for a full-service agency like Olympus. "Besides knowing the ins and outs of the airline industry," Galieti explains, "our people must now develop expertise on cruising; European tours; Hawaiian resort vacations; Utah ski, bike, or whitewater adventures; or on any other vacation or recreation experience you can think of."

Although Olympus is growing along with Utah, Billman says that when it comes to service, bigger is better only so long as it means more service, not less personal service. "With some travel agencies, you may have trouble getting the same person on the phone twice in the same day," he says. At Olympus, a live voice answers your phone call and puts you in touch with your own personal travel agent.

CLOCKWISE FROM TOP: OLYMPUS TOURS & TRAVEL'S CLIENTS TRAVEL TO EXOTIC DESTINATIONS ALL OVER THE WORLD.

"WITH SOME TRAVEL AGENCIES, YOU MAY HAVE TROUBLE GETTING THE SAME PERSON ON THE PHONE TWICE IN THE SAME DAY," BILLMAN SAYS. AT OLYMPUS, A LIVE VOICE ANSWERS YOUR PHONE CALL AND PUTS YOU IN TOUCH WITH YOUR OWN PERSONAL TRAVEL AGENT.

PETER BILLMAN (RIGHT) AND HIS PARTNER, MICHAEL GALIETI, OFFER TOP-NOTCH SERVICE TO A GROWING CRUISE, LEISURE, AND FAMILY MARKET.

▲▶ DAYBELL PHOTOGRAPHY

S ummit Destinations takes Utah's Olympic motto seriously—The World is Welcome Here. Summit, however, does more than just extend an invitation—it takes its customers by the hand. More than just a travel agency, Summit is a destination management company that specializes in its own backyard. ▩ "Madagascar may seem a lot more exotic than

Salt Lake City," says Donna Dick, the agency's leisure promotions and operations director. "But only if you've never visited Utah."

Like most of her coworkers, Dick is a Utah native with many years' experience in the travel business. Before becoming operations director, she spent more than 11 years teaching and translating in Israel, Greece, Europe, Puerto Rico, Mexico, and Canada, as well as in southern Florida. Realizing how much she missed all that the Salt Lake City area has to offer, she came home. Dick soon joined Summit, which is a division of Travel Zone, and now specializes in group tours ranging from 10 to 8,000 people, including convention, meeting, and incentive program planning.

Since its founding by Jon Christopher Jones, Travel Zone has grown to be Utah's third-largest independent travel agency. Travel Zone's agents are versed in cruises, as well as group, corporate, leisure, and adventure travel, including international itineraries that encompass museum exhibitions.

TRAVEL KNOW-HOW

B ut Summit does more than inbound, full-service individual and group travel planning. Its agents turn the agency into a school, inviting university professors, historians, geologists, sociologists, architects, and other experts on Utah to educate the agents, making sure they are as informed about their state as they are about the world of travel.

"It's not just a matter of making reservations," says Neil Jacobsen, Summit's inbound services manager. "It's also attending to every detail of transportation, accommodation, and itinerary. And that means knowing the lay of the land and having strong relationships with hotels, chambers of com-

merce, the convention and visitors bureau, national parks, ski resorts, arts and cultural institutions, even the Olympic venues for the 2002 Winter Games."

Supporting that agent know-how is an agency wired into the latest in the world of travel. Travel Zone is an affiliate of the Leisure Travel Group, Inc. and a member of CorpNet International, both of which provide Summit agents the opportunity to consult with other travel experts to gain new ideas and insights and to update knowledge and skills. CorpNet's hotel program ensures significant cost reduction in more than 65,000 hotels worldwide. Summit also uses the CoRRe quality control system for the lowest possible fares prior to departure, even after ticketing. It provides detailed flight and fare options through ResFax, and allows customers to view live computer reservations through RemoteLink and the Internet Travel Network. Wanting to make life easier for its corporate clients as well, Summit also provides a comprehensive program of detailed, tailored management reports in

formats compatible with the clients' accounting needs.

But even with all its high-tech tools, Summit's distinction still comes down to its staff. Says Dick, "Jon gathers the people and makes the partnerships to help us diversify and give us the background, experience, and expertise to serve our clients. It's common in this industry for people to claim to be experts at everything from cruises to conventions. Jon makes sure we have the people who are experts at what they do."

And for Summit Destinations, that begins with knowledge of its own backyard.

More than just a travel agency, Summit is a destination management company that specializes in its own backyard (top).

But even with all its high-tech tools, Summit's distinction still comes down to its staff. Says Summit's leisure promotions and operations director Donna Dick, "Jon makes sure we have the people who are experts at what they do" (bottom).

WHEN BUSINESS OR VACATION TRAVELERS COME TO SALT LAKE CITY, they often choose the Salt Lake City Marriott as their home away from home. On any given day, the lobby of the hotel is crowded with business travelers preparing to venture out on sales calls, vacationers planning their tour for the day, and conventioneers

attending conferences or shows at the Salt Palace Convention Center.

"From a name standpoint, we are the most recognizable hotel in the community," says Dan Boyer, director of marketing for the hotel. "We've got a great reputation in the hotel community, and our reputation in the Salt Lake City community speaks for itself."

MORE THAN JUST A GREAT LOCATION

Boyer says the reason why people choose the Marriott is simple: "In the hotel business, location is everything, and we have the most desirable location downtown. We're across from the Salt Palace, which goes a long way in our marketing efforts, and the fact that we're connected to Crossroads Mall is another big advantage."

But, as Boyer quickly points out, location alone is hardly enough to propel a hotel's success. Another factor is consistency, and the Salt

WITH A HISTORY OF QUALITY SERVICE, A WEALTH OF AMENITIES, AND A COMMITMENT TO CONSTANT IMPROVEMENT, THE SALT LAKE CITY MARRIOTT HAS TRULY MADE A NAME FOR ITSELF IN THE AREA'S HOTEL INDUSTRY OVER THE YEARS (TOP).

THE UNDERLYING OBJECTIVE AT THE SALT LAKE CITY MARRIOTT IS TO SET ITSELF APART BY OFFERING CONSISTENTLY EXCELLENT CUSTOMER SERVICE (BOTTOM).

Lake City Marriott is tops in that area too. "We've been a Marriott since the day we opened our doors in 1981," says Boyer. "People recognize that. If you're a meeting planner, you know you can go to a Marriott Hotel in Salt Lake City or Portland and receive the same quality service and accommoda-

tions. And the customer knows if he or she is traveling 50 to 100 nights a year, they're going to get the same services and amenities from one Marriott Hotel to another."

These amenities in Salt Lake City include 515 modern guest rooms; a health club with an indoor/outdoor pool, sauna, and whirlpool; three restaurants and lounges; and eight different meeting rooms with a total of 17,000 square feet of flexible space. The 14,000-square-foot Grand Ballroom, which seats as many as 1,400 people, has also proved popular with organizations as varied as the University of Utah, Dyno Nobel, Novell, the Utah Dental Association, and the Utah Farm Bureau—all of which regularly book the Marriott's facilities for their conventions and meetings. The hotel also hosts meetings of smaller organizations, including some gatherings of as few as a dozen people. But regardless of the customer, the commitment to high-quality service remains the same.

The Marriott's amenities alone are enough to attract guests, but Utah's vibrant nightlife and large variety of restaurants are also a major draw. "Outside of skiing, you don't hear that much about Salt Lake City, but meeting planners are very pleasantly surprised by the range of recreation, nightlife, and dining options available here," Boyer explains.

"More and more," Boyer continues, "this is a year-round destination. There's a lot going on. The city doesn't roll up and go to sleep when the sun goes down. When you're planning a meeting for 2,000 to 5,000 people, you don't necessarily want to send your attendees to a sleepy town."

Visitors to Salt Lake City won't be disappointed: New restaurants and bars—comparable to some of the finest establishments in the country—lend themselves very well to the city's cosmopolitan atmosphere.

LOOKING AHEAD

With the Salt Lake Valley currently experiencing explosive growth, Marriott recognizes the opportunity to build a headquarters hotel suitable for housing dignitaries and VIPs, as well as hosting specialty functions. In fact, as the city demonstrates its commitment to expanding its convention business, Marriott hopes to construct an 800-room hotel as a further incentive to holding larger meetings. "With Marriott's presence in this community, we're fortunate to be in a position to do this," says Boyer. "We recognize the excellent opportunities in the convention business for Salt Lake City."

As organizations increasingly choose Salt Lake City to host their shows, Marriott is committed to being there to help that growth. "With our nearby mountains, canyons, and deserts, we're in the perfect location to host year-round trade shows," says Boyer. "If needed, exhibitors can demonstrate their products right in our backyard."

Even as it looks toward the future, Marriott remains focused on the day-to-day realities of the hospitality and convention business. With that in mind, the underlying objective at the hotel is to set itself apart by offering consistently excellent customer service. Boyer explains, "By some estimates, 80 percent of all future jobs are going to be service-related. The quality of service is what will distinguish one organization from another. Everything we do, from offering a breakfast and a newspaper to providing an executive meeting manager to take the fuss out of planning a meeting, is designed to distinguish the Marriott Hotel."

With a history of quality service, a wealth of amenities, and a commitment to constant improvement, the Salt Lake City Marriott has truly made a name for itself in the area's hotel industry over the years. And as the company enters the next millennium, it is poised to set the standards by which all other Salt Lake City hotels will follow.

*A*TTRACTED BY A NUMBER OF FACTORS—INCLUDING A LARGE population of well-educated and multilingual residents, a convenient geographical location, and an outstanding quality of life—American Express established a significant presence in Salt Lake City in 1982. ▨ Many of the company's 2,000 Utah employees

now work around the clock in the American Express Service Center in Salt Lake City, which houses the operations for the company's worldwide Travelers Cheque business and boasts a 32-language capability. Other Salt Lake City team members focus on the company's consumer card services group, new business research and development, American Express Centurion Bank, American Express Financial Advisors, retail and business travel offices, and HRICS-West, which handles salary and benefit questions for American Express employees in the United States.

But regardless of their department, the Salt Lake City staff is excited about the company's direction. American Express has achieved strong performances in all its major businesses, including growth in spending on American Express cards, increased assets under management, and gains in market share in travel and Travelers Cheques.

The company has introduced a wide range of new products, significantly increased the number of merchants accepting the card, and broadened the number of alliances with financial institutions and travel businesses. The company has also returned to the money order business after a five-year absence and plans to begin offering its money orders in retail locations as well as financial institutions.

MANY OF AMERICAN EXPRESS' 2,000 UTAH EMPLOYEES NOW WORK AROUND THE CLOCK IN THE AMERICAN EXPRESS SERVICE CENTER IN SALT LAKE CITY, WHICH HOUSES THE COMPANY'S WORLD-WIDE TRAVELERS CHEQUE OPERATIONS AND BOASTS A 32-LANGUAGE CAPABILITY (TOP).

AMERICAN EXPRESS IS THE LARGEST CORPORATE SPONSOR OF THE ECCLES CENTER IN PARK CITY (BOTTOM).

EMPLOYEE INVOLVEMENT

When American Express moved into Salt Lake City, employees immediately became active in community affairs. According to a company spokesperson, that commitment has recently been renewed and expanded. On both the community and the employee levels, a lot of work has been done recently. The company is much more visible in the community.

Employees serve on a wide variety of nonprofit and cultural organizations' boards in Salt Lake City. For example, company executives currently sit on the boards of a variety of organizations, including the Salt Lake Area Chamber of Commerce, Utah's Hogle Zoo, the Salt Lake Acting Company, and Traveler's Aid Society. American Express is also the largest corporate sponsor of the Eccles Center in Park City, and is very involved in Repertory Dance Theatre, as well as a lecture series at Westminster College.

American Express also boasts a program to encourage employee involvement in community service. In 1996, the company's Utah staff contributed more than 14,000 hours to the program. Also that year, American Express launched its popular Culture Card program. Under this initiative, the company makes donations to a number of Salt Lake City's artistic and cultural organizations. In turn, those organizations offer free or dis-

counted admission to places such as Utah's Hogle Zoo, the University of Utah's museums, the Utah Symphony, and the Repertory Dance Theatre.

CELEBRATING DIVERSITY

American Express has an Employee Appreciation Month program as well as a Diversity Week. The company sponsors a diversity fair each spring, and employees are encouraged to staff booths, provide entertainment, and share information. Among the groups that participate in the annual event are employee networks representing various minority groups—all of which offer support for employees throughout the year.

But the company's celebration of diversity goes far beyond a one-week fair. A full-time manager is dedicated to integrating diversity into company culture, and each employee goes through diversity awareness training. The company's Blue Box Values include a specific tenet to treat each other with respect and dignity. Examples of the company's attempts to recognize and reward employee contributions include a generous tuition reimbursement plan, an on-site fitness center, and the REACH (Resource Education and Career Headquarters) Center—a 24-hour library that opened in 1994.

THE IMPORTANCE OF COMMUNICATING

As a means of further encouraging dialogue and employee involvement, American Express celebrates its own holiday each January, which organizers have dubbed National Communication Month. Activities include an information fair designed to provide employees with details about new services and products offered by the company, as well as Leader 2 Leader, in which team leaders communicate with one another about strategies and initiatives. The month's activities have been so successful that they are now carried on throughout the year, including Talking on Tuesday, which gives employees the opportunity to offer feedback on company issues in an informal lunchtime setting.

Looking to the future, growing its businesses continues to be the highest priority and American Express is pursuing three themes that hold great potential for that expected growth: opening the American Express network to other card issuers by signing significant partners in key markets; expanding its brand presence in financial services; and deepening its penetration of markets outside the United States. All of these build on the company's traditional businesses from which contined growth is expected.

AMERICAN EXPRESS BOASTS A PROGRAM TO ENCOURAGE EMPLOYEE INVOLVEMENT IN COMMUNITY SERVICE. IN 1996, THE COMPANY'S UTAH STAFF CONTRIBUTED MORE THAN 14,000 HOURS TO THE PROGRAM, INCLUDING INVOLVEMENT IN THE TRAVELER'S AID HOMELESS SHELTER, MEALS ON WHEELS, AND THE UTAH FOOD BANK.

ROLF KAY

ROLF KAY

THE LARGEST VENDOR OF LIBRARY AUTOMATION SYSTEMS IN THE WORLD, Ameritech Library Services is on a mission to move libraries to the cutting edge of information technology and, in the process, change the way users view these hallowed founts of information, enlightenment, and entertainment. ▣ "Our focus," explains Vice President of Marketing Carl Grant, "is to connect people with the information resources." Ameritech does this by bringing together what Grant terms a "unique set of core competencies," connecting users to networks and providing the software, on-line cataloging, and videoconferencing, so the client can conveniently connect to the library via the Web.

Ameritech Library Services is a subsidiary of Ameritech, one of the world's largest communications companies, boasting more than 13 million customers. Ameritech Library Services serves more than 9,000 client libraries around the world, including academic, public, school, and special libraries. Its Utah library clients include the Salt Lake City School District, Orem Public Library, American Fork Public Library, and Weber County Public Library. The company also provides its customers with database services, content delivery, and information access.

In 1996, Ameritech and the Utah Academic Library Consortium signed a partnership that allowed the installation of the company's Horizon automated library system at all 11 academic institutions in the state. The implementation of the system greatly expanded faculty, student, and public access to electronic information held by the state's universities and transferred across the Internet.

COMMUNITY ACTIVITIES

As part of its outreach to the community, Ameritech employs some 35 inmates from the Utah State Correctional Facilities to work on basic information conversion. In this division, called Retro Link, inmate employees convert library card catalogs into computer-compatible records. The program benefits library patrons who use computer searches to find out whether the title being searched for is available. Grant is enthusias-

tic about the program. "It helps inmates rehabilitate themselves," he says, "so they can find employment upon release." The money the inmates earn is funneled back into the state through a victim-restitution program, contributions to inmates' families, taxes, and a fund that helps cover the costs of the inmate's own incarceration.

Ameritech makes contributions on the national level. In 1996, the company donated $2 million to the Library of Congress to set up digitization projects to record and preserve American history. Many major libraries have received financial contributions from Ameritech to contribute to the project.

Closer to home, the company's 400 Provo employees enjoy a liberal benefits package, including a 401(k) program, educational reimbursement, and adoption assistance. Additionally, the company has participated in programs sponsored by such organizations as the

THE LARGEST VENDOR OF LIBRARY AUTOMATION SYSTEMS IN THE WORLD, AMERITECH LIBRARY SERVICES IS ON A MISSION TO MOVE LIBRARIES TO THE CUTTING EDGE OF INFORMATION TECHNOLOGY AND, IN THE PROCESS, CHANGE THE WAY USERS VIEW THESE HALLOWED FOUNTS OF INFORMATION, ENLIGHTENMENT, AND ENTERTAINMENT.

United Way. And, Grant says, "We do a lot of things on the department level from the employees up. This last year, the staff went out of its way to adopt families to ensure they had a good Christmas."

VIRTUAL LIBRARIES

As Ameritech approaches the 21st century, Grant says the company is planning for changes in the way individuals and businesses gather information. "We are trying very hard to move libraries away from physical locations visited by a patron into a virtual location accessible no matter where you are. Our goal is that you can be in a mall at a kiosk or on the beach with your battery-powered laptop and get what you need. We want to position libraries as the places to visit on the Web." But for that to happen, the guardians of information—librarians—will have to be fully prepared for the changes in information systems. "Librarians are a value-added service," Grant allows. "Having people who understand how information is stored, retrieved, and delivered will be vital if libraries are to remain meaningful to the user."

As for businesses, Grant's opinion is that they are similar to individual consumers, only on a much larger scale; they need to know

about pricing, competition, marketing, and changes in product lines. "Right now, most companies have only small libraries, if they have libraries at all," says Grant. "They're looking for people who can help them filter out the information they need."

No one is in a better position to introduce librarians and business owners to one another than Ameritech. "We're trying to bring together librarians on the basis of subject expertise, trying to help the businesses make better deci-

sions and be better competitors in whatever marketplace they're functioning in," says Grant. "What businesses need is to realize that libraries are information-rich and -wise."

Grant says Ameritech is committed to the importance of the information industry. "We will contribute to the future by helping people enrich their personal and professional lives by getting the information they need out of all the information that's available."

ELISA COMINS

EIGHTY-THREE YEARS AGO, WHEN O.A. FLEMING STARTED A SMALL GROCERY wholesale business in Topeka, the world was a different place: computerized inventory lists had yet to be invented, stock was transported on small trucks, and most grocers were independent operators who owned one or, at most, a handful of stores. Getting groceries to stores and serving customers well was a pretty straightforward proposition.

Times have changed. Food distribution and marketing have become increasingly challenging in a world with more places to shop than ever before and more intense competition for consumers' food dollars.

Despite the many changes that have occurred, however, the values Fleming espoused in the early 20th century remain vital to success today for the company bearing his name. "Even though a lot of things have obviously changed, we still follow traditional practices based on values that have endured since our company's inception," says Patrick Sorensen, human resources manager of Fleming's Salt Lake City Division. "Our motto here is to tell the truth and do the right thing."

Working according to this simple and direct philosophy clearly supports Fleming's ability to meet its overall mission: "To excel at meeting the needs of consumers who shop at each Fleming-supported retail store."

On a national level, Fleming currently serves customers in 42 states and has more than 39,000 employees working in its 43 product supply centers and its corporate headquarters in Oklahoma City. The Salt Lake City Division has 350 employees working out of a 400,000-square-foot warehouse and office, serving retail customers in a five-state area that encompasses more than 1,000 square miles and includes Utah, Idaho, Wyoming, Nevada, and parts of Oregon.

In addition to marketing and distributing grocery and household products to more than 3,100 supermarkets around the country, Fleming also operates approximately 270 of its own retail supermarkets. In Utah, the company owns several stores and has plans to open more.

A larger part of Fleming's business comes from its strategic partnerships with independent supermarket stores and chains. With Fleming's help, many smaller grocers find it easier to compete with larger chains in the fiercely competitive supermarket wars. The company offers retailers a full-service approach, providing them with everything from product delivery to retail services support.

"We support retailers by helping them keep their stores up to date, their products in step with what consumers want, and their prices competitive. Fleming's team of experts provide the latest technologies, recommend effective promotions, and even help build effective in-store displays," Sorensen explains. "Our goal is to get more consumers in the stores we serve by working with our retail customers on better ways to meet their needs."

Recently Fleming took a new direction to offer customers more value by focusing on building five key store brands—BestYet™, Rainbow™, IGA™, Piggly Wiggly™, and Marquee™. BestYet store brands rank as the largest store brand Fleming offers today. Now 100 years old, the BestYet name is more than a catchy marketing slogan;

CLOCKWISE FROM TOP:
WITH FLEMING'S HELP, MANY SMALLER GROCERS FIND IT EASIER TO COMPETE WITH LARGER CHAINS IN THE FIERCELY COMPETITIVE SUPERMARKET WARS. THE COMPANY OFFERS RETAILERS A FULL-SERVICE APPROACH, PROVIDING THEM WITH EVERYTHING FROM PRODUCT DELIVERY TO RETAIL SERVICES SUPPORT.

THE SALT LAKE CITY DIVISION OF FLEMING HAS 350 EMPLOYEES WORKING OUT OF A 400,000-SQUARE-FOOT WAREHOUSE AND OFFICE, SERVING RETAIL CUSTOMERS IN A FIVE-STATE AREA THAT ENCOMPASSES MORE THAN 1,000 SQUARE MILES AND INCLUDES UTAH, IDAHO, WYOMING, NEVADA, AND PARTS OF OREGON.

MEETING THE NEEDS OF CONSUMERS THAT SHOP AT FLEMING-SUPPLIED RETAILERS IS A KEY PART OF THE COMPANY'S MISSION. FOOD 4 LESS IS ONE OF MANY FORMATS SUPPLIED BY FLEMING NATIONALLY.

it's a reflection of Fleming's commitment to its retailers and consumers. "These brands offer consumers high-quality, competitively priced alternatives to national brands, and they give retailers another way to differentiate their stores in the marketplace," Sorensen says.

In addition, Fleming continues to find ways to offer more efficient service at a reasonable price. Increasingly, this means relying on automated systems in diverse areas, such as reordering product, managing inventory control, and establishing effective promotions. The company's innovative, interactive communications system, known as VISIONET™, now links retailers, vendors, and Fleming together for the fastest possible updates on new promotional opportunities.

Another area constantly being reevaluated is logistics. "We have a huge network of equipment—tractors and trailers—on the roads. We want to utilize them to the greatest extent possible and in the most efficient way we can," says Sorensen.

THE SALT LAKE CITY DIVISION

The Salt Lake City Division has consistently ranked in the top 10 among Fleming's divisions in terms of productivity. Sorensen believes the high productivity can be traced to a highly skilled, dedicated workforce. In fact, the local product supply center recently celebrated five years without a single lost-time accident.

Sorensen also credits Fleming's success to a positive attitude that is fostered through all levels of the company—from order selectors to managers. "We try to create a culture that's pro-family and to recognize associates' outstanding contributions with rewards like Utah Jazz, Grizzlies, or Buzz tickets and associate appreciation days and luncheons."

The division is also heavily involved in Utah charities. "We have a monthly luncheon where all proceeds go to the Utah Food Bank. We also support Sub for Santa and give generously to the United Way. We like to contribute to local charities that address specific needs in the community," says Sorensen.

ANOTHER AREA CONSTANTLY BEING REEVALUATED IS LOGISTICS. "WE HAVE A HUGE NETWORK OF EQUIPMENT—TRACTORS AND TRAILERS—ON THE ROADS. WE WANT TO UTILIZE THEM TO THE GREATEST EXTENT POSSIBLE AND IN THE MOST EFFICIENT WAY WE CAN," SAYS SORENSEN (TOP).

THE COMPANY'S INNOVATIVE, INTERACTIVE COMMUNICATIONS SYSTEM, KNOWN AS VISIONET™, NOW LINKS RETAILERS, VENDORS, AND FLEMING TOGETHER FOR THE FASTEST POSSIBLE UPDATES ON NEW PROMOTIONAL OPPORTUNITIES (BOTTOM).

"We're committed to making the communities we serve better places in which to live and work."

Along with this spirit of involvement and the importance placed on individual initiative, there are other constants at Fleming. "We've always had the same business goals—to provide quality, service, and price to our customers—in that order," says Sorensen. "The only difference today is that we must be even more in tune with the changing needs of retailers and consumers. Along with competitive pricing, retailers need assistance in bringing meal solutions to busy consumers and in creating business-building promotional activities like frequent-shopper loyalty programs. Creating ads that bring shoppers into their stores and remodeling stores to upgrade their appeal are also important. Effectively managing finances of these much more sophisticated business enterprises is essential. Fleming has experts who support retailers in all these areas with ideas and answers that pack a real competitive punch.

"Customer-focused solutions were important more than 80 years ago," Sorensen concludes, "and they're even more important today in our business."

NIGHTIME PEDIATRICS CLINICS, INC.

N 1977, WHEN DR. RODNEY POLLARY BEGAN PRACTICING IN PEDIATRICS, he sought to balance his personal life with his dedication to professional service. At the time, he saw many of his peers practicing medicine as a competitive, rather than a cooperative, enterprise. His goal was to develop an alternative model that would meet patient needs

with compassion and individual attention.

In 1983, Pollary opened the first Nightime Pediatrics Clinic. Originally envisioned as an alternative to the stress and long hours associated with seeing patients seven days a week, 24 hours a day, the clinic provided urgent care during the hours when regular practitioners were off duty. Open from 5 p.m. until midnight, with a rotating staff of part-time nurses, receptionists, and pediatricians, the clinic was able to handle almost any conceivable situation. As the concept grew in popularity, Pollary's patient base began to grow.

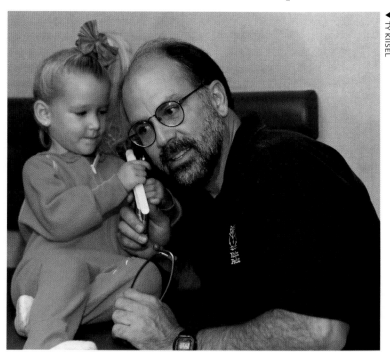

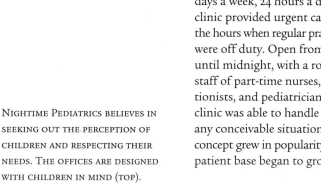 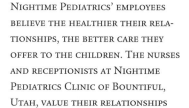

NIGHTIME PEDIATRICS BELIEVES IN SEEKING OUT THE PERCEPTION OF CHILDREN AND RESPECTING THEIR NEEDS. THE OFFICES ARE DESIGNED WITH CHILDREN IN MIND (TOP).

NIGHTIME PEDIATRICS' EMPLOYEES BELIEVE THE HEALTHIER THEIR RELATIONSHIPS, THE BETTER CARE THEY OFFER TO THE CHILDREN. THE NURSES AND RECEPTIONISTS AT NIGHTIME PEDIATRICS CLINIC OF BOUNTIFUL, UTAH, VALUE THEIR RELATIONSHIPS WITH EACH OTHER (BOTTOM).

EXPANDING ON SUCCESS

In 1998, Nightime's 45 providers expect to see some 90,000 children, or an estimated one-fifth of the youth population, in the Wasatch Front. Nightime has clinics located on the campuses of most Salt Lake City-area hospitals, and operates five freestanding

clinics. A facility that recently opened in the southern end of the valley has met with overwhelming success.

There is a simple reason for this success: Nightime's clinics

provide a reasonable alternative for parents of sick children. Instead of taking a child to an emergency room for nonemergency illnesses such as otitis, viral infections, bronchitis, or urinary tract infections, parents can have their child seen by a pediatrician, who is better equipped to diagnose and treat childhood illnesses.

Pollary's focus remains on caring for his young patients. "We want to be open when people need us," he says. "We want to support working parents, community pediatricians, and, of course, the children."

HIGH-QUALITY, PERSONALIZED ATTENTION

Although other factors have changed for Nightime Pediatrics, a constant factor has been its emphasis on high-quality, personalized attention. In the early 1980s, this was a unique departure from the doc-in-a-box model prevalent at the time. According to Pollary, "When we started, other entities were open which, like the ER, didn't cater to the needs of children."

In contrast, Pollary points out, "By hiring a staff specifically trained as pediatricians, we were—and are—uniquely positioned to take care of all children who need our help. People often say our doctors provide as much or more love and care as their regular pediatricians. That was our goal from day one. We provide after-hours services so pediatricians aren't so stressed out or tired. Nightime contributes to the quality of life in the community."

Nightime has stressed flexibility in order to better serve its clients. In early 1998, Nightime inaugurated after-midnight pediatric care. The new Starlight Clinic, located in the Murray Nightime Pediatrics office, is open between midnight and 7 a.m. All of Nightime's clinics are open 365 days a year and see patients by appointment or on a walk-in basis.

Nightime is also working to develop a strategy for dealing with peak sickness periods during cold-weather months. In addition, the company has opened a daytime clinic, called Access, to serve overflow patients from other physicians and those without primary care providers. And Nightime works with entities as varied as insurance companies, school districts, and Medicaid to provide care.

CARING INSIDE AND OUT

Nightime empowers its employees as well. "We're trying to walk our talk and follow our philosophy inside the company as well," CEO Teresa Lever-Pollary explains. "We've taken a pause in our growth to develop internal relationships. Our efforts have been rewarded because our employees do feel cared for."

The company's 146 flexible-time (the equivalent of 60 full-time) employees include physicians, nurses, receptionists, and financial and human resource specialists. Recognizing the fact that employees are the company's most valuable resource, Nightime devotes significant time, energy, dollars, and heart to training and development. In addition, employees are eligible for a competitive benefits package that includes health insurance, retirement planning, and bonuses.

WHAT'S AHEAD

Nightime is positioned for growth," says Lever-Pollary. "We're positioned to respond to change." The company hopes to eventually expand beyond Salt Lake City and the Wasatch Front, and is already identifying the kinds of individuals it would like to see take the company into the next century.

The company will also continue to focus on serving the area's various communities. That service includes participation in charity events such as Christmas Box House and Cerebral Palsy's Casual Day activities, and the recent publication of *Nightime Stories*, which emphasizes the company's ethos of caring. Nightime is also planning to put a mobile van into service, providing alternate access points for care, and is actively pursuing greater involvement in the community's health.

Pollary is confident that Nightime will continue to thrive by sitting out the all-too-frequent battles between providers over patients, and by focusing on creating healthy relationships and fulfilling its mission of caring for children.

▶ TY KIISEL

▶ TY KIISEL

AT THE COMPANY'S 15TH ANNIVERSARY CELEBRATION, LIEUTENANT GOVERNOR OLENE WALKER PRESENTED TO NIGHTIME PEDIATRICS AND DR. RODNEY POLLARY A DECLARATION FROM GOVERNOR MICHAEL LEAVITT HONORING NIGHTIME PEDIATRICS FOR SERVICE TO CHILDREN. NIGHTIME PEDIATRICS IS RECOGNIZED AS THE INNOVATOR IN AFTER-HOURS URGENT CARE FOR CHILDREN ACROSS THE COUNTRY (TOP).

NIGHTIME PEDIATRICS PROVIDES SERVICES FOR INFANTS, CHILDREN, AND TEENAGERS, AND OFFERS APPROPRIATE AFTER-HOURS URGENT CARE, WHICH INCLUDES A WIDE RANGE OF PROCEDURES NEEDED BY CHILDREN FOR ACCIDENTS AND INJURIES. DR. RODNEY POLLARY APPLIES A SPLINT TO THE ARM OF ONE OF HIS PATIENTS (BOTTOM).

RESIDENCE INN BY MARRIOTT-
TROLLEY SQUARE

To Barbara Hughes, Salt Lake City's Residence Inn by Marriott-Trolley Square isn't just a home away from home; it's like family. "I still drop by once a month just to say hi," says Hughes, who lived at the Residence Inn for nine months after a fire devastated her home. "I miss them. They took care of me. They still send me little tubs of their egg salad just because they know I like it."

Opened in 1983, the Residence Inn-Trolley Square is the city's original extended-stay hotel, appealing to travelers who need a room for five or more consecutive nights. The property is part of Marriott International, Inc., which—in addition to its traditional hotels around the world—operates 224 Residence Inns in 43 states and Canada, totaling 120,800 rooms.

"We're committed to meeting the needs of every guest," says General Manager Valerie Unger. "We focus on our long-term guests, but we try hard to be a great hotel for short-term visitors as well."

CENTRAL LOCATION

What distinguishes the Residence Inn-Trolley Square is not just the courtesy that guests like Hughes appreciate so much. The hotel is also centrally located in a safe area of downtown, only seven miles from the Salt Lake City International Airport and within 45 minutes of seven major ski areas. "We're also an Olympic partner," Unger adds. "We've set aside a block of our rooms for visitors and dignitaries planning the 2002 Winter Games."

For business travelers and guests attending corporate events, the Residence Inn is conveniently situated within blocks of the Salt Palace Convention Center and the University of Utah. Nearby businesses include American Stores, Kennecott Utah Copper, Unisys, U S WEST, Chevron, Evans & Sutherland, and IBM.

The Residence Inn is also perfect for visitors who are interested in everything but business. Nearby sites and attractions include Utah's Hogle Zoo, the Delta Center (home of the Utah Jazz), and the Latter-day Saints Genealogy Library. Also in close proximity is Temple Square, the 10-acre block that contains the visitors centers, monuments, sculptures, and Assembly Hall and Tabernacle of The Church of Jesus Christ of Latter-day Saints.

And only a block away is Trolley Square, a historic shopping mall that features nearly 100 retailers, four movie theaters, and popular restaurants scattered amid the landmark water tower and remodeled red-brick barns that once housed the city's turn-of-the-century trolley system. The mall's proximity means that the Residence Inn is only a short stroll from a primary hub of local nightlife.

A LONG LIST OF AMENITIES

Despite the countless entertainment options nearby, Unger and the staff do their share to keep guests indoors. The Residence Inn's 128 studio and penthouse suites, spread throughout 16 separate buildings, provide significantly more space than ordinary hotel rooms for about the same price.

Each studio suite measures 540 square feet and includes a queen-size bed and sleeper sofa; a living room with a fireplace and cable television; a full-size kitchen equipped with a coffeemaker, microwave, cookware, and complete

CLOCKWISE FROM TOP:
THE RESIDENCE INN-TROLLEY SQUARE IS THE CITY'S ORIGINAL EXTENDED-STAY HOTEL, APPEALING TO TRAVELERS WHO NEED A ROOM FOR FIVE OR MORE CONSECUTIVE NIGHTS.

THERE IS A SEASONAL OUTDOOR SWIMMING AREA (WITH POOLSIDE BARBECUES EVERY WEDNESDAY DURING THE SUMMER), ACCOMPANIED BY A YEAR-ROUND HOT TUB.

AT THE GATEHOUSE, GUESTS CAN ENJOY THE COMPLIMENTARY BREAKFAST AND EVENING SOCIAL, OR JUST RELAX.

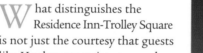

EACH STUDIO SUITE MEASURES 540
SQUARE FEET AND INCLUDES A QUEEN-
SIZE BED AND SLEEPER SOFA; A LIVING
ROOM WITH A FIREPLACE AND CABLE
TELEVISION; A FULL-SIZE KITCHEN
EQUIPPED WITH A COFFEEMAKER,
MICROWAVE, COOKWARE, REFRIGERA-
TOR, AND STOVE; AND A FULL BATH
WITH EXTRA-LARGE VANITY.

place settings; and a full bath with extra-large vanity. The two-bed, 840-square-foot penthouse suites offer twice as much space as comparably priced conventional hotel rooms. Each unit includes an upstairs loft with a king-size bed; a downstairs sleeping area with a queen-size Murphy bed and sleeper sofa; two televisions with cable; two full baths; a full-size, fully equipped kitchen; and a living room with a fireplace.

The amenities available within the Residence Inn are many. A complimentary continental breakfast buffet is served daily, including free morning editions of the *USA Today*, the *Salt Lake Tribune*, and the *Wall Street Journal*. When the sun sets on another busy day,

the Residence Inn's evening hospitality hour features complimentary beer, wine, soft drinks, and hors d'oeuvres. The on-site fitness room is equipped with stationary bikes, stair steppers, universal weights, and a court area for racquet sports, basketball, and volleyball. There is also a seasonal outdoor swimming area (with poolside barbecues every Wednesday during the summer), accompanied by a year-round hot tub. Other highlights include a complimentary grocery shopping service, on-site laundry and dry cleaning, extended cable with HBO and CNN, an in-suite safe, room service privileges at many local restaurants, complimentary curbside parking, and ski shuttle pickup.

The unique combination of services offered by the Residence Inn-Trolley Square has been enough to entice guests to stay an average of 24 nights. "Our motto is really true," says Unger. "We really try to be as close to home as we can make it."

This attitude—the staff's unwavering commitment to please every guest—is certainly what impressed Barbara Hughes during her stay. "They all pitched in whenever I needed anything," Hughes recalls. "The housekeeping staff remembered details that made me feel at home. The kitchen staff prepared my breakfast just the way I prefer it. They were attentive. I just knew they really cared, and they still do."

THE ON-SITE FITNESS ROOM IS EQUIPPED
WITH STATIONARY BIKES, STAIR STEPPERS,
UNIVERSAL WEIGHTS, AND A COURT AREA
FOR RACQUET SPORTS, BASKETBALL, AND
VOLLEYBALL.

Salt Lake Convention & Visitors Bureau

WHEN BRIGHAM YOUNG FIRST SAW THE EXPANSIVE SALT LAKE VALLEY in 1847, he is said to have propped himself up on his sickbed in his wagon and announced, "This is the right place." More than 150 years later, Salt Lake has become a destination for millions of visitors from all over the world who are drawn by the mountains,

deserts, national parks, inland sea, and thriving social scene. And with the city's honor of hosting the 2002 Olympic Winter Games, more and more visitors will learn the truth of Salt Lake's motto: The World Is Welcome Here.

In 1966, when Salt Lake made its first bid to host the Olympics, visitor information was provided by several sources, including Salt Lake County. In the early 1980s, as Salt Lake came into its own as a year-round travel destination and the number of visitors continued to grow, the county reorganized its tourism promotion program, striking strategic alliances with the private sector. The resulting public/private partnership was directed by a board of community leaders who established the Salt Lake Convention & Visitors Bureau (the Bureau) in 1984.

The Bureau is a private, non-profit organization with more than 900 members. Operating as an independent contractor to Salt Lake County, the Bureau derives most of its funding from room taxes paid by visitors staying in the county's 14,000 hotel and motel rooms. Additional revenue is generated through membership dues, the sale of advertising in Bureau publications, and the sale of mer-

▲ ALAN YORGASON

chandise in the gift shop. The Bureau is governed by an executive committee chaired by R. Steven Romney, with Richard E. Davis as president/CEO. In addition to the Salt Lake office located in the Salt Palace Convention Center, the Bureau operates satellite offices in New York City and Washington, D.C., and employs a full-time staff of 57.

Since its founding, the Bureau has been committed to establishing Salt Lake as a premier destination. Tourism is a $3.8 billion industry in Utah, accounting for nearly 10 percent of the state's economy and employing 92,000 people. The Bureau endeavors to sustain that trend in three ways: by attracting conventions, meetings, and group travel; providing information to visitors; and supporting its members in the hospitality and service-related industries.

The Bureau was recently awarded *Meetings and Conventions* magazine's Gold Service Award, the ultimate symbol of excellence for convention and visitors bureaus throughout the world. In addition, the creative advertising campaign "It's Salt Lake. Honest." was honored with the prestigious PRIMA Award

▲ DOUG BARNES

from the American Society of Association Executives. The print series addresses stereotypes of Salt Lake with tongue-in-cheek ads highlighting the area's attributes.

The Bureau attracts such high-profile conventions as Outdoor Retailers, Veterans of Foreign Wars, and Novell BrainShare, to name just a few of the trade show, association, and corporate groups that convene in Salt Lake. More than 700,000 visitors utilize the Bureau's visitor information centers each year to obtain information about Salt Lake and the state of Utah. With a growing membership base and a dedicated, professional staff, the Bureau will continue to promote Salt Lake as the right place.

◄ STEVE GREENWOOD

A S DOCTORS, HOSPITALS, AND INSURANCE COMPANIES WORK TO improve patient care and control costs, one Salt Lake City company has pioneered a line of electrosurgical tools that does both. MegaDyne® Medical Products, Inc., founded in 1985, has developed surgical blades that save both time and money in the

operating room (OR). Studies show that the average OR procedure may cost as much as $40 a minute. If a surgical team saves even five minutes in the OR, savings can be as much as $200. Surgeons definitely save time in the OR with MegaDyne's E-Z Clean® cautery tip.

Says Matt Sansom, MegaDyne's executive vice president and chief operating officer, "We help clinicians do their jobs better, and that means more effective delivery of patient care. We are committed to providing the health care industry with products that increase the quality of care and hold down costs."

Medical Breakthrough

It's no accident that the original idea for MegaDyne's breakthrough had its beginnings with a respected Salt Lake City surgeon. Dr. G. Marsden Blanch had grown impatient with traditional cautery blades. Using the blades, surgeons must periodically halt a procedure to scrape the eschar—dried tissue that forms from the heat generated during electrosurgery—from the blades. These disruptions slow the procedure and increase operating room costs.

Blanch enlisted the assistance of biomedical engineers to solve the problem. Working together, they experimented with several

substances to coat the surface of traditional blades. Finally, they discovered a high-tech coating process that reduces the amount of eschar on regular blades. Blanch was soon awarded a patent on his product—the E-Z Clean tip with PTFE coating.

That was the beginning of MegaDyne. Surgeons nationwide soon discovered that one MegaDyne blade, simply wiped clean, could last the duration of a surgery. And as it turned out, the blades had other advantages. The coated blades produce the same or better results at lower power settings, reducing damage to surrounding tissue. This means the incision heals quicker with less scarring.

This innovation did not go unnoticed. In 1995, *Surgical Products* magazine profiled MegaDyne's product. Soon surgeons who had used the basic blade were requesting coated versions of other surgical tools. So MegaDyne developed a full line of E-Z Clean tips—including standard blades, needles, balls, specialty tips, and a line of laparoscopic instruments for minimally invasive surgery.

Commitment to Innovation

MegaDyne is working hard to help practitioners meet the rapid advances in the medical

field," says Sansom. "We want health care professionals to look to MegaDyne to help them control costs and effectively treat patients."

In keeping with this goal, MegaDyne has continued to develop new products. Under the guidance of President Gary R. Kehl, the company recently crafted a specialized line of laparoscopic instruments called the All-In-One®. The All-In-One provides cautery, suction, and irrigation for laparoscopic procedures. By combining suction, irrigation, and electrocautery into one device, the number of instruments required for a laparoscopic procedure is reduced—again saving time and money in the operating room.

MegaDyne's interest in serving the medical community is also evidenced in its number of patents. MegaDyne currently has 12 issued patents and several more pending.

"New patents are a good indication of our commitment to developing innovative products that meet the needs of a changing health care environment," Sansom says. "MegaDyne views innovation as the key to shaping the future of health care and the company's long-term success. Through our commitment to research and development, we have expanded our product line from a single niche product to a full line of electrosurgical accessories, and look forward to a continuing stream of innovative products."

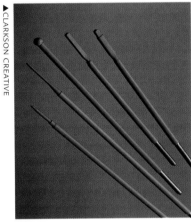

CLOCKWISE FROM TOP: MEGADYNE'S HEADQUARTERS IS LOCATED IN THE SUBURBS OF SALT LAKE CITY.

E-Z CLEAN ELECTRODES ARE CLEANER, FASTER, AND SAFER IN THE OPERATING ROOM.

THROUGH INNOVATION, MEGADYNE CONTINUES TO EXPAND ITS PRODUCT LINE, OFFERING CLINICIANS A BROAD ARRAY OF PRODUCTS TO MEET THEIR NEEDS.

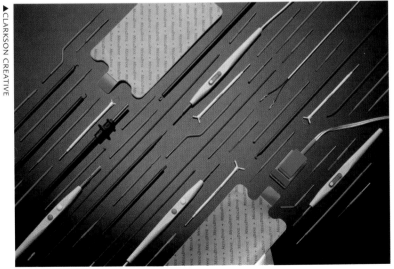

COLVIN ENGINEERING ASSOCIATES, INC.

COLVIN ENGINEERING ASSOCIATES HAS DRAWN ON ITS INITIALS TO CREATE a slogan to illustrate the company's philosophy: Communicate! Evaluate! Act! The company's motto encapsulates Colvin Engineering's attitude toward providing an array of mechanical engineering services for hospitals, manufacturing facilities, office buildings, laboratories,

recreation facilities, convention centers, and large public facilities, such as hockey rinks. Client satisfaction is evidenced by the fact that approximately 90 percent of Colvin's clients are repeat customers. This ongoing client relationship enhances the company's ability to effectively respond to client issues.

The company's services include the analysis, design, and commissioning of HVAC (heating, ventilating, and air-conditioning), plumbing, process piping, fire protection, smoke control, and environmental quality/pollution controls. Other engineering services include the formulation of energy management strategies for heating, air-conditioning, ventilating, and refrigeration systems. Colvin's engineers have the ability to provide hour-by-hour computer simulation of any proposed building to estimate energy consumption and a payback analysis to determine the optimum system based on a building's projected construction and operating budgets.

The founder of the company, Tom Colvin, relocated to Salt Lake City with an engineering firm out of Denver and quickly grew fond of the area. When the firm he worked for left the area, Colvin stayed, founding his company in 1985 with a handful of employees. Every year since, the company has registered considerable growth and now has several principals and more than 25 employees. Plans are under way to expand from its current office space to accommodate its increasing staff.

BIG ENOUGH TO SERVE; SMALL ENOUGH TO CARE

We pride ourselves on our innovation and our ability to design projects that will be contemporary into the 21st century," Marketing Director Marion Cook explains. "If you were to ask other design professionals about our reputation, you'd find that we're known for embracing leading-edge technology and for being specialized across the board in a lot of different areas."

To back up her claim, Cook proudly points to client evaluations filled with glowing superlatives. Terms like "responsive" and "diligent" turn up regularly. A Utah software company commented: "They are big enough to serve; small enough to care. They give us progressive designs, not the status quo. They are cost-conscious and responsive to answering questions and solving problems."

A large, local developer described one of the strengths of the firm as "the ability to work with architects, other engineers, and owners for a good system for the project within a reasonable budget."

One general contractor rates the quality of Colvin's work as "very good, and its systems always work when they are constructed." Another said, "The quality of its work is excellent. They are also great team players."

A representative for a governmental entity complimented the company on the quality of its work. "They are value-conscious and easy to work with, with any budget."

COLVIN REMAINS COMMITTED TO ITS MISSION STATEMENT: TO PROVIDE UNIQUE, COST EFFECTIVE DESIGN SOLUTIONS TO CLIENTS' NEEDS THROUGH CLEAR COMMUNICATION, INNOVATIVE THINKING, SOUND ENGINEERING, AND PROACTIVE MANAGEMENT, WHILE CONTINUALLY STRIVING TO EXCEED ALL CLIENT EXPECTATIONS. SOME OF THE COMPANY'S PROJECTS INCLUDE (CLOCKWISE FROM TOP) WEST VALLEY CITY E CENTER, GATEWAY TOWER, AND ST. ALPHONSUS HOSPITAL.

VALENTINER CRANE BRUNJES ONYON ARCHITECTS AND HOK SPORT

MHTN ARCHITECTS

GERALD R. NICHOLS & ASSOCIATES ARCHITECTS

Although most of Colvin's work still originates in Utah and Idaho, the company is licensed in most Western and Midwestern states. The company's diversity is evident in a list of its recent projects, which include the Ogden Conference Center; Provo City Ice Rink; Franklin Quest Field; NuSkin corporate headquarters; One Utah Center; Broadway Center; Novell corporate headquarters; Alta View Hospital; St. Alphonsus Regional Medical Center; The E Center in West Valley; IHC corporate headquarters; Fresenius USA; Compeq International; Gateway Tower West; Huntsman corporate headquarters; Blue Cross and Blue Shield; HealthRider corporate offices; and River Run Day Lodge in Sun Valley, Idaho, among many others.

A CONCERNED CORPORATE CITIZEN

Colvin Engineering is a strong supporter of volunteer organizations, and employees participate in events such as United Way's annual Day of Caring. As part of that event in 1997, employees worked on a Habitat for Humanity house, and a Colvin engineer partnered with a volunteer architect to design a radiant heating system that is energy-efficient and minimizes utility and maintenance costs.

The company is also very concerned about homeless issues and offers matching contributions for employee donations to organizations like Traveler's Aid. Instead of sending Christmas cards, Colvin Engineering sends each client a letter explaining that the company has made a contribution to charity in that client's name. "It's been very well received," Cook reports.

In addition, Colvin is on the board of directors of the Ronald McDonald House and has volunteered his services to help upgrade the house's mechanical systems. He has also done volunteer engineering work on the air-conditioning system of a Salt Lake City elementary school.

In the future, Cook believes Colvin Engineering's combination of teamwork and technical expertise will allow the company to take advantage of the burgeoning design/build trend where engineers and contractors pair up to expedite construction. But she adds that regardless of whatever changes the company encounters, it will remain committed to its core values. "We haven't changed at all since we started, as far as commitment to quality. We feel we provide the most service for the dollar and go the extra mile to assure our clients' optimum satisfaction. Our goal is pretty solid: We want to continue to expand our technical expertise and remain at the forefront of the industry." The company remains committed to its mission statement: To provide unique, cost-effective design solutions to clients' needs through clear communication, innovative thinking, sound engineering, and proactive management, while continually striving to exceed all client expectations.

COLVIN ENGINEERING ASSOCIATES HAS DRAWN ON ITS INITIALS TO CREATE A SLOGAN TO ILLUSTRATE THE COMPANY'S PHILOSOPHY: COMMUNICATE! EVALUATE! ACT! THE COMPANY'S MOTTO ENCAPSULATES COLVIN ENGINEERING'S ATTITUDE TOWARD PROVIDING AN ARRAY OF MECHANICAL ENGINEERING SERVICES FOR OFFICE BUILDINGS, LABORATORIES, RECREATION FACILITIES, HOSPITALS, CONVENTION CENTERS, AND LARGE PUBLIC FACILITIES, SUCH AS HOCKEY RINKS. EXAMPLES OF THE COMPANY'S WORK INCLUDE ONE UTAH CENTER (LEFT) AND TANKS AND PROCESS PIPING FOR FRESENIUS USA.

*W*HEN FIDELITY INVESTMENTS OPENED ITS SALT LAKE CITY OFFICE IN 1986, the company had a total of 110 employees on one floor of one building. Today, Fidelity boasts a local workforce of 1,400, operating out of four separate facilities in the downtown area. These four locations represent a variety of nine business units that

make up the local presence of Fidelity Investments. Such employee growth is a reflection of the company's tenfold increase in the marketplace. However, one thing about Fidelity has never changed: "As technologies have expanded, so have our services," says Site General Manager Scott Gygi. "But one main focus we've maintained is customer service."

Fidelity Investments was initially attracted to Utah for several reasons, including its central location in the western United States. "We wanted an office where we could cater to the West Coast without necessarily being on the coast," Gygi explains.

The company was also drawn by the reputation the Utah labor force enjoys for its devoted work ethic, quality education, and foreign language skills. More than 26,000 employees cover the worldwide reaches of Fidelity Investments, presenting the need for a customer service staff that is versatile in many foreign languages. Mandarin Chinese, Japanese, French, and Spanish are just a few of the languages overheard in the local Fidelity setting as employees continually strive to deliver excellent customer service. "Fidelity puts a big emphasis on incremental increases in quality until you reach your goal," Gygi says. "The employees

here are dedicated to the same principles."

A HALF-CENTURY OF HISTORY

Fidelity Investments' corporate history reaches back to 1943, when a Boston attorney Edward C. Johnson assumed the presidency of a small investment fund called the Fidelity Fund. Johnson proved to be a shrewd investor, and grew the fund's assets from $3 million to $10 million in two years.

By 1996, Fidelity Investments was the nation's largest mutual fund company, the leading provider of 401(k) retirement plans, and the second-largest discount brokerage firm. With more than $681.7 billion in assets—including 241 mutual funds—the company's customer base now exceeds 12 million people. Along the way, Fidelity has been a consistent innovator in areas as wide-ranging as on-line customer service and trading, open-end municipal bond funds, and discount brokering.

NATIONAL SCOPE, RANGE OF SERVICES

Fidelity's national stature benefits both its customers and its employees. Company employees nationwide have the chance to explore different opportunities within the design of Fidelity. Though primary focus is in the financial arena, a variety of divisions contribute to the diversity. With software development divisions, data centers, a transportation division, a hotel, and more, Fidelity Investments continues to build its unique structure. And customers benefit from Fidelity's cutting-edge perspective on technology and training.

Fidelity Investments' list of firsts is long and impressive. The company was the first to offer a check-writing feature on a mutual fund and the first to offer services 24 hours a day, seven days a week.

FIDELITY INVESTMENTS' SALT LAKE CITY INVESTOR CENTER PROVIDES A FACILITY WHERE CUSTOMERS CAN ENJOY A VARIETY OF INVESTMENT OPPORTUNITIES.

STEPHEN SMITH

TIME, TALENT, AND TECHNOLOGY ALL
CONTRIBUTE TO FIDELITY EMPLOYEES'
DEDICATION TO CUSTOMER SERVICE.

In addition, Fidelity has also been a leader in offering 800 numbers for information retrieval, Touch-Tone telephone trading, on-line computer quotes and trading, retirement services, college-savings plans, annuities, and life insurance. While other companies now offer these features, Fidelity was a leader in providing simplified transactions and building one-step investment opportunities for customers' needs. The company also offers 79 Investor Centers in 65 major cities where customers can transact business while enjoying a personal as well as professional atmosphere.

ENHANCING SALT LAKE CITY

Fidelity is justifiably proud of its company culture, which is an ongoing interpretation of Johnson's 50-year philosophy. In his management strategy, Johnson believed in hiring bright, motivated employees and giving them the tools to make money for the company's shareholders. Fidelity remains a privately held company with management now entering the third generation. Each generation will be remembered for its contribution to the improvement of customer service.

An additional component of servicing the customer involves enhancing the community. Fidelity

offers its employees a cornucopia of choices for becoming involved in civic, educational, and other volunteer activities. Employees may participate in food drives, fund-raising walks for nonprofit groups, donations to homeless shelters, and telethons for public television, to name a few.

The company attempts to pinpoint projects that emphasize volunteerism and that focus on long-term positive effects for the community. The annual literacy campaign is a prime example. Each year, Fidelity holds a literacy event stressing that reading is fun, and books are donated to employees' children as well as to children in the community. The children have an opportunity to select the

books they want and take ownership of them. The company believes this decision process will encourage the child to read books.

Like many other professional organizations in the area, Fidelity is bullish about the future of the Utah market. With the growth and changes occurring in Utah, the area is on track for worldwide review and scrutiny in the near future. Fidelity's goal is to strengthen its customer base, continue to enhance the lives of employees and their families, continue to be a contributing corporate citizen, and remain a leader in providing financial services. The company has quality personnel and professional standards that it's proud to demonstrate to the rest of the world.

FIDELITY EMPLOYEES VOLUNTEER THEIR
TIME TO RAISE FUNDS IN SUPPORT OF
PUBLIC TELEVISION.

NPS Pharmaceuticals is a drug research and development company dedicated to providing products that relieve suffering and improve health. The early days of NPS' drug research involved the extraction and exploration of components of venom from spiders, scorpions, and centipedes. On the basis of that formative work,

Clockwise from top: NPS Pharmaceuticals' corporate management team includes (seated) Hunter Jackson, Ph.D., CEO, president, and chairman of the board; Thomas B. Marriott, Ph.D., vice president, development research; James U. Jensen, J.D., vice president, corporate development and legal affairs, and secretary; (standing) Robert K. Merrell, CPA, vice president, finance, chief financial officer, and treasurer; Derek Hook, Ph.D., director, discovery research; David Clark, MBA, director, corporate communications; Doug Reed, M.D., vice president, business development; N. Patricia Freston, Ph.D., vice president, human resources; and Edward F. Nemeth, Ph.D., vice president and chief scientific officer.

NPS Pharmaceuticals is a drug research and development company dedicated to providing products that relieve suffering and improve health.

Originally founded in 1986 by a pair of researchers from the University of Utah, NPS has grown from the time when its two founders crowded into a one-room laboratory to a thriving business today, with more than 100 employees.

today's NPS engages in discovering and developing novel, small-molecule drugs that address a variety of conditions, including osteoporosis, stroke, head trauma, hyperparathyroidism, and diseases of the central nervous system.

Originally founded in 1986 by a pair of researchers from the University of Utah, NPS has maintained its close ties to the research staff at the university, and has grown from the time when its two founders crowded into a one-room laboratory to a thriving business today, with more than 100 employees.

Drug Candidates

NPS' initial research on arthropods has had a significant impact on its current discoveries, aimed at improving human health. "This early work was very difficult," says David Clark, director of corporate communications. "There were hundreds of compounds, most of them biologically active in unique ways. It was necessary to figure out which are useful and how."

As a result of this research, the company was able to model compounds after venom, including one drug that is now being tested for the treatment of stroke. Clark is enthusiastic about the prospects. "It's wonderful for us

to be in human trials with a drug that was the result of what started us off," he says. "We're all very excited."

NPS is focusing on identifying novel receptors and channels in cell membranes, and beginning to look for drugs that act on those targets. "Because of our experience, we're uniquely positioned to look for novel targets on the surface of cells," Clark notes. "We've also been able to discover small molecules that produce therapeutic effects to a range of disorders."

Pharmaceutical research—while exciting and innovative—is a competitive business. "This is a business as difficult as it is miraculous," says Chief Executive Officer, President, and Chairman Hunter Jackson. "Nature does not easily yield to intervention. For all its excitement and reward, it is also competitive, it is a business, and it is hard work."

On the business front, NPS has established collaborative agreements with SmithKline Beecham, the pharmaceutical division of Kirin Brewery Company of Tokyo, and Amgen Inc. The company expects to continue collaborations as scientific progress is made.

Community Involvement

Of equal importance to its business endeavors is NPS' involvement in the Salt Lake community. "In addition to being a

company that provides a significant payroll and is involved in developing drugs, we're also actively involved in community causes," says Clark.

Those causes include sponsoring a transitional housing unit through the Travelers Aid Society; the unit is specifically dedicated to assisting homeless families. NPS also supports the Ronald McDonald House and the United Way. In addition, NPS is working with the neighboring Residential Treatment Center of the Primary Children's Hospital to support programs for abused children.

In a very competitive industry, NPS is taking steps to ensure its role in the future of pharmaceutical research. "We have a commitment to becoming an enduring company," says Clark. "We see ourselves as a large pharmaceutical company in its early years."

EXPANDING UPON THE TRADITIONAL SCOPE OF COMMERCIAL BROKERAGE services, Colliers CRG (Consolidated Realty Group) sets new standards of service to tenants, landlords, developers, and investors. ▨ The group's full-service approach to commercial real estate is grounded in a simple philosophy: To anticipate and identify the needs of a diverse clientele and

to provide the experience and tools necessary to ensure each client's needs are met. The company's success in accomplishing these goals is evident in the Salt Lake City skyline, and Colliers CRG now stands as one of the largest commercial brokerages in the state.

PERFORMANCE THROUGH EXPERIENCE

Founded in 1987, Colliers CRG has grown from seven to more than 75 employees, building on a strong core of commercial brokerage services centered on retail, office, industrial, and land leasing and sales. The company's cadre of licensed agents have more than 400 years of combined experience in the industry, a foundation Colliers CRG utilizes to expand its scope and accommodate the ever changing needs of a thriving marketplace.

Colliers CRG Realty Advisors, the company's development services arm, concentrates on providing fee-based services for a broad range of commercial projects. Staffed by professionals experienced in all aspects of commercial real estate, the group encompasses complete project management from initial site selection and acquisition through design, construction, and marketing assistance for leasing and disposition.

In response to the needs of its clientele for a dedicated property manager, the company formed Colliers Consolidated Realty Management Group (Colliers CRMG) as a natural extension of its spectrum of brokerage services. Colliers CRMG now manages more than 1.7 million square feet of commercial real estate, including office, retail, and industrial properties. Colliers CRG has also positioned itself to serve the investment client, with the addition of experienced specialists who employ the most technologically advanced marketing and analysis systems available.

AN INFORMATION LEADER

Colliers CRG Information Services Group (ISG) is widely recognized as a leader in providing the most comprehensive market data available in Utah. Based on the premise that up-to-the-minute, accurate information is crucial to real estate transactions, Colliers CRG has made a major investment in the equipment, personnel, and technology necessary to track vital market conditions, and to provide in-house graphic design and mapping. A growing number of government and private agencies rely on the group's data for nationally published surveys and newsletters, and Colliers CRG's Internet home page at www.collierscrg.com was recently ranked among the top five commercial real estate sites on the World Wide Web by the *Commercial Investment Real Estate Journal.*

Most recently, the company broadened its horizons on a national and international scale through affiliation with Colliers International, an alliance of leading real estate firms providing comprehensive service in more than 215 offices in 47 countries. As a member of this internationally recognized organization, Colliers CRG's commitment to consistently superior service is reflected in access to the experience and relationships of more than 4,400 professionals worldwide.

Colliers CRG's agents actively participate in the top professional associations in the industry, including the International Council of Shopping Centers (ICSC), Building Owners and Managers Association (BOMA), and National Association of Industrial and Office Properties (NAIOP). Many of the group's agents have the professional designations of Certified Commercial Investment Member (CCIM) and Society of Industrial and Office Realtors (SIOR). On a local level, the company is a contributing member of the Economic Development Corporation of Utah (EDCU), Salt Lake Area Chamber of Commerce, and Utah Information Technologies Association (UITA).

COLLIERS CRG'S SUCCESS IN ACCOMPLISHING ITS GOALS IS EVIDENT IN THE SALT LAKE CITY SKYLINE, AND THE COMPANY NOW STANDS AS ONE OF THE LARGEST COMMERCIAL BROKERAGES IN THE STATE.

ONE OF THE WORLD'S LEADING INFORMATION TECHNOLOGY (IT) SERVICES companies, EDS is expanding its presence in Utah. EDS employs more than 110,000 people worldwide, and during the last decade, the number in Salt Lake City has grown to more than 160, making EDS an important area employer. A combination of factors has fueled the company's

growth. First, EDS applies IT in ways that fundamentally improve the economics of its clients' businesses. As those clients have grown, EDS has grown with them. Second, Utah's educated workforce led the company to relocate groups here that serve EDS clients around the world. Third, as a global leader in IT, EDS brings world-class resources to Utah that will help companies here thrive in the coming digital economy.

A HUNGER FOR EXCELLENCE

EDS first came to Salt Lake City to serve Smith's Food and Drug Centers, Inc. in 1992. Since then, EDS has helped Smith's become a dominant force in this region by using IT in ways that have held down costs while improving customer service.

For instance, EDS has developed an item tracking system that uses hand-held scanning units to speed up inventories. The system also tracks incoming and outgoing items to calculate quantities on hand. Another example is Smith's frequent shopper program. Supported by EDS, it rewards Smith's loyal customers with significant discounts and added value incentives. EDS was involved in the launch of this program, and is now working with Smith's to enhance its customer-specific marketing efforts and to take its frequent shopper program to the next level.

EFFICIENCIES OF ELECTRONIC BUSINESS

Financial institutions these days are caught in a squeeze. On one hand, they must deliver more and better services to meet national competition. On the other, they must keep costs down to offer competitive rates.

To resolve this conflict for credit union clients like America First, EDS has developed a comprehensive suite of software and services that includes direct payroll deposit, ATMs, home banking, and more. Automated voice response systems installed by EDS handle customer inquiries seven days a week, 24-hours per day—without adding payroll. Transactional Internet sites developed by EDS make credit union services available around the clock, around the world. In effect, they turn members' personal computers into millions of brickless, mortarless branches—resulting in highly competitive credit unions.

IMPROVING SPEED WITHOUT REDUCING QUALITY

One of the paradoxes of information technology is that it can help companies achieve benefits once thought mutually exclusive. For instance, IT can help designers improve both time to market and quality.

Along the I-15 Corridor, EDS is helping the Reconstruction Design Team of the Sverdrup/De Leuw

CURRENTLY OPERATING IN 44 COUNTRIES, EDS IS EXPANDING ITS PRESENCE IN UTAH. NOT ONLY WILL EDS MAKE WORLD-CLASS INFORMATION TECHNOLOGY AVAILABLE TO UTAH COMPANIES, IT IS HELPING MARKET UTAH TALENT TO THE WORLD.

Joint Venture meet accelerated construction schedules. The team is able to design roads, drainage, signage, lights, and bridges that comply with Utah Department of Transportation specs—within budget, without delay.

BRINGING JOBS TO UTAH AND UTAH TO THE WORLD

Much of EDS' growth in Utah can be attributed to the state itself. Utah's educated workforce, spectacular environment, and reasonable cost of living led EDS to locate one of its Technology and Engineering Solution Centers here. These centers give EDS' highly skilled specialists the freedom to focus on making the best systems possible in an atmosphere removed from day-to-day client pressures. They provide best-in-class solutions that EDS can tailor for customers anywhere around the world.

Another factor responsible for the growth of EDS in Utah is the ability to bring world-class resources to companies here. For instance, the EDS Virtual Reality Center provides an ideal environment for companies to "test" product designs before prototypes are developed. This results in lower development costs, higher quality, and faster development cycles. Virtual stadiums created by EDS put 2.5 million 1998 World Cup tickets on sale—two years before actual stadiums were completed.

EDS also offers advanced crop forecasting systems that help assure the quality of fruit, reduce spoilage, and improve profits; Call Centers that provide technical support for technology companies, subscriber services for publishers, and roadside assistance for stranded motorists; and adapted ATMs that create new channels of distribution for a wide variety of products from postage stamps to theater and airline tickets.

CARING FOR THE COMMUNITY

As a company that has benefited from being in Utah, EDS recognizes its obligation to give back to the community.

This year, EDS made it possible for students at Mountain View Elementary to participate in the JASON Project. Through a technology called "telepresence," kids were able to interact with world-leading scientists such as Dr. Robert Ballard, discoverer of the *Titanic*. Many discovered something unexpected: the joy of scientific learning.

EDS employees also mentor area students in a variety of subjects. This year, on their annual Global Volunteer Day, EDS staffers helped restore public areas in cooperation with the Salt Lake City Parks and Recreation Department. EDS also supports charitable organizations including the March of Dimes, Shriners Hospitals for Children, and the Sub for Santa program.

The men and women of EDS work in a cutting-edge environment where possibilities are limitless. They harness the power of information technology to improve the performance of thousands of businesses worldwide. For EDS and Utah, this is just the beginning.

FROM ITS TRADEMARK CHOCOLATE CHIP COOKIES TO ITS LUXURIOUS feather pillows to its gracious staff and wealth of amenities, the Doubletree Hotel in Salt Lake City is a home away from home for business and pleasure travelers alike. The reason is simple: great service in a homelike atmosphere. There is no detail of operation too small or too trivial to merit attention.

"There are as many as 7,000 hotel rooms in town, depending upon whom you ask," says Steve Lindburg, general manager of the Doubletree Hotel. "We want to go beyond providing clean pillows. Our goal is to build ongoing relationships with customers. We try to determine what our guests' expectations are and then do everything we can to exceed them."

One way in which the Doubletree exceeds guests' expectations is to encourage a spirit of camaraderie among the hotel's staff. "When it comes right down to it, our goal is to be sure all 385 members of the team enjoy coming to work," Lindburg explains. "If you like your job, you automatically do a little bit more. You greet guests with a smile. You're happy to drop everything to answer a question."

According to Lindburg, the hotel's goal can only be realized by drawing on perhaps the most used of 1990s buzzwords—empowerment. The difference at the Doubletree, however, is that the entire staff really subscribes to the philosophy. The hotel maintains an environment where any member of its team can step forward and speak his or her mind without fear of retribution. "We want our staff to be recognized for their contributions," says Lindburg. "If we catch someone doing something right, we reward them."

PLENTY OF AMENITIES

The Doubletree name means more than just good service. With downtown Salt Lake City anticipating a flurry of hotel construction in time for the 2002 Winter Olympics, the Doubletree is actively involved in building a loyal customer base. Part of its strategy involves cultivating what the hotel calls a "winning interface" between staff and guests.

Just as important is the Doubletree's variety of facilities. Currently, the property boasts a 2,500-square-foot ballroom, 11 meeting rooms, an executive room equipped with leather chairs and a walnut table, and a 4,000-square-foot workout facility with lap pool, aerobic equipment, weights, dry saunas, and a massage therapy clinic. The 17th floor caters to business customers, with 30 rooms equipped with desks, fax machines, scanners, and office chairs. The 18th-floor concierge level features a private lounge, and includes complimentary breakfasts, afternoon cocktails, and light hors d'oeuvres. Additionally, an independent group of restaurateurs have taken over the in-house dining space and opened a fine destination restaurant.

Throughout the hotel, guest rooms are equipped with hair dryers, full-sized ironing boards, voice mail service, coffeemakers, and pay-per-view movie access. "There aren't many amenities people ask for that we don't offer," Lindburg says.

These amenities have been satisfying customers since February 1997, when hotel management removed the old Red Lion sign from the property and replaced it with the familiar Doubletree logo. Although they recognized right away there would be challenges, the experience has been overwhelmingly positive. "The team

FROM ITS TRADEMARK CHOCOLATE CHIP COOKIES TO ITS LUXURIOUS FEATHER PILLOWS TO ITS GRACIOUS STAFF AND WEALTH OF AMENITIES, THE DOUBLETREE HOTEL IN SALT LAKE CITY IS A HOME AWAY FROM HOME FOR BUSINESS AND PLEASURE TRAVELERS ALIKE (LEFT).

SPENCER'S OFFERS DOUBLETREE GUESTS A CASUAL DINING ATMOSPHERE (RIGHT).

DAVID PAPAZIAN

remained whole throughout the conversion," says Lindburg. "We've actually expanded on the service-staff end, and we're now seeing a broader cross section of national and international travelers as a result."

Another change since the hotel's reopening is an increasing awareness that the Doubletree is serving two distinct markets. "During the middle of the week, we are mostly a businessperson's hotel," Lindburg explains. "But Friday rolls around and 50 percent of our guests come from the surrounding counties. Then we try to be a leisure spot and weekend retreat. A businessperson is here with an itinerary, whereas a weekend traveler is here to have fun."

As guests' motivations change, so does the hotel atmosphere. On weekends, staff members wear golf shirts. Menus offer kids' meals, and rooms are stocked with crayons. "The last thing we want to do is be stuffy," Lindburg adds.

INVOLVED IN THE COMMUNITY

Going beyond merely striving to please its guests, the hotel has made a commitment to civic and community affairs. "We've been partners with Ballet West

DAVID PAPAZIAN

and the Utah Symphony for years," Lindburg says. The hotel has also supported the Downtown Alliance, the mayor's Clean Cities program, and Midnight Basketball, and even made an in-kind contribution of a half million dollars to the Salt Lake Organizing Committee's Olympic bid.

But in the end, a hotel's success or failure is tied directly to how welcome guests feel. As an

example, Lindburg points to the now-famous chocolate chip cookies that have been presented to incoming guests at all Doubletree locations since 1992. "They're an icon, a symbol of the warmth and hospitality of checking into the hotel," he says. "They reinforce the message that we're glad guests have chosen us. The cookies are a little bit of home, and that feeling is what really brings guests back."

CLOCKWISE FROM TOP LEFT: SPENCER'S FOR STEAKS AND CHOPS IS THE STANDARD FOR STEAKS IN SALT LAKE CITY.

CURRENTLY, DOUBLETREE BOASTS A 4,000-SQUARE-FOOT WORKOUT FACILITY WITH LAP POOL, AEROBIC EQUIPMENT, WEIGHTS, DRY SAUNAS, AND A MASSAGE THERAPY CLINIC.

THE 17TH FLOOR CATERS TO BUSINESS CUSTOMERS, WITH 30 ROOMS EQUIPPED WITH DESKS, FAX MACHINES, SCANNERS, AND OFFICE CHAIRS.

*I*RONICALLY, THE FOUNDER OF ONE OF THE WEST'S HOTTEST FOOD FRANchises hit upon the idea for his business while sitting around the family dinner table. ▣ That was in 1989, when Michael Clayton worked as a certified public accountant. Clayton had spent the previous six years balancing the books for fast-food operations: snack shops at amuse-

ment parks, hamburger chains, even Colonel Sanders' Kentucky Fried Chicken. Now, he was looking to go into business for himself.

"There were a lot of submarine sandwich shops, bagel shops, places like that," says Clayton, a graduate in accounting from Brigham Young University with a master's degree in taxation. "And ice-cream shops started serving frozen yogurt. These two items—submarine sandwiches and frozen yogurt—were the hot food items."

Clayton started thinking about the potential market for the combination of these two popular food segments in the fast-food industry. "This dual concept was the first of its kind ever," he says. "It would appeal to the lunch and dinner crowd, as well as the snack and dessert diners. And it was my family who helped come up with the name—Hogi Yogi."

CLOCKWISE FROM TOP RIGHT: STORE DECOR REFLECTS THE FUN, MODERN IMAGE OF THE HOGI YOGI CORPORATION.

HOGI YOGI SANDWICHES ARE AS HEALTHY AS THEY ARE DELICIOUS.

HOGI YOGI YOGURT IS CUSTOM BLENDED WITH MORE THAN 50 MIX-INS TO CHOOSE FROM.

ANDREW CHASE

◄ ANDREW CHASE

A FRESH IDEA

*H*ogi Yogi's legacy began in 1989, when Clayton opened two stores. Both served up made-to-order submarine sandwiches

ANDREW CHASE

and custom-blended frozen yogurt. The hoagie submarine sandwiches are still made from fresh-baked white or wheat bread; lean cuts of beef, chicken, or turkey breast that are 95 percent fat free; and eight vegetable toppings. And the nonfat vanilla or nonfat chocolate yogurt still can be blended with any combination of 50 fruits, nuts, candies, or cookies.

The concept proved so popular that a third store was opened in 1990, another in 1991, and another in 1992. To keep up with demand, Clayton started to franchise in 1993, opening nearly 40 stores. Now, more than 100 Hogi Yogis dot the landscape in 10 states, including Utah, Arizona, California, Colorado, Nevada, Oregon, Washington, and Texas. And Clayton has his eyes set on international expansion, with franchises planned in Canada, Japan, and several countries in Europe.

"I personally try to help open every franchise," Clayton says. "We look for exceptional individuals to be our franchise owners, people committed to their customers, employees, and the community."

In 1997, Hogi Yogi responded to its customers' requests for a low-fat, icy cold, nutrient-packed line of real fruit smoothies. These 24-ounce drinks are made of natural, unsweetened fruits and the finest sherbet, frozen yogurts, and fruit juices available. Customers may also add supplements that include a range of healthy additives— from oriental herbs to fibers, proteins, carbohydrates, and vitamins.

The summer of 1997 also saw the completion of a new corporate headquarters in Provo. The campus includes an 18,000-square-foot multiplex with offices, training facilities, and a showcase store to support and train Hogi Yogi's more than 2,000 employees nationwide.

"We provide a delicious, healthy alternative to the typical fast-food offering," Clayton says. "Hogi Yogi and its franchise owners are out to do nothing less than help change the way America dines."

Owen "R" Black is a Utah native, and his home state's natural wonders are the subjects for much of his photography. As the director of food services and housekeeping at the Utah State Hospital in Provo, he pursues photography as a hobby, developing the images in his own darkroom. Black's work is on permanent display at the Salt Lake City International Airport, and has appeared in local newspapers, advertising publications, the *Utah Sports Guide*, and *Persimmon Hill* magazine. He is the recipient of numerous awards, including Best of Show honors from Brigham Young University's Bean Museum and the Springville Museum of Art.

John Blodgett came to the Salt Lake area in 1996 from Portland, Maine. Employed at CitySearch, Inc., he specializes in newspaper and documentary photojournalism. He graduated from Boston University and received a master's degree in journalism from the University of Missouri-Columbia. Blodgett has worked for five daily newspapers and does freelance work for the Associated Press and Knight-Ridder/Tribune Business News.

Patrick Cone is from Park City and received a bachelor of fine arts degree in photo design from Utah State University. A former geologist and helicopter navigator, he is now a self-employed photographer specializing in travel and aerial images and portraiture. His work has appeared in *National Geographic World, Sunset, The Magazine of Western Living, Arizona Highways, Snow Country,* and *Flying,* among other publications.

Lee Foster is a veteran travel writer and photographer who lives in Berkeley, California. His work has been published in a number of major travel magazines and newspapers, and he maintains a stock photo library that features more than 250 worldwide destinations. Foster's full travel publishing efforts can be viewed on his Web site at www.fostertravel.com.

Ewing Galloway, Inc., based in Rockville, New York, opened in 1920 as one of the country's original stock agencies. During its almost 80 years of operation, the company has provided images for advertising agencies, design studios, corporations, publishers, and record companies.

John P. George has been photographing the American landscape for 25 years, specializing in seasonal panoramas, intimate close-ups and abstracts, early and late light, and mood and long exposures. He has covered western deserts, mountains, and coastlines, as well as the boreal forests of the Northwoods and New England states. Widely published in North America and Europe, George has accumulated more than 1,500 photo credits including calendars, books, magazines, postcards, advertising, and travel-related material. He has participated in many group, traveling, and solo exhibitions throughout the country, and his images have appeared in *National Geographic, National Wildlife, Natural History Magazine, Nature Conservancy Magazine,* and other publications.

Wayne Gillman, a lifelong resident of Utah, has been interested in capturing the beauty of the state on film for many years. A former attorney, Gillman began studying with photographer Linda Delay-Joseph of California-based Silver Moon Photography in 1994, and decided to make the medium his profession. He has also participated in the Santa Fe Photographic Workshops and worked with photographers Nevada Weir, Linde Waidhoffer, and Brenda Tharp.

Sean Graff is an associate instructor of black-and-white photography for the University of Utah's communications department. A native of Missoula, Montana, he moved to Salt Lake City from Boston in 1993, after graduating from Amherst College with a bachelor's degree in English. The recipient of various awards and grants, he has had images published in *Salt Lake City Magazine* and *Catalyst*.

Hillstrom Stock Photo, established in 1967, is a full-service stock photography agency based in Chicago. Its image catalog features subjects such as architecture, agricultural backgrounds, classic autos, gardens, and high-risk adventure/sports.

Frank Jensen, a Salt Lake City photographer, began his career as bureau manager for the *Salt Lake Tribune* in Cedar City. In 1956, he was part of a Pulitzer-prize-winning team that covered the midair collision of two airliners over the Grand Canyon. He spent 15 years working as a freelance television photographer and reporter, producing two award-winning documentary films. Since 1975, he has devoted himself to still photography, publishing images in *Time, Newsweek,* the *New York Times, National Geographic Traveler, Outside,* and *Better Homes and Gardens.*

Rick McClain became interested in photography while traveling with the United States Army Marksmanship Training Unit. Originally from Texas, he moved to Salt Lake in 1971, where he is owner of Rick McClain Photography. Using both traditional photography and digital manipulation, McClain supplies images used in brochures, magazines, and catalogs for a client list that includes members of the industrial, architectural, advertising, and publishing industries.

Mary E. Messenger resides in the Sacramento, California, area and specializes in stock photography with a photojournalistic slant. Her subjects include people, portrayed in their daily lives and activities, as well as sports and travel.

Rod Millar is a Wisconsin native who moved to the Salt Lake area in 1965. In addition to work in computer imaging and art, he specializes in 360-degree, panoramic photography, focusing on subjects such as landscapes, scenics, cities, and crowds. His images have appeared in numerous publications and his client list includes Questar Corporation and Richardson Design.

include the Utah Travel Council, Utah Film Commission, Salt Lake Area Chamber of Commerce, and Blue Cross and Blue Shield of Utah.

Scott Smith, born and raised in Salt Lake City, received a master's degree in meteorology from Utah State University. A self-taught freelance photographer, he specializes in landscapes, cityscapes, people in nature, and historic buildings. In addition to his two books, *Nevada: Magnificent Wilderness* and *Stories to Gather All Those Lost*, his images have been published in *Sierra, Sunset, The Magazine of Western Living, Nevada Magazine*, National Geographic books, and numerous calendars. Smith lives in northern Utah's Cache Valley with his wife and their three cats, and most summers he can be found packing with his llamas somewhere in the high country of the western United States.

Dan Miller is a self-taught photographer specializing in photojournalism and outdoor and scenic subjects. His images have appeared in *Life, Sports Illustrated*, and *Rock and Ice*. Miller is married to photojournalist Diane Bush and is currently at work on two books—a hiking guide to Utah's high peaks for the University of Utah Press, and a book for Utah State University on Antelope Island.

Photophile, established in San Diego in 1967, is owned and operated by Nancy Likins-Mastern. An internationally known stock photography agency, the company houses more than 1 million color images, culled from more than 90 contributing local and international photographers. Subjects range from extensive coverage of the West Coast, business and industry, to people and lifestyles, health, medicine, travel, scenics, wildlife, and adventure sports.

Craig Pozzi, is a resident of Vancouver, Washington, where he is an adjunct instructor for Portland State University in Portland, Oregon, and Clark College in Vancouver. His education consists of a bachelor of arts degree in psychology from Brown University, a bachelor of professional arts degree in motion picture production from the Brooks Institute, and a master of fine arts degree in photog-

raphy from the California Institute of the Arts. His work has been featured in solo, two-person, and group exhibitions across the country, and has been published in numerous exhibition brochures, catalogs, and magazines. Pozzi has received a variety of awards, grants, and fellowships, and his images are part of the permanent collections of Coos Art Museum, Evergreen State College, Middle Tennessee State University, the Salt Lake Art Center, Seattle Art Museum, the Utah State Collection of Fine Arts, American Express Corporation, and Microsoft Corporation, among others.

Richard J. Quataert is an award-winning photographer from Rochester who specializes in still and fine art photography, as well as large-scale infrared black-and-white photos and small-scale Polaroid image transfers. His work has been displayed at the Metropolitan Museum of Art in New York City, and one photograph remains as part of the museum's permanent collection. Quataert's photography is represented by the Elizabeth Collection and the Austin-Harvard Gallery in Rochester, and by Conversation Pieces in Manchester, Connecticut.

André Ramjoué moved to Salt Lake City in 1970 from Nuremberg, Germany. He specializes in architectural

and editorial images for T&A Photography, and his work has appeared in *Mountain Living* magazine. The recipient of a Utah Addy gold award in 1992, he spends his free time fly-fishing and traveling.

Barbara Richards has been exhibiting her images for more than 20 years and is the recipient of numerous awards. A Minnesota native, she moved to Salt Lake City in 1965, but travels extensively in the United States and abroad to find the subjects for her photographs.

Kay Shaw moved to the Salt Lake area in 1990. Her images have been featured in numerous books and magazines, as well as on calendars, note cards, and postcards. The recipient of a bachelor's degree from Hamline University in St. Paul, and a master's degree from the University of Chicago, Shaw has been on assignment in Haiti for Habitat for Humanity, and in South Korea for the Korean Tourist Commission. Her travels have taken her to 27 countries and many states.

Jerry Sintz, a resident of Sandy, Utah, is employed by the U.S. Bureau of Land Management. He is a part-time photographer with an emphasis on landscape, building, street scene, and historical structure images. His clients

Nicholas Sokoloff, a part-time instructor at the University of Utah, is also the photo director and a Web site designer at CitySearch, Inc., an international multimedia company. Originally from Boston, he received a master's degree from the University of Missouri School of Journalism and moved to the Salt Lake area in 1995. A former staff member of the *Santa Fe New Mexican* and the *Ogden Standard-Examiner*, he specializes in documentary photography, portraiture, and digital illustration, and his images have appeared in numerous local and national publications.

Other photographers and organizations that contributed to *Salt Lake City: Welcoming the World* include Bill Baptist, Andrew D. Bernstein, Nathan Butler, Richard Cummins, David Cutts, Tim Defrisco, Mark Keller, Terry Newfarmer, Cheyenne Rouse, Fred Wright, the National Basketball Association, the Ririe-Woodbury Dance Company, Root Resources, the University of Utah, and the Utah Opera Company.